PEKKA KORVENMAA

FINNISH DESIGN
A CONCISE HISTORY

Published in this revised edition by Aalto ARTS Books
in association with V&A Publishing, London

Aalto ARTS Books
Helsinki, Finland
books.aalto.fi

Victoria and Albert Museum
South Kensington
London SW7 2RL
www.vandabooks.com

Distributed in North America by
Harry N. Abrams Inc., New York

Text © Pekka Korvenmaa
© Aalto ARTS Books in association with
Victoria and Albert Museum, London

Translated from the Finnish by Jüri Kokkonen
Design and layout by Jani Pulkka and Camilla Pentti
Paper 150gsm Yulong pure
Type set in Swift, Interstate
Printed and bound by C&C Offset Printing Co. Ltd

ISBN (Finland) 978-952-60-5600-5
ISBN (UK & US) 978 1 85177 812 6

Library of Congress Control Number 2014932332

10 9 8 7 6 5 4 3 2 1
2018 2017 2016 2015 2014

A catalogue record for this book is
available from the British Library.

Pekka Korvenmaa

**FINNISH
DESIGN**

A CONCISE HISTORY

CONTENTS

INTRODUCTION

Applied art and design have long been a central aspect of the culture and economy of Finland. They have also had significant international exposure. Despite this, there has been no recent general work on the subject aimed at a broad readership. The present work seeks to respond to this need.

This book outlines the development of applied art and design in Finland from the 1870s to the beginning of the 21st century. The initial stages took place in the Grand Duchy of Finland, a part of the Russian Empire. Around the middle of the 19th century, significant changes began in economic policy in Finland, both permitting and requiring improved quality in the products of crafts and industries. The last stages described here are as close to the time of writing as possible. The beginning and end of this period of approximately 140 years are marked by significant, programmatic developments in the field. Many of the main institutions for the purposes of training, promotion and display in applied art and design were launched in the 1870s. Prominent developments in recent history are measures that were introduced in the late 1990s and were included in the five-year national design policy programme from 2000.

This book focuses on the 20th century, and specifically the period after the Second World War. This is because the late 19th and early 20th century have been presented and discussed extensively in several previous works on the subject, and accordingly this period is presented in a condensed manner here. This provides more space in this otherwise succinct overview for the phenomena of the last decades of the 20th century, which have hardly been discussed in general works.

The present book is a general presentation of the main structures, phenomena and courses of development of applied art and design in Finland. It naturally includes the leading individuals, designers and products, but only part of the rich heritage of this field can be presented here. Therefore, references have been added to the end of the book to help the reader explore in further detail the periods and phenomena that are discussed only briefly. Research concerning the field has gained pace especially since the 1990s, and books and catalogues published for exhibitions offer a great deal of new information. The present work would not have been possible without the recent contributions of many scholars and researchers. Because of the nature of the presentation, notes are used to only a small degree and therefore the bibliography seeks to give the main published sources in a comprehensive manner.

To place the phenomena of Finnish applied art and design in a broader national and international context, I recommend to the reader two works alongside the present book. *The History of Finland* by Jason Edward Lavery (2006) gives an overall view of developments in Finland to which applied art and design also belong. Jonathan M. Woodham's extensive *Twentieth-Century Design* (1997), in turn, helps relate the matters discussed here to the international context – to which applied art and design in Finland have made a significant contribution.

The previous general work in Finnish on this subject, Erik Kruskopf's *Suomen taideteollisuus. Suomalaisen muotoilun vaiheita* (1989) appeared two decades ago. Since then, research into the history of applied art and design has progressed significantly in both quality and quantity. Research has been activated by the originally British, and now world-wide, orientation of design history, the ideas of which have been spread especially by the *Journal of Design History*. Annual conferences and symposia in this area of research are also well known. Since the late 1980s, the *Scandinavian Journal and Design History*, published in Denmark, has been an organ of the Nordic research community in this field. Methodological emphasis in design history has clearly shifted from focuses on individuals, styles and objects to approaches of a broader basis, including those of the history of technology, consumer studies and social history.

So-called material culture studies have questioned the separation of selected objects and phenomena from the abundant world of goods into a distinct area defined as applied art and design. Also the approach known as design studies underscores, among other considerations, the importance of social and cultural factors as a basis for analyses. In recent years there has been increasing emphasis on viewing applied art and design as cultural activity, as an active factor shaping our material and visual environment. This perspective is expressed, for example, in *An Introduction to Design and Culture – 1900 to the Present* (2004) by Penny Sparke, and the contributions published in the *Journal of Design and Culture*, which was launched in 2009. The sphere of research and researchers has also expanded from its previously dominant Eurocentric bias to the Far East and South America.

Finnish design history has developed through impulses provided by an international field of research that has rapidly expanded and gained depth. The recent Finnish studies that provide a basis for the present work employ a wide range of perspectives and approach their subjects through various disciplines and methods. Art history, consumer studies, cultural history, gender studies, and the history of professions among other fields have explored phenomena falling under the rubric of applied art and design. What then is meant by 'applied art' and 'design'?

Without entering into any deeper terminological discussion, it should be noted that, in the Finnish context, the term 'applied art' (FI. *taideteollisuus*), which was previously used almost exclusively began to be replaced in the 1970s by the blanket term 'design' (FI. *muotoilu*), largely because of the emergence of industrial design. The term design has later been extended to older phenomena, making the terminology somewhat overlapping. The situation is similar in Sweden (*formgivning/design*) and Germany (*Formgebung/Design*). The word 'design' as an English loan is used universally – also in Finland. The terms 'applied art' and 'design' are used here depending on the period and context concerned.

What then is the subject of design history, especially in a concise general work? Our whole culturally shaped environment, from regional plans down to the items of the home, is explicitly designed. Today's design expertise ranges from papermaking machines to potholders. But looking at history we notice that many excellently designed devices and objects that make everyday life easier nonetheless have an anonymous background, without any information on who designed them. The designers were often without any training in the field. Although the numbers of design professionals have significantly grown over the past decades, our material and visual environment even today is only partly the work of professionals in design and applied art.

The design sector is always bounded by numerous broader factors, such as the economy, cultural policy and technological innovation. The results, the applied art and design of specific periods, depend on these external parameters. In addition, multi-disciplinarity and fragmentation are characteristic of the sector. The internal developments of different fields and the terms under which design and manufacturing have been pursued have differed considerably. The examples chosen here are intended to be historically illustrative and representative. The important bearing structures of applied art and design in Finland, and the public and private background forces that maintain them, necessarily remain without any detailed discussion.

A history of applied art and design in Finland will self-evidently include certain phenomena, objects and individuals. They outline in different ways what we regard to be representative and meritorious. It must be remembered, however, that in distinguishing phenomena from the flow of history, choices are made that are based on values bound to the author's culture and aims and, of course, his own time. The tension between a wealth of phenomena and a limited presentation leads to choices that may arouse discussion. The graphic design sector, which has a strong and varied impact on our everyday lives, is present only as briefly mentioned and as examples in the illustrations. The reason for this is that the wide scope and varied sectors of this field require a broader discussion which cannot be undertaken here. The same concerns fashion design. Digital data processing, which has fundamentally changed our lives, and its designed media world, are mentioned here only in passing.

Despite its concise manner of presentation I hope this book and its index will serve as an introduction to Finland's rich heritage of applied art and design. It is a solid basis for creating things to come.

This second edition of my book, which was originally published in 2009, is the product of collaboration between V&A Publishing, London, and Aalto ARTS Books, the publishing unit of Aalto University School of Arts, Design and Architecture, Helsinki.

PEKKA KORVENMAA
Helsinki, February 2014

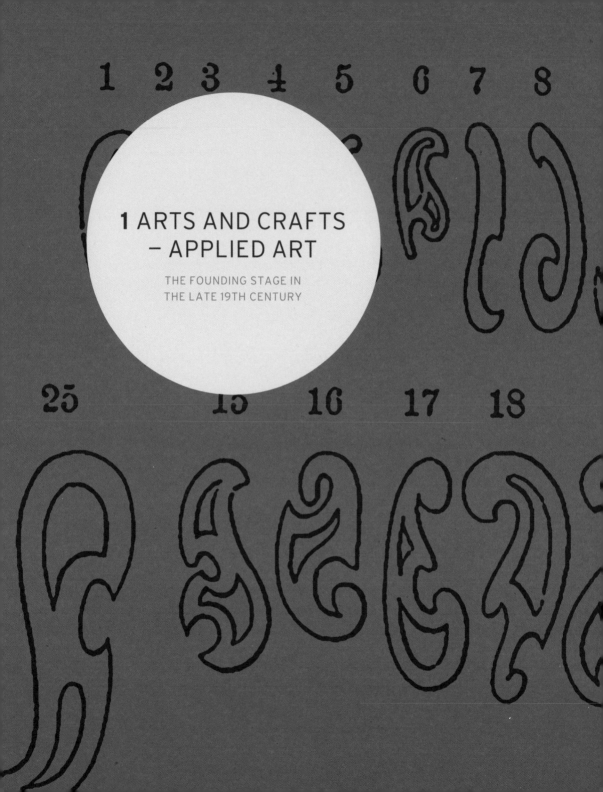

1 ARTS AND CRAFTS – APPLIED ART

THE FOUNDING STAGE IN THE LATE 19TH CENTURY

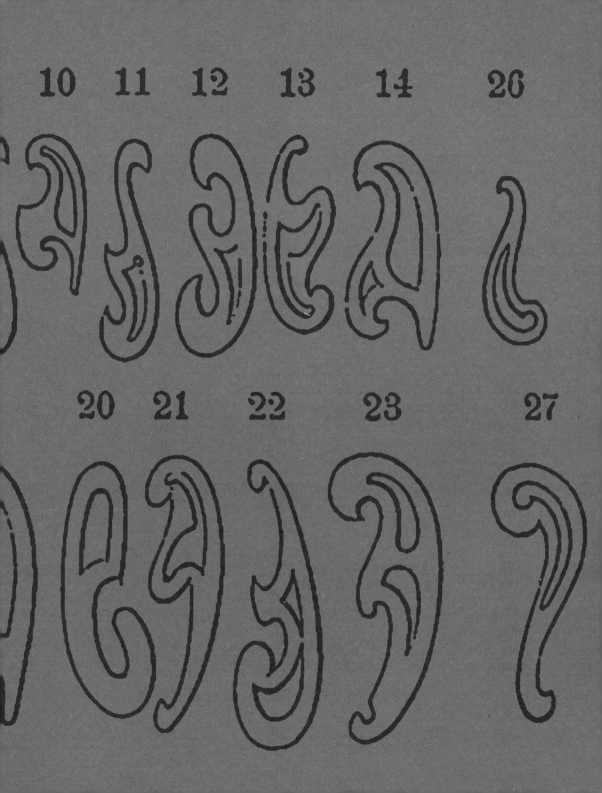

ARABIA
Helsingfors

| 1865 | 1874 | 1881 | 1887 |

The Grand Duchy of Finland is granted its own currency, the *markka* (mark)

The Arabia porcelain factory begins operations

Finland's first exhibition of applied art

Completion of the Ateneum building for the collections and schools of the Finnish Art Society and the Finnish Society of Crafts and Design

The founding stage of the applied arts in Finland is difficult to outline, because the products in question do not stand out from the past in the same way as the material culture of later years. For this reason, among others, the period is described mostly in terms of ideology, politics, industry and institutions rather than actual material results. The period's main views and positions on industry, applied art and competitiveness, however, live on. From time to time, they have dominated discussion and decisions concerning the raison d'être and future of the whole field of design

The history of Finland is conventionally divided into politically defined stages, due no doubt to the importance of separation from Sweden and incorporation into the Russian Empire in 1809, national independence in 1917 and the war years of 1939–1945. But where in the course of history did applied art begin to emerge? Does it have any distinct point of departure?

This book begins its account in the 1870s, the period when the institutions that were to be significant for the later evolution of applied art and design in Finland were established. This took place in the wake of recent industrialization and the resulting growth of the economy and international contacts. These institutions were involved with training, promoting the field, holding exhibitions and documentation. Their basis had been laid by the political and economic reforms of the previous decade. Official permission for steam-powered sawmills in 1857 opened the floodgates for the utilization of Finland's forest resources, soon followed by the emergence of the paper industry which was to be of prime importance for the country's exports. In 1865, Finland obtained its own currency, the Finnish *markka* (mark), which stabilized the economy and provided independence from the Russian rouble in both domestic and international trade. In the 1860s, Finnish was decreed the official language of the Grand Duchy of Finland alongside Swedish. This fanned rapidly growing patriotism that gained nationalist overtones within a few decades and would also give achievements in applied art a distinctive character. The developments of the 1870s were part of broader processes at the national level that had begun earlier, but it was only now that they also launched the development of applied art.

The Finnish word *taideteollisuus* (literally 'art industry' or 'the industry of art') translates into English as 'applied art' or 'industrial art'.[1] The literal meaning brings to mind industry utilizing artistic skills to improve the aesthetic and functional quality of products. In Finland, however, items of material culture produced in such a manner were exceptional in the late 19th century. Everyday implements and ornaments and even more valued items were hand-made, partly on an organized craft or cottage-industry basis. The crafts corporations, the heirs of the closely regulated guild system of the Middle Ages, were already disintegrating, but were not dissolved until freedom of occupations was legislated in 1879. Industrialization had begun rapidly and concerned sectors such as the production of groundwood pulp, which had no use for skills in the applied arts. As for products falling within applied or industrial art, such as the cotton fabrics of the Finlayson mills in Tampere, their patterns and designs came from abroad.[2] This situation continued for a long while.

Finland was a predominantly agricultural nation until the Second World War. In the late 19th century, it had only a small urban middle and upper class that would demand and, as consumers, pay for skills in applied art. The dominance of the countryside and the related hand-crafting of objects for household needs were the main factors creating items for everyday life and festive occasions until the twentieth century. Gradually, however, awareness and finally activities began to emerge for explicitly improve the quality of products, first handcrafted and later made in larger workshops and ultimately in factories.

Crafts and applied art products of the late 19th century, the actual world of objects and artefacts, do not generally meet the criteria by which later achievements were included in the canon of applied art, exhibitions and books. The qualities of originality, innovativeness, creation of style or aesthetic boldness hardly describe, for example, furniture design of the 1880s or the Arabia factory's tableware, which was produced in remarkable quantities.[3] Nonetheless, there were products that can be classed as applied art, partly industrial but mainly handcrafted, that were bought and used by consumers.

In the late 1860s Finland experienced catastrophic famines caused by several years of crop failure. This, too, speeded the efforts of the decision-making elite to develop rural livelihoods with the aid of crafts. At the same time, conditions began to be created to improve skills in the applied arts. From the late 1870s to the First World War, the applied arts sector was included in a process that almost trebled the gross national product of Finland. This meant increased consumer demand, in turn fuelling the need for both industrial and applied arts skills. These skills now had to be developed further through explicit training.

The beginning of systematic training

Training launched in 1871 was the most far-reaching and influential measure for developing the field in its early stages. In that year, the Craft School was founded, the predecessor of the University of Art and Design Helsinki. Training and education play key roles in the professional development of all fields. The Craft School[4] made it possible to create a system replacing the former crafts corporations with apprentices progressing through journeyman rank to the status of master craftsman.

Work along similar lines had begun earlier in the other Nordic countries. Sweden provided a template for Finland in this respect until the post-war years. Applied-art education had already begun in Sweden in 1844 and the Svenska Slöjdföreningen society (the predecessor of the Swedish Society of Industrial Design)[5] was founded a year later. Sweden abolished the crafts corporation system in 1846. In Finland the Finnish Society of Crafts and Design[6] was established in 1874 and the crafts corporations were officially dissolved in 1879.

Similar processes had taken place much earlier in more industrialized countries, such as England and France. The establishment of Finland's institutions of applied art followed examples from abroad. The Craft School was founded to serve industries, mainly on a handicraft and small-scale basis, making, among other products, furniture, tableware, wooden and metal utility objects, woven fabrics and ornamental objects. There was an obvious need to raise the quality of domestic manufactured goods, as was learned from the international exhibitions where Finnish products were also displayed.

A leading role in creating the system of training was played by Carl Gustaf Estlander (1834–1910),[7] Professor of Aesthetics at the University

— Käsityökoulu Helsingissä. Sittenkun asianomainen lupa on annettu käsityökoulun perustamiseksi tänne, tarkoituksella hankkia suurempaa taiteellisuutta käsityöläisillä ja tehtaissa työskentelewille, awataan tämä laitos ensi tammikuun 11 p:nä.

Opetusaineet owat: A. 1. Wiiwan ja pallonpiirrustus wapaalla kädellä; 2. Koristeenpiirrustus; 3. Kaunokirjoitus ja tekstaaminen; 4. Kuwion- ja maisemanpiirrustus; 5. Tawallinen ja koristeenmaalaus sekä 6. Mallitus. B. 1. Fysiiki ja Kemia; 2. Mittaustieteen muoto-oppi; 3. Lasku-oppi sekä 4. Kirjanpito. Lukutunnit owat maanantaina, tiistaina, keskiwiikkona, torstaina ja perjantaina kello 7—9 j. pp. sekä sunnuntaina kello 9—10 e. pp. Kansakoulun huoneissa Kasarmitorin warrella.

Kouluun pyrkiwältä waaditaan todistus siitä, että hän osaa lukea äitinkieltä, kirjoittaa wälttäwätä käsialaa sekä jokseenkin käyttää yksinkertaiset laskutawat, ynnä myöskin mainetodistus luotettawalta henkilöltä. Niiltä, jotka owat nauttineet opetusta toisessa koulussa tahi owat jäseniä käsityöläisten yhdistyksessä, waaditaan näiden laitosten antama todistus. Oppilaan tulee olla 13 wuotta täyttänyt. Opetuksesta maksaa kukin oppilas 50 penniä wiikossa.

Kouluun pyrkiwät ilmoittakoot itsensä koulun esimiehelle, tehtailija L. J. Källström, joka sitä warten on kotosella joka päiwä Joulun ja Uudenwuoden wälillä kello 5—7 j. pp. Helsingissä 17 p. joulukuuta 1870.

◄ Official announcement
issued on 24 December
1870 concerning the
launching of the future
Craft School in Helsinki.

of Helsinki and a central figure of Finland's art and applied arts community throughout the latter part of the 19th century. Together with other
influential cultural figures at the Finnish Art Society,[8] such as the author Zachris Topelius (1818–1898), he discussed ways of furthering the
issue of training. The Russian authorities soon granted permission for
the school and teaching could commence on the 11th January 1871. Together with his other analysis *Vid konstflitens härdar* (By the Hearths of
Craft) from 1875, his earlier writings from 1871 outlined the vision and
aims that would guide the field in the years to come.

As the future system of training was being drafted, the mutual relationship of the arts, craftsmanship and industry had to be addressed.
Estlander's ideal was a synthesis in which crafts and industry would
be "articized" – in other words refined through artistic skills. The arts
– i.e. painting and sculpture – should in turn humble themselves to
acknowledge the value of crafts. This would spread artistic skills among
broad sectors of the populace. The contemporary Finnish art world and
its institutions, however, were not ready to make any major concessions
towards what they regarded as the "lower arts". Nonetheless, art teaching was to play an important role in training in crafts and applied art at
the Craft School and its successors. Art education provided by the Finnish Art Society and training in the applied arts offered by the Finnish
Society of Crafts and Design remained separate even when both were
housed in the Ateneum building (built 1887).

In 1871, when the Craft School began its work, i.e. systematic training in crafts and applied art, it initially had 64 pupils. The teachers were
volunteers and instruction took place in the evenings. Before the Ateneum[9] was completed in 1887, the school was in rented premises. Both
its curriculum and enrolment grew quickly and by the 1880s it had up
to 171 students, over 70 of whom were women. Although the large proportion of women seems completely natural today, it was no means
typical in Finland at the time. As noted by Kerstin Smeds (1999), this new
sector was not burdened, even from the outset, by the genderized conventions that applied to previously established areas of education and
divisions of labour.[10]

Initially established to guide and support the poorly equipped Craft School, the Finnish Society of Crafts and Design took control of it. These two central institutions of applied art and design, which are still active today, thus began their work, one in training and the other in promoting the field in general. Dating from the establishment of institutions in the 1870s is today's Design Museum (formerly the Museum of Applied Arts).[11] Its primary task was to serve the teaching of the Craft School with displays of foreign products of crafts and applied art that were considered exemplary. At present, we understand museum activities to mean the display of collections telling us about the past. In the applied arts, museums originally served the educational use of presenting the best examples of the contemporary world of artefacts. This was the underlying idea of the Victoria & Albert Museum of London, among other institutions.

The Craft School became the Central School of Arts and Crafts in 1886 with a regularly revised curriculum and a wider range of subjects. The architect Armas Lindgren (1874–1929),[12] of the renowned Gesellius (1874–1916), Lindgren, Saarinen office of architects, began work as the school's first Artistic Director in 1902, when the curriculum was revised and A.W. Finch (1854–1930),[13] originally of Belgium, began to teach ceramic art. By this time the school had some 600 students.

The introduction and consolidation of professionalism
The school was headed by architects for many years. In 1912, Lindgren was succeeded as artistic director by the architect Rafael Blomstedt (1885–1950).[14] Werner von Essen (1875–1947),[15] also an architect, began his long period of service as the head of the school in 1915. The leading role of architects continued with minor exceptions until the 1970s. This involved both the clientele of professional skills in applied art and the hierarchy of the arts. For many years major public and private building projects were a major source of employment for professionals in crafts and the applied arts. Moreover, the cultural and social status of architects was clearly higher than that of professionals in applied art. Although the education of architects began in Finland around the same time as training in arts and crafts, it could benefit from being part of training in engineering, whereby it gained the status of tertiary education as early as 1908.

Architects had been active for a long while in applied art and design, especially as designers of furniture and lamps.

The deepening scope and expansion of training from its modest beginnings in the 1870s to the broad and high-standard curriculum of the 1910s led to professionalism in crafts and applied art. Signs of professional distinction are organizations specific to individual fields and a trade press. In 1911 Finnish professionals in arts and crafts were among the first in the world to establish their own professional and ideological association, originally called the Ornamo Association of Ornamental Artists – the present-day Finnish Association of Designers Ornamo.[16] Several magazines on crafts, applied art, design and interior decoration began to appear already in the early 1900s. In the background of these developments were a long economic boom and a marked process of urbanization. The new building stock created a demand for both objects for home interiors and the finishing of buildings by craftsmen. By the First World War, several public building projects of national importance had been completed, such as the Ateneum, the House of the Estates, the National Theatre and the National Museum in Helsinki and numerous churches, all of which provided work for craftsmen. For a long while, however, individuals trained in crafts and applied art realized the ideas of others, often architects, rather than working as independent designers in their fields.

Discussion on the relationship of art and craftsmanship

The most visible and permanent achievement in establishing the field of applied arts in the late 19th century was the Ateneum building, inaugurated in 1887. Discussion of the purpose of the building, its complement of space and facilities, and the building itself, with its elaborate decorative programme and works of sculpture, had crystallized the will and means of the Grand Duchy of Finland, now in the process of industrialization, to provide an impressive setting for education and exhibitions in the applied and fine arts. Although the path to realizing this project was partly contradictory and full of compromises, the importance of the Ateneum building then and now cannot be underestimated. The Ateneum bears permanent witness to purpose and commitment unparalleled later in the independent republic of Finland at least in applied arts and design.

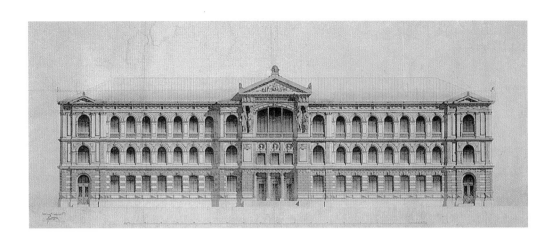

The nature of the planned building had been discussed since the 1860s and a central issue was the relationship, separateness and coexistence of the fine arts with crafts and applied art. The different camps of the discussion were represented by the Finnish Art Society and the Finnish Artists Association on the one hand and the Finnish Society of Crafts and Design on the other. Estlander desired the unity of all arts and crafts in training. Shared training in the initial stage would then lead to either the fine or the applied arts. Practitioners of either domain would have a shared understanding of the role of skilled craftsmanship in the fine arts. After prolonged disputes and political manoeuvring a joint building project was chosen instead of a separate art academy and school of applied art. The leading architect of the time, Theodor Höijer (1843–1910)[17] was commissioned in 1882 to design the Ateneum. Permission to build was granted by the Emperor of Russia in 1885, and two years later the building was completed. The agreement – or compromise – that was ultimately achieved is also expressed in the motto on the building's façade: "Concordia res parvae crescunt" – in concord even minor things will grow.

The Ateneum expressed the growing significance of the field of applied arts and training in it. But as noted by Pekka Suhonen,[18] it also reflects the ideological trends and views of the industrial policies of its day. Finnish industry and its further development through the applied arts was a cause that was dear especially to liberal and internationally oriented circles in Helsinki. Strengthening domestic industries was also a patriotic activity linked to the objectives of export policies aimed at increasing national wealth. Modern economic life, which was enriched by the applied arts, embodied a new kind of patriotism aimed at the future. Home industries involving craftsmanship were regarded as the task of the inland regions and the countryside.

Tensions between the international and the domestic prerogatives and manufacturing for export and the home market respectively would define training in applied arts and craftsmanship and its political interests until the end of the 20th century. The late 19th century thus created the situation on which discourse in the field, in its various forms, was to be based for the century to come.

Exhibitions as a measure of quality

In the late 19th century international exhibitions became a permanent means for the applied arts in Finland to build international momentum and to present the county's own achievements. These "showcases of the nations" held at regular intervals in different parts of the Western world became prime occasions for countries to display the achievements of their industries and applied arts. Finnish applied arts circles visited these exhibitions, gathering influences and reporting to decision-makers in Finland. In most cases it was observed that the quality of Finnish products could be greatly improved.

These comparisons provided impetus, among other things, for Estlander's wide range of activities. Finland was to earn its place among the civilized Western nations in applied arts. Although this small and relatively poor part of the Russian Empire had been granted autonomy, it was still a minor actor on the international arena, without political independence. As a whole, efforts to develop the country, which began in the late 19th century and led to national independence in 1917, had the aim of evolving into a nation by creating national institutions, culture, education and the economy – with the applied arts as part of it. Neither then nor later could Finland compete in terms of quantity, only in quality, which was specifically gauged at the world expositions.

International exhibitions, such as the Vienna World's Fair of 1873[19] which was of importance for the applied arts, provided objects regarded as exemplary for the teaching collection of the Museum of Applied Arts. This allowed students, whose opportunities to travel abroad were limited, to study artefacts, which could be copied and adapted to keep teaching abreast of international trends.

The exhibitions also permitted Finnish industries and craftspeople to display their products. Individual companies and exhibitors could participate as part of a larger national entity, once they were chosen by the exhibition committee. Works by students of the Craft School were also on display in the exhibitions. Finland participated in, among others, the Paris World's Fairs of 1878 and 1889, and most successfully in 1900[20] in Paris – although the latter occasion was not only a display of Finnish industries but also a cultural and political effort.

◀ Interior view of an exhibition of Finnish industries held in Kaivopuisto Park in Helsinki in 1876. This exhibition demonstrated the industrial and technological progress that the applied arts and recently launched education in this field were intended to support.

▶ Finland's first exhibition of applied arts was held in 1881. The exhibits were mainly related to high-standard home interiors and were in revived historical styles.

These major exhibitions displayed an immense array of objects, and the venues were of considerable size. They were not exhibitions of applied arts, nor did the departments of the various countries explicitly showcase items of a related character. Exhibits ranged from steam engines to tableware – or wooden spoons as in the Finnish department at the Paris World's Fair of 1889.[21] The important consideration was the quality of the products as such. In handcrafted artefacts, the skills of craftsmanship and applied art rather than individual expression were evident in the execution of pieces. When the Arabia Porcelain Factory of Helsinki displayed its products in Paris in 1878, they did not differ in any way from the mainstream in form or decoration. On the contrary, the factory sought the same results as the European centres of the industry. Towards the end of the century, the styles reflect a distinct national character, often adapted from ethnographic material. This was particularly the case with woven textiles. An important aspect of Finn-

Konstindustriutställningen i Helsingfors 1881
N:o 11.

ish applied arts was to be the objective of creating something national and characteristic for display on the international scene.

Exhibitions were also important at the national level. In 1875 an exhibition of home industries and crafts[22] was staged in Helsinki. But it was not until the General Finnish Exposition,[23] an industrial exhibition held in the following year, that broad public interest was generated and large numbers of people attended. Held in Helsinki's Kaivopuisto Park in a large wooden pavilion designed by Theodor Höijer, it featured a large selection of exhibits and permitted the public to see domestic products in particular and to draw conclusions regarding their quality. Reactions were not consistently positive: training in the applied arts had begun in the same decade, and its results could not be enjoyed until later.

The exposition was followed by an exhibition devoted to the applied arts in 1881 in Helsinki. [24] It focused on handcrafted products such as furniture and ornamental objects and was dominated by revived historical styles alluding to the Renaissance, Baroque and Rococo. The applied arts in Finland have often been described as having emerged from developing an original "Finnish" form of expression. This, however, was not the case. The overwhelming majority of objects that can be classified as the applied art of the late 19th century were based on adaptations of leading historical styles created in accordance with international examples. But even so the quality of work in the applied arts – or arts and crafts – improved. Independent expression regarded as national and distinctive was to come later. But even at this stage, the turn of the 19th and 20th centuries, the leading role was taken by artists and architects and not by graduates of the Craft School or the subsequent Central School of Arts and Crafts.

National designs and patterns – a Finnish style?

The actors promoting training, work to develop the field, collections and exhibitions, rarely addressed any ideological, symbolic or stylistic content that applied art or industrial products might have. Instead, these aspects were underscored by the Friends of Finnish Handicraft,[25] founded in 1879. Its work was to be marked by the promotion of general crafts skills and the culture of crafts and the aim of creating a world of

▶ Founded in 1897 and still operating, the Friends of Finnish Handicraft began to produce woven fabrics with designs and patterns based on vernacular textile ornament from Finland and Karelia in particular.

forms adapting and reforming the vernacular tradition that could be understood as national, Finnish, in terms of content.

Fanny Churberg (1845–1892)[26] was one of the charter members of the Society and its leading figure until her death. She rejected her former career as a renowned painter and concentrated for the rest of her life on creating a national style, with woven textiles in particular as her medium. Appreciation of national motifs and their adaptation to contemporary needs, for which Churberg and the Friends of Finnish Handicraft campaigned, were associated with the so-called national awakening that had emerged earlier. The cultural and literary symbol and flagship of the nationalist ideology that it engendered was the *Kalevala*[27] folk poetry epic, originally published in 1835. Now, the impulses of the heritage of vernacular material culture became involved. Its most prominent re-interpretations were to be created in the 1890s and around the turn of the century.

The Friends of Finnish Handicraft first began to copy "ancient Finnish" and mainly East Finnish, Karelian, motifs. In this respect, it opened the way for the Karelianism[28] that made a deep imprint on cultural life in Finland towards the end of the century. Copies gradually made way for new interpretations, combining folk heritage with the latest trends in applied art. In Europe the use of national material regarded as "authentic" characterized architecture and the applied arts on a broad scale around the turn of the century, not only in Scandinavia but also in countries such as Hungary and even Poland. Not only activating the topical use of heritage, the Friends of Finnish Handicraft introduced internal competition and debate into the Finnish applied arts community. The society's handicrafts products were also well received in national and international exhibitions. The successful products were especially those whose design differed from prevailing international counterparts. As an agent of creating and reforming style, the society took the role that could have been assumed for the Central School of Arts and Crafts. In the 1890s the School still concentrated on crafts skills, acquired through copying examples, rather than developing independent expression.

Munakori.

Ovikyltti.

Parsaheinasäilytin.

Pesukaapin laakoja.

A-malli.

B-malli.

C-malli.

D-malli.

Purkkeja.
Apteekkipurkki.

Hillopurkki.

A-malli.

B-malli.

Pönttö.

B-malli.

Rasioita.
Hammasharjarasia.

B-malli.

N-malli.

O-malli.

Saippuarasia.

B-malli.

F-malli.

G-malli.

H-malli.

◄ ▶ The 1893 catalogue of the Arabia factory points to the long-standing importance of household and sanitary ceramics in the company's product line. This aspect of applied art and design has been overshadowed by products displayed in museum collections and exhibitions. On the right, a tableware service from 1920s with decoration by Thure Öberg portrays castles of Finland, thus continuing the patriotic themes established already in the late 19th century.

The quest for the "Finnish", national, style that was regarded as important remained the task of visual artists and architects in the 1890s. Some of them were of foreign background. Moreover, this "Finnishness" was not achieved until the latest international currents were incorporated as part of the national project. This way of merging the most recent international motifs into the applied arts of Finland and presenting them successfully in the international context as something "Finnish" would remain a permanent factor of success for the field in Finland.

In histories of culture and the arts in Finland the period from the early 1890s to the early 1900s has, in retrospect, come to be called a "golden age". The flourishing of the arts in these years and the quality of achievement are obvious. The nationalism that fuelled the overall mood and the growth of the economy as a background factor fostered innovation. There was a desire for something that would permit a cultural distinction with regard to the metropolises of east and west alike, in between Stockholm and St. Petersburg, while presenting the original and progressive character of the Grand Duchy of Finland to Continental Europe. The applied arts also played a role in this process. Many of the artefacts and interior designs that have now achieved iconic status were created in these years.

THE FINNISH PAVILION AT THE PARIS WORLD'S FAIR OF 1900

The competition held in 1898 for the design of the Finnish Pavilion at the Paris World's Fair was won by the office of the young architects Herman Gesellius, Armas Lindgren and Eliel Saarinen. Their project combined adapted medieval Finnish motifs with the latest trends in architecture. The pavilion was positively received, with an exterior displaying motifs of Finnish flora and fauna, such as bears and squirrels, framing the entrance. The exhibits and visual material of the interior portrayed the industries and culture of Finland. Applied art was mainly present through works of handicraft, because mass-produced items, such as the products of the Arabia factory, were in a separate hall of industrial exhibits. The greatest interest was aroused by the so-called Iris Room in the semi-circular end of the pavilion. The furniture of the room was designed by Axel Gallén, as were also the textiles woven by the Friends of Finnish Handicraft. Placed on the mantelpiece of the stove made by the Iris company and the shelves of the room were ceramics designed by A. W. Finch and also made by Iris. Like the architecture of the pavilion, the interior combined motifs regarded as national, such as bare wooden surfaces and the ryijy textile technique with a contemporary idiom of form interpreted in an individual manner.

1

1. The pavilion resembled a masonry building but was mainly built of wood.

2. The main entrances were framed with steatite friezes of animal motifs.

3. & 5. The Iris Room, with furniture and textiles designed by Axel Gallén, ceramics by A. W. Finch. The Friends of Finnish Handicraft later made several replica versions of the *Liekki* (Flame) ryijy weave covering the wall, bench and floor.

4. The main vaulted interior space of the pavilion contained paintings by Axel Gallén of subjects from the *Kalevala*.

3

4

5

2 INTERNATIONAL
ON A NATIONAL BASIS

THE COLLABORATION OF THE ARTS

·TUVA·

SISUSTA.

1900

1902

1903

1911

1917

The Paris World's
Fair

The teaching of ce-
ramic art begins at
the Central School
of Arts and Crafts

Completion of the
Hvitträsk studio
and residential
complex

Founding of the
Ornamo Associa-
tion of Ornamen-
tal Artists

The Russian revo-
lution, Finnish in-
dependence

The quest for a national form of expression gained pace towards the turn of the 20th century. In the background were the aims of the Romanov empire to curtail the autonomy of the Grand Duchy of Finland. As public political activities were banned, culture became a channel for emerging nationalism.

Finnish architecture and applied art were now involved in currents of reform that had emerged in various parts of Europe in the 1890s. Among these trends, Central European Art Nouveau became mixed with influences from the British Arts and Crafts movement. In Finland, these international orientations merged with so-called Karelianism and the strong interest of the young artistic generation in the world of the *Kalevala* epic and monuments of the Middle Ages.

The contemporary conception of the arts underlined their unity, implying that the visual arts, architecture and handicraft were to be synthesized into comprehensive and stylistically coherent entities. In this atmosphere, emphasizing the collaboration and equality of genres, applied art rose to accompany the visual arts and architecture in a more complete way than before, now as part of high culture. Alongside the considerations of benefits for livelihoods and industries that had been presented in such an emphasized manner before, there was now focus on the "art" of "applied art". At the same time, individuals emerged who were instrumental to reforms in the field. They had not been trained in the applied arts, or if they had such training it had not been acquired in Finland. The personification of works in terms of their authors, which was established practice in architecture and the visual arts, was now followed in applied art.

Folklore merging with international trends

As mentioned above, the Friends of Finnish Handicraft first began to copy and later to adapt embroidery and woven designs mainly originating from Karelia. Karelianism, i.e. enthusiasm for the "authenticity" of the traditions of vernacular architecture and material culture of East Karelia, on the Russian side of the border, was one of the main sources for those seeking the elements of a "Finnish" style in the 1890s. This was interspersed with broader interest in the country's historical, mainly me-

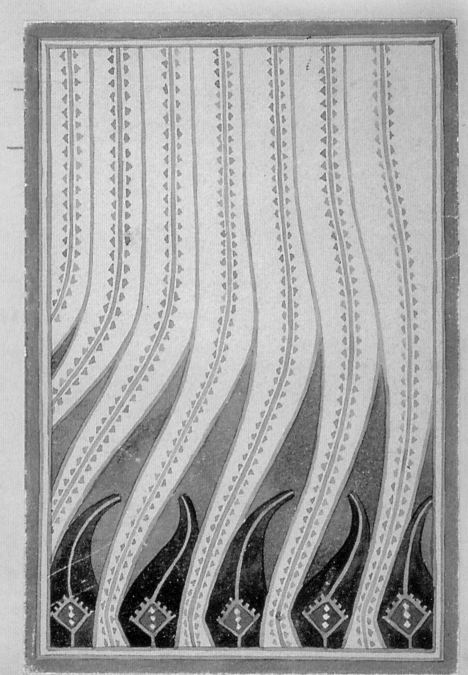

Kopia eft. A. Galléa.   Gewebt in Nr. 2.

Grösse 180 cm × 350 cm Preis...

dieval but also vernacular, architecture and material culture. The trailblazers were leading architects and artists of the young generation, especially Axel Gallén (later Gallen-Kallela) (1865–1931).[29] At the same time there was awareness of the achievements and principles of the British Arts and Crafts movement. They were presented in publications such as *The Studio*, which was avidly read in Finland. Many of the goals of the movement were excellently suited to the needs of high culture as new inspiration was sought for shaping the architectural and material culture of wood, employing simple forms.

Axel Gallén was one of the leading names of the 1890s in a movement freely combining real folklore and a mythologized and *Kalevala*-inspired ancient Finnish past with international orientations. This trend produced works that have gained a central role in the history of Finnish art. While Gallén's main area was of course visual art, his wilderness studio and home, Kalela, which he had designed for himself in 1894, and its interior, also pointed the way for architecture and handicraft of the end of the century. This building corresponded to the principles of the Arts and Crafts movement while freely interpreting vernacular log architecture. It also included a few carved ornamental figures that reflected a primitivist exoticized approach. Gallén also experimented with the applied arts in the symbolist spirit of the period, making small objects, including a cupboard, and later small stained-glass works with lead frames.

Expression regarded as Finnish was mainly based on the effects of the texture and structure of timber. Further influences were sought from regionalism drawing upon the folk tradition and a romanticized concept of national history. Towards the end of the 1890s these ideas merged with the new Continental European currents of reform that were known under the umbrella term of Art Nouveau. This Belgian-French style was soon joined by movements developing across Europe, such as Jugendstil in Germany, Viennese modernism and Charles Rennie Mackintosh's (1868–1928) own iteration of the style in Glasgow. They all provided influences for Finnish art, architecture and applied arts, which now interacted more than before with the international scene. A new feature was also the fact that this exchange increasingly worked

in two directions. Finland was no longer a passively receptive province but a kind of miniature centre whose achievements interested the international field to a growing degree.

The contemporary conception of art underscored the collaboration of the arts and the artist as a multi-skilled individual. Gallén began his career in oil painting, but went on to printed graphics, woodblock work, architecture and applied art. The architect Eliel Saarinen (1873–1950)[30] painted in oils and designed furniture. Alfred William Finch (1854–1930), a Belgian representative of avant-garde visual art who moved to Finland and spent the rest of his career here, shifted his focus to ceramic art, while the Swedish painter Louis Sparre (1863–1964),[31] who worked in Finland for fifteen years, became a designer of furniture and interiors. In 1897, Finch, Sparre and the latter's wife Eva Mannerheim-Sparre (1870–

▲ The *Koti* chair designed in 1898 by Eliel Saarinen. The backrest contains motifs from the vernacular wooden architecture of East Karelia. This chair sought to capture the "Finnish style" that was regarded as central to the period.

1957)[32] established the Iris company[33] specializing in applied arts. Iris opened its salesroom in Helsinki in the same year, offering the latest achievements of modern international applied art. The company had a furniture and ceramics factory in the town of Porvoo east of Helsinki. Iris also provided complete interior designs, for which there was demand in the nearby metropolis of St. Petersburg. The Iris company followed an uncompromisingly modern and international line but was unable to generate a sufficiently large Finnish clientele. Although Iris was discontinued in 1902, the Sparres continued to design and make furniture until 1908.

Iris is a good example of how a few members of the artistic elite with a broad-minded international attitude and enthusiasm could establish an applied arts enterprise of high standard. The line followed by Iris,

however, did not sufficiently inspire the middle- and upper-class matrons who decided what was to be bought for their homes. Finch's unique ceramics of simple design required aesthetic expertise in order to be appreciated and these products could not compete with the Arabia factory's tableware with its traditional floral motifs. Even Helsinki could not provide a so-called critical mass of sufficient size, an affluent clientele versed in modern applied art that could be found in metropolises such as Vienna, who would have been the precondition for the success of a company of this kind. Something similar, but more enduring, was not achieved until some forty years later when the Artek[34] company was launched.

Breakthrough in Paris in 1900

In its own day and in later writings the Finnish pavilion at the Paris World's Fair of 1900 has been regarded as an epoch-making display of Finnish architecture, fine art and applied art, and as their international breakthrough. It is hard to overestimate the national and international importance of the pavilion. Designed by the young architects Herman Gesellius,[35] Armas Lindgren and Eliel Saarinen, the pavilion freely combined medieval themes with the most recent international trends. The nation's leading names in their respective fields participated in the artistic finishing work of the building, its interior decoration and the design and execution of the exhibits. The pavilion was intended as a framework of information on the industries, educational pursuits and culture of the small Grand Duchy of Finland, now under Russian political oppression, and its artworks and applied art made a deep impression on visitors and the experts who wrote about the exhibition.

In later years the pavilion and its department of applied art have been mentioned as a kind of leading example of innovation and a special regional, i.e. Finnish, quality. Finland had participated with its own pavilion in the previous Paris World's Fair in 1889, but without any exalted overtones. How could have the exhibited works of applied art have achieved the "originality" that they lacked a decade earlier – assuming that they had ever striven for it?

The display in Paris was a culmination of the developments of the 1890s. It would also provide impetus for some of the best achievements of the early 20th century. A similar effect was had by later success in international exhibitions of applied art and design in the 1950s, the second "golden age" of Finnish design. Firstly, the whole Finnish art world had become international in the 1890s, while, paradoxically, taking on a national identity. It was precisely this combination of national and international that spurred reforms in the visual arts, architecture and the applied arts, as well as other cultural domains, such as literature and the music of Jean Sibelius (1865–1957). These were the successful tactics of a culturally peripheral country, whereby it utilized the ideas of major centres that created style while avoiding provincial plagiarism. Skilled individuals and the economic and cultural structures on which they relied were able to create an internationally distinctive quality to the works.

The 1900 World's Fair pavilion leads the way

The activation of art, architecture and applied art that took place and the emergence of younger generations in the 1890s came to fruition in the Finnish pavilion at the Paris World's Fair of 1900. Combining the Middle Ages with the latest trends, the exterior had motifs taken directly from the Finnish countryside, such as squirrels, pine cones and bears. Inside, on the vaulting under the high central dome were Axel Gallén's famous paintings of subjects from the *Kalevala* epic.

This time, the main exhibits of the Finnish pavilion were not mass-produced items of applied art, such as Arabia tableware, which were on show in another part of the exposition. Arts and crafts, however, had a visible presence in many ways. The exhibitors included the Friends of Finnish Handicraft and the Central School of Arts and Crafts. In 1898, when an architectural competition was held for the Finnish pavilion, there was also a competition for the design of a suite of furniture in a Finnish style. The furniture of the winning design, by Eliel Saarinen, was also on display in the pavilion. The so-called Iris Room[36] at the end of the building received the greatest amount of attention both from contemporaries and in later histories of design. It was a total interior design prepared by Gallén in association with the Iris factory of Porvoo and the Friends of Finnish Handicraft association, which was responsible for the textiles. The furniture by Gallén with its feel for wood as a material and the *Liekki* (Flame) ryijy (piled weave) with its fern motif ,along with ceramic art, textiles of highly simplified design by Albert Finch and the ceramic kiln of the Iris factory created a successful synthesis. This combination of themes, forms and materials that were of Finnish origin while internationally topical was felt to be something of both new and local, i.e. Finnish, character.

Although these works were created by architects and visual artists instead of professionals in the applied arts, this did not reduce the influence and appeal of the results for the international public and the future development of applied art and design in Finland. The pavilion also promoted the integration of the applied arts as part of the art world, an area offering room for individual artistic expression no less than the other arts. This introduced a new dimension for the utilitarian aims of the late 19th century, which were associated with industrial policies and underlined skills in applied art as a factor in adding value to objects. One of the overriding themes of later applied art in Finland, related discussion and exhibitions was to be the coexistence and tensions of crafted objects made as unique, one-off pieces or in small editions in relation to industrially manufactured products. The finishing work of the Iris Room with its emphasis on natural materials and the far-reaching simplification of the design would markedly define what was to be felt to be authentic, correct and Finnish.

Towards a unity of style

Success at the Paris World's Fair demonstrated the possibilities of distinctively original art and crafts and how architecture, furniture and other interior design objects could operate in concert when aiming at results of an aesthetically comprehensive nature. This approach found support in the international stylistic climate of the turn of the century and the early 1900s. Art Nouveau and *Jugendstil* underscored the way in which the variety of materials, forms and colour, extending from architecture to the small items of the home, was to be subordinate to a uni-

fied objective of style. It was in this manner that the 19th-century eclectic principle, employing the layers of history and leading to a stratification of styles in interior decoration was rejected. The quest for new form, liberated from history, provided opportunities for an individual approach. On the other hand, the aims of unity and harmonization could limit furniture, textiles and ornamental objects to serve only as an accompaniment to the whole, thus eroding their artistic individuality and the interest aroused by it.

In the early 20th century the creation of complete entities was specifically the task of architects, who could extend their design of the material world from town plans to buildings and their interior space and artefacts. The architectural profession also felt this to be the goal of professional identity. This trait became a permanent aspect of architectural professionalism in Finland – a later example being Alvar Aalto (1898–1976).[37]

The role of architects in the applied arts in early 20th-century Finland, as stressed here, does not exclude the growing significance of graduates from the Central School of Arts and Crafts. The fact remains, however, that it was not until the 1910s that a broader group of independent domestically trained design professionals began to emerge. An example of earlier training is Eric O.W. Ehrström (1881–1934),[38] an important ornamental artist of the early 20th century who was particularly known for his embossed and chased metalwork. In addition to collaborating with many of the leading architects of the period, Ehrström was also an independent designer and manufacturer. He had attended the school of the Finnish Art Society, trained as an apprentice with Gallén at Kalela, the latter's studio and home at Ruovesi, and completed his studies in Paris. Ehrström achieved professional competence in arts and crafts in addition to artistic independence and status. This gave him a place in the design teams of buildings and their interiors – not just as someone who executed the designs of architects.

The situation described above began to change as instruction diversified and specialized at the Central School of Arts and Crafts. In 1902 the architect Armas Lindgren became the school's Artistic Director, a newly established position. In the same year, Albert Finch, who had become unemployed following the discontinuation of the Iris company, began to teach ceramic art at the school. The teaching of furniture design began in 1909. This meant that by the mid-1910s a group of furniture designers with training in the applied arts was evolving and was to emerge soon alongside architects. Partly fanned by success at the Paris World's Fair of 1900 and partly because of artistically based views, the training gained an increasingly artistic emphasis, in which decorative art gradually superseded considerations of utility. A direct result of this emphasis in education was the founding of the Ornamo association of ornamental artists in 1911. This association would later become a unifying factor among professionals in the applied arts. As noted by Smeds,[39] the long-term emphasis on decorative art in teaching separated the school and its graduates from the overall improvement of quality in industry and crafts that had been emphasized when the school was founded – i.e. "utility art". Nonetheless, this laid the basis for the international success of Finnish applied art or arts and crafts that began in the 1930s.

The new collaboration of architecture and applied art

The demand and provision of applied art always depend on economic trends. The boom that began in the mid-1890s and even gained pace in the 1910s, created affluence that the middle and upper classes could also direct towards applied art, in both interior design and decorative art. The home was where some of the most ambitious entities of architecture and applied art were realized. It was a space in which the educated and wealthy bourgeoisie of the younger generation met professionally aesthetic ambition.

In early 20th-century Finland, the influence of the Arts and Crafts movement and new English applied art and interior decoration combined with other Continental European trends such as Art Nouveau. Finnish architecture and applied art in Finland were distinctively regional while at the same time markedly oriented towards achieving something that was internationally new and unprecedented. This situation proved to be positive for experiments and the innovative skill of architects and the artisans who supported them. These skills resulted in a few private environments that were exceptional in the Finnish context, with

▶ Louis Sparre's work in design also contained references to a simple vernacular language of form. Shown left is furniture designed for the building of the Students Union of the University of Helsinki, published in 1902 in *Kotitaide*, a magazine that presented new interior decoration.

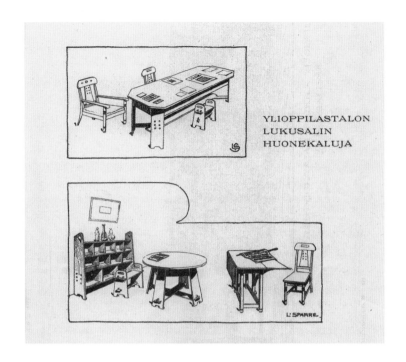

YLIOPPILASTALON
LUKUSALIN
HUONEKALUJA

seamless entities of architectural design, interior fixtures, furniture, other objects and decoration. The most brilliant examples include Hvitträsk (1903)[40] at Kirkkonummi in South Finland and the main building of Suur-Merijoki Manor (1903)[41] near Viipuri. Both were designed by the architects Gesellius, Lindgren and Saarinen. Hvitträsk was their combined working and living environment, where all three architects lived with their families. These works had been preceded by the architect trio's apartment buildings in Helsinki from the early 1900s. Urban apartments sought a new way of organizing middle-class family living. A new aspect was emphasis on the family connection instead of the previously underlined requirements of representation. All these works were clearly marked by arts and crafts combined with architecture.

Aims merging contemporary considerations of reform, aesthetics and the social aspects of habitation and the home also had considerable impact on the applied arts. They marked the beginning of a movement that was to influence the design of homes in the 1930s and even in the post-war period. The writings of the Swedish reformer Ellen Key (1849–1926) on social and aesthetic issues and the position of children were read widely. They were reflected in the design of the Saarinen family's nursery room at Hvitträsk in Finland and in the design of Frank Lloyd Wright's (1867–1959) home and studio in Chicago. In their ambitious aims and scale, Hvitträsk and Suur-Merijoki were magnificent exceptions. Their objectives were present in smaller scale in villa communities built in the environs of Helsinki after the beginning of the 20th century. Young members of the middle class moved to communities such as Kulosaari [42] and Kauniainen to enjoy a way of life defined by a close connection with nature, privacy and an aesthetically complete personal home.

Private milieux employing a large amount of craftsmanship were expensive exceptions. On the average, objects of applied art in homes did not consist of separately ordered furniture and textiles. Instead, such items were bought ready-made. Early 20th-century public architectural projects, however, favoured sumptuous craftsmanship in both the exteriors and interiors of buildings. Since the architecture of the period had rejected historical examples, the briefs for decorating buildings and their details had to be generated independently. Pre-existing motifs, such as the Renaissance features of previous decades, were no longer permissible. Nonetheless, studies at the Central School of Arts and Crafts involved the copying of precisely these motifs. New themes and motifs included nature, animals and pure fantasy. Churches, bank premises and the head offices of insurance companies involving a great deal of craftsmanship – such as carving, textile work, embossing and decorative painting – were demanding yet rewarding projects, because considerable sums of money were invested in their hand-crafted finishing work. They raised the standard of requirements in the field and provided demand for entrepreneurs specializing in this work, such as Salomo Wuorio's (1857–1938) [43] and Carl Slotte's (1878–1946) decorative painting firms.

In most cases, the architect of a building would also prepare a plan for its decoration to be carried out by craftsmen. In some cases, as for exam-

▲ The main hall of the Privatbanken bank in Helsinki designed by Lars Sonck, 1904.
The scheme of decoration,
employing several materials,
such as granite, steatite and
wood, and techniques in-
cluding fresco painting and
glass mosaic work was by the
architect Valter Jung. This
project is an example of how
positive economic trends
of the early 1900s together
with the work of professionals in architecture, decorative art and crafts could
create total works of art that
were of even international
significance.

ple in the Privatbanken bank project (1904) in Helsinki its architect, Lars Sonck (1870–1956)[44] collaborated with another architect, Valter Jung (1879–1946)[45] in the plan for the decoration. The artisan and craftsman Eric O.W. Ehrström, in turn, designed and realized some of the period's most significant works in metal, such as the outer doors of the Pohjois-maiden Osakepankki bank building in Helsinki. Sculptors were also employed in the decoration of buildings. The male figures flanking the main entrance to the Helsinki Railway Station were designed by the sculptor Emil Wikström (1864–1942).[46] Unlike in the late 19th century, markedly stylized sculpture was now made an integral part of the actual building.

Early 20th-century architecture provided a rich area of work with innovative briefs of visual elements and motifs for design in the applied arts, and for executing these designs. The decoration of the exterior and inner surfaces of buildings, the furniture of spaces and other moveable items were included in this area. Arts and crafts flourished in this period, when the preferences of clients and their desire to invest combined with the skills of designers and the quality of execution to produce numerous integrated works that are still regarded as exemplary. This situation prevailed until the mid-1910s, after which ornament became more abstract and limited. At the same time, features from the strata of style history once again began to be adapted for decoration and furniture. Recourse was first made to the Biedermeier style, followed by Baroque and finally by Antiquity and Neo-Classicism. A classicizing approach was to significantly characterize architecture, furniture design and other applied art during the following decade.

A mainstream of anonymous products

Economic growth, which had maintained a brisk pace of building and consumer demand continued during the First World War, to end in the Russian Revolution of 1917, the closing of the eastern border and finally the traumatizing Finnish civil war of 1918 that followed in the wake of independence gained in December 1917. A rising trend of some two decades that had promoted the applied arts in many ways now came to an end. After this, the leading names of the period no longer had the same presence as before.

The applied arts had been involved in the major social and cultural effort with which national identity and even international awareness of Finland had been created. Originally a utopian aim, national independence had been gained in the chaotic late stages of the First World War.

Apart from the prime examples, we know less about general applied-art and hand-crafted production during the period, the contemporary business world, channels of distribution or consumption. Finland was still a predominantly rural nation with a modest overall standard of living. The degree of urbanization was low, although cities like Helsinki, the capital, began to grow rapidly in the late 19th century. But even Helsinki had a population of only 170,000 in 1914, and only a small proportion of its inhabitants could be consumers of the latest trends in arts and crafts, or were interested in them. The fate of the Iris company was described above. Nonetheless, the supply of products of applied art had developed in Helsinki as part of the overall expansion of trade and the specialization of industries. Founded in 1911, Kotiteollisuusliike Pirtti (Pirtti Home Industries) was a retailer of home-made rural craft products, such as staved wooden vessels and woven fabrics. In 1913, the Stockmann trading company opened its refurbished department store with spacious, roofed courtyards next to Senate Square in the city centre. The success of the department store inspired the company as early as 1916 to hold an architectural competition for a new department store to be built at the end of Aleksanterinkatu street. The planned department store was of gigantic size for contemporary conditions and was not completed until 1930.

What for example in Stockmann's range of products was domestic applied art and what were imported items? This question is valid in view of middle- and upper-class consumption of applied art in general. What was the proportion of domestic products in the material environment chosen for their homes by the civil servants and bourgeoisie of the cities and smaller industrial communities with an affluent managerial class? This question leads to a consideration of what we mean by Finnish applied art during the period in question. Should it be understood as products created by Finnish designers and manufacturers, or more broadly as the world of artefacts, some domestic, some imported,

that were acquired and consumed here? And should it consist solely of objects designed or made explicitly with applied-art or artisanal skills?

Since the 18th century, the Fiskars[47] ironworks had made implements of excellent functional properties, such as spades and axes. These, however, are not included among applied art of the early 20th century or even industrial product design, unlike present-day Fiskars products. The same is true of the items mass-produced at the time by the Nuuta-järvi[48] glassworks and Finnish textile products employing patterns acquired from abroad. Of the output of the Arabia ceramics factory, which was considerable even by international standards, the Fennia tableware by Thure Öberg (1872–1935) is generally mentioned in the context of the early 1900s. Fennia, however, was produced in limited volume and it was thus an exception among the more traditional models that dominated Arabia's sales of products.

▲ Design by Max Frelander for the furniture of a gentleman's den, 1906–1908. Until the 1930s, upper middle-class homes included genderized space of this kind. The den was matched by the boudoir, a dressing and reception room for women. The furniture for these spaces was commissioned, first mainly from architects, but from the 1920s also from trained professionals in applied art.

▶ Sketch by Väinö Blomstedt for the ryijy-rug *Horses* (1906–1907). The ryijy was made by the Friends of Finnish Handicraft. Motifs from the *Kalevala* epic and folk tradition had now given way to a more abstract, international approach (cf. design by Blomstedt on page 52).

Owing to technological innovation, the production of utility objects and furniture for the home developed just before the First World War. The designers of these products, such as beds with frames of metal tubing, remain anonymous. These aspects of technological innovation, the companies utilizing them and their ultimately anonymous designers must be borne in mind throughout the account given in the present book. Finnish manufacturing and material culture gradually gained an "applied-art identity" towards the modern era. But discussion of high-quality examples of applied art must be related to a broader stream of goods and visual material than the samples of this book. Then as now, only a part of this material environment was designed by individuals with professional training in the applied arts and design.

▲ The shop of the Pirtti Home Industries shop in Helsinki in the 1910s. This firm was a distributor of handcrafted wooden utility and ornamental objects and woven fabrics from the countryside. These products were made in considerable volume alongside the above-discussed examples of arts and crafts.

From low technology production to industrial product design

The developments of the 1870s into the 1890s and thence to the late 1910s highlight two basic factors that defined the applied arts in Finland. One was the relationship of its products with technology, and the other was the evolution of styles and the underlying design of form and use of materials. Both are linked by their movement along the axis of innovation, adaptation and copying.

Around the turn of the century the products of applied arts, the work of artisans and craftsmanship in general did not share any particular technological or material properties. This has also been the case later owing to the connections of applied art with a wide range of uses and types of objects. Finnish industries primarily operated in the area of so-called low technology. Timber was the main material, and handwoven fabrics were also an important category. Where 19th-century Continental Europe and Great Britain, in particular, were marked by an abundance of goods provided by industrialism, this was not the case in Finland even at the end of the century. Furthermore, at this time the originally British Arts and Crafts movement was influential here, with its explicitly anti-industrialist bias and appreciation of craftsmanship and the specific properties of materials. Mass production in the applied art sector was mainly represented by the Arabia porcelain factory and the textile industry.

Finns, and especially the country's urban population, were gradually surrounded by an increasingly complex technological infrastructure. Its products represented the kind of product design that would now be called industrial design. Telephones came into widespread use in Finland at an exceptionally fast pace around the turn of the century, although the actual equipment was made by the Ericsson company of Sweden. Trains were already a familiar feature and electric-powered trams now came in to use. They were soon followed by automobiles, which would become the most important examples of industrial design. Electrical appliances, such as vacuum cleaners, were acquired for the home, and electric lighting and related lamp design became a new area of design.

Except for lamps, hardly any of these classes of objects were yet designed or manufactured domestically. Products of applied art that were

made in Finland were not characterized by merging technological innovation with related manufacturing and applied art skills. This was to come later. Progress in technology and production techniques does not necessarily lead to devices or products that are innovative in terms of applied art. Adapting and copying international examples can readily lead to large-scale output of products that can be included in applied art, as noted above in the case of the Arabia factory and the Finlayson mills.

From adaptation to dialogue

The evolution of the arts and applied art is often presented as a series of original and stylistically innovative solutions, in which artistic competence, the skill of execution and response to practical problems merged to become something new that had not been experienced before. The applied arts scene of the late 1890s and early 1900s was dominated by individual and collective achievements of this kind, such as the Finnish Pavilion at the Paris World's Fair or the work of Finch or Gallén. This had not been the case in previous decades, when neither training nor production in applied art stressed innovation, much less individuality. In addition, Finland was in a provincial, adaptive or imitative relationship with the major centres of style, such as Paris and Berlin. While the period of so-called revived styles was by no means stylistically uniform, its eclectic principles were applied almost universally. Architectural ornaments drawing upon the Renaissance or Neo-Rococo sofas were made in Finland and Spain alike.

The situation changed when states that had remained aside from the mainstream or nations incorporated into leading powers began to develop so-called national styles, which freely combined elements of folk heritage with international materials. At the same time, artistic thinking of the 1890s and early 1900s underlined innovation and the individual. Although Art Nouveau and Jugendstil sought to be dominant styles overturning eclecticism and providing liberation from repetitions of history, they inspired, particularly in Finland, results blending national and the most recent international material in an individual manner. But now Finnish art, architecture and applied art were part of the international field in a completely new way, as an actor and no longer as a

party adapting and replicating received material. Accordingly, contemporary applied art in Finland, with its quest for things new, managed to emerge from its geographical periphery to be in real-time in terms of style and even a forerunner. Finland – Helsinki – had become a regional centre similar to Glasgow or Barcelona, whose achievements were also noted "in the wide world". The process of adopting and developing had created a new kind of applied art, in which the impulses of several centres merged to become elements of aims and skills on a local basis. In this respect, Finland had changed its role from that of a province to that of an active periphery.

Finland looked to the West for influences and opportunities to emerge, with Sweden a consistently important mediator and reflection of design ideas. In this Western sphere were the Continental European centres, Paris and Berlin, along with Vienna which was becoming increasingly

▲ Students at the Central School of Arts and Crafts in the late 1910s.

important in the early 20th century, not to mention the multi-layered example of England, both ideologically and at the level of material culture. World's Fairs and other important displays took place within this context. But on the other hand, Finland was in the vicinity of St. Petersburg, one of the world's largest metropolises, with a wide range of industries and an active art world, and it was even part of the same empire. There were rail and boat connections to St. Petersburg. Did the applied arts in Finland completely lack an Eastern dimension, natural contacts with colleagues and institutions in St. Petersburg and Russia in general?

Finnish applied art was often on display in Russian exhibitions of which the All-Russian Exposition held in 1896 in Nizhniy-Novgorod[49] was the largest. Finland had its own pavilion at the Paris World's Fair of 1889, because Russia did not participate. The national pavilion was thus a practical necessity and not a political gesture. By the Paris World's Fair of 1900, however, the political climate had dramatically changed. The exhibits of the Finnish pavilion clearly reflected Finland's desire to mark its territory in cultural terms. From the perspective of St. Petersburg, the Grand Duchy of Finland had acquired a singular degree of autonomy, and conflicts now arose from Russian attempts to incorporate it more closely into the Russian Empire as a whole. The political and cultural repercussions of these attempts continued until Finland gained independence in 1917. This, however, did not prevent the young art circles of Russia, such as the Mir Iskusstva group from being interested in Finnish fine and applied art. But at the time and after the birth of the Soviet Union, Finns were oriented strictly towards the West almost unanimously.

Finland, and Helsinki in particular, could have had an important role in combining the impulses of East and West and as a melting pot. But Finland chose the West, permanently. Through this choice, the applied arts gained the role of an active participant with the task of emphasizing the Western heritage and future of Finnish culture.

THE HOME AS A WORK OF ART

The concepts of the Arts and Crafts Movement came to Finland from England in the 1890s. Together with many other currents of the turn of the 20th century, these ideas were expressed most clearly in the interior design of upper-middle-class homes. In these dwellings the architects of the building were generally responsible for the design of furnishings, and often of other features of the interior. The period had a preference for the total work of art, in which the setting, the building itself and its interior were steered by an all-encompassing stylistic approach that assembled the parts into an integrated whole. In Finland this aim was achieved most impressively in two works by the office of Gesellius, Lindgren, Saarinen. Hvitträsk (1902–1903) at Kirkkonummi, west of Helsinki, was designed by the trio as their joint residence and working environment and provided an opportunity for a synthesis of this kind. It involved a great deal of artisanal work in features such as chased stove and oven shutters, vault paintings, and fixed and movable furnishings. All the items were designed specifically and uniquely for this project. Even more finished in its details was the main building of Suur-Merijoki manor near Viipuri (1901–1903, destroyed), which was commissioned by Maximilian Neuscheller, an industrialist from St. Petersburg. Carried out almost without any with any financial restrictions, this project was also a brilliant example of high-standard contemporary arts and crafts.

1

1. Hvitträsk, the combined residences and working environment of the Gesellius, Lindgren, Saarinen office of architects, was built in 1903 at Kirkkonummi, west of Helsinki.

2. View from the main room towards the lounge area with vaults decorated in fresco technique.

3. The combined tiled stove and open fireplace of the main room.

4

4. Coffee service designed by Eliel Saarinen, Hvitträsk.

5. Unrealized villa design by Eliel Saarinen, 1901.

6. Eliel Saarinen, project for the library of Suur-Merijoki manor, 1903.

7. The library clock of Suur-Merijoki manor, Eliel Saarinen 1903.

8. Sconce from Hvitträsk.

5

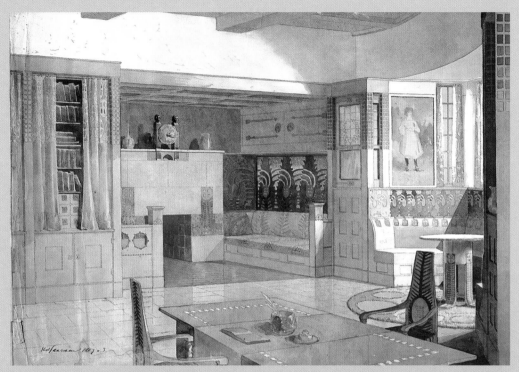

6

7

8

3 HERITAGE AND
THE MODERN

A NEW STATE WITH NEW SYMBOLS

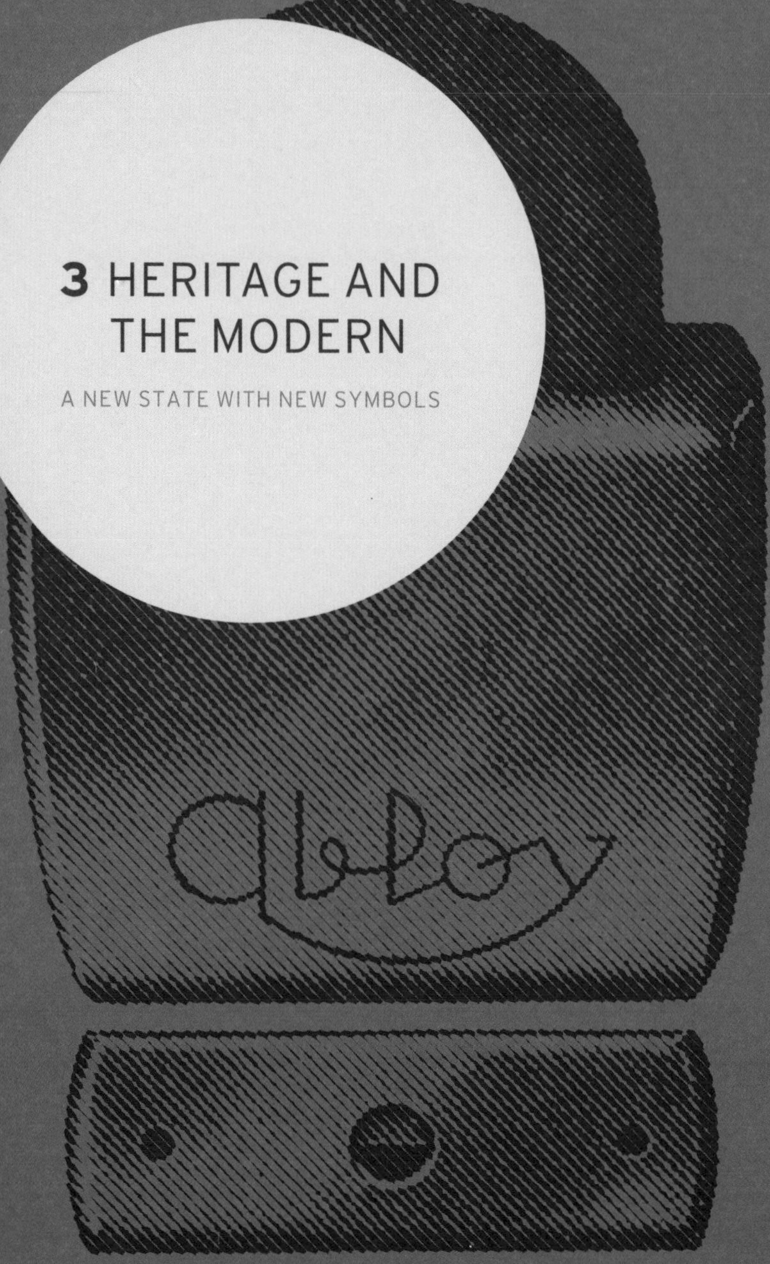

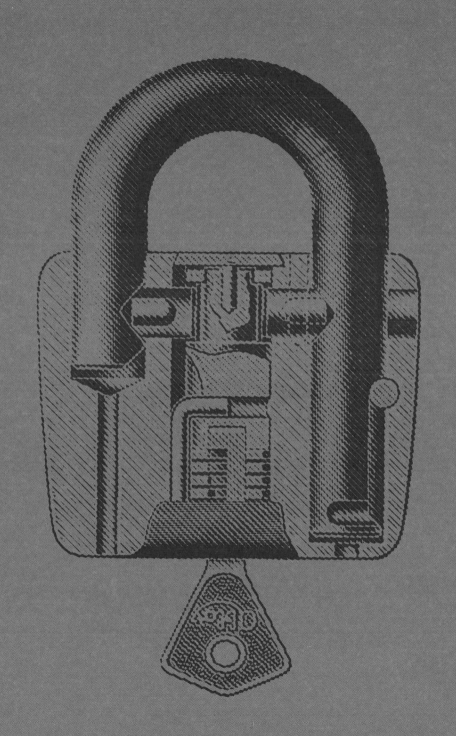

1918

1927

1930

1935

1939

The civil war of 1918

The founding of the
Lahden puuseppä-
tehdas (later Asko)
furniture factory

Finland's first
furniture fair
held in Helsinki

Inauguration of
Parliament House
in Helsinki

The founding of the
Artek company

The New York
World's Fair

Finland's first
housing fair

W hen the Grand Duchy of Finland became the independent Republic of Finland in December 1917 a profound change took place that marked a break with the past and led to reorientation. In the nation-state that was evolving after the civil war of 1918, it became the task of the applied arts to create official symbols. Finland became a constitutional democracy headed by an elected president. It differed thus from the other Nordic countries – monarchies with courts providing conditions for a different array of designed items and a different visual world than newly independent Finland, beset with economic problems. Finland had to emphasize its young democracy and its Western orientation. The situation gained further emphasis as Russia became the Communist Soviet Union and the previously open eastern border was closed both politically and economically.

Finnish architecture and interior decoration in the 1920s were generally dominated by classicist approaches, while the visual and material world of the decade was otherwise highly mixed. Then, and in the 1930s, there was a strong undercurrent of national – and rural – culture. This did not involve any kind of historical retrospection, for Finland was clearly an agrarian county where the ideal of a free land-owning farmer and rural dweller was strong. Even in the 1920s, 80% of the population lived in the countryside, in a predominantly self-sufficient economy.

Towards the end of the decade, new trends from Continental Europe and America influenced the lifestyle of Finland's largest cities, further emphasizing differences between the rural and the urban, and, accordingly, differences with regard to the objects and experiences of applied art. While the cultural avant-garde in the larger cities turned increasingly outward, towards the international scene, the contemporary cultural atmosphere and along with it the products of art and other visual expression largely maintained an introverted nationalist attitude.

In the 1910s classicism came to have increasing influence on building, interiors and furniture. This took place in a fairly general way, without any repetition of the features of particular periods or monuments. This trait was reinforced in the public and private milieux of the new republic: in churches, the halls of the paramilitary civil guards, and

TAIDETEOLLISUUS
NÄYTTELY
TAIDEHALLI   24 · XI − 8 · XII 11−5

homes alike. References to the forms of Ancient Greece blended with the Neo-Hellenism that influenced Finnish culture in general. Politically, use of the style was intended to highlight the values shared by the original homeland of democracy and its latest torchbearer, Finland. This involved the idea of Finland as an outpost of Western civilization against eastern barbarism, i.e. the Bolsheviks *cum* Persians. Classicism was an orientation that dominated the 1920s in other Nordic countries. The choice was thus justified by the example of nearby Western democracies that were felt to be close and served as relevant models.

It is thus no surprise that the main symbolic building of this new democracy, Parliament House in Helsinki, a monument of independent parliamentary rule, was given a classicist appearance both externally and internally. Built according to Johan Sigrid Sirén's (1889–1961)[50] winning entry (Borg, Sirén, Åberg architects) in a competition in 1924 and officially opened in 1930, it was to be an important project for the applied arts, and decorative art and interior design in particular. Although Sirén participated in preparing the brief for the decoration of the building and partly even in the design of the furniture, this large project on a generous budget involved numerous leading designers, artists and artisans. The building was to be a milestone of Finnish skill in all respects. Its ambitious goals and the high-standard results raised the appreciation of the applied arts sector both within the country and abroad.

Despite prevailing classicism, the interiors and furniture of Parliament House were not uniform in their style. They included obvious Art Déco influences as well as the results of modernism, which had made its breakthrough as the building was being finished. Obvious examples of the latter are the tables and chairs of metal tubing designed by Werner West (1890–1959)[51] for the cafeteria. In their immediate context of architectural classicism they are a good illustration of the arts in the 1930s, with classicism making way for modernism. A year earlier Alvar Aalto had won the competition for the Paimio Tuberculosis Sanatorium (1929–1933) with an extremely modernist project. Parliament House was a monument of architecture and arts and crafts executed in the spirit of classicism, and the termination of trends that had emerged in the 1910s. In style, the turn of the 1930s again involved innovation and

◀ Glassware designed by Rafael Blomstedt from the 1918 exhibition of the Finnish Society of Crafts and Design. Originally educated as an architect, Blomstedt was for many years a teacher and artistic director of the Central School of Arts and Crafts, and finally its rector.

◀ Dining-room suite designed by Werner West from the early 1920s. A pioneer of furniture design in Finland, West applied design features of the heavy Baroque style, which was regarded as dignified.

a trailblazing role in relation to tradition. However, the heavily classicist, dark-toned furniture characteristic of the 1920s, and perceived as prestigious, remained popular long after modernist chairs of steel tubing and curved birch laminate had come on the market.

Applied art defined by the family and the home

Quantitatively, the symbolic world of the new state, its heraldry and milieux of representation and prestige were a small sample of applied art produced and consumed in the period. The main sphere for such objects was still private – the home. After the turn of the century, discussion of practical design work for the home and the family had become increasingly important in architecture and interior design. Evaluation of living conditions and reformist propaganda increased, first for the upper middle class, followed in due turn by the broader society and, ultimately, the working class.

In 1919, 70% of all dwellings in highly populated areas were small homes of one or two rooms. The Puu-Käpylä (Wooden Käpylä) section of Helsinki, planned in 1916 but not built until the 1920s, is a good example of the efforts of the city authorities to improve the standard of habitation for workers and to provide opportunities for a spacious and healthy environment. The recent civil war, fought in the spring of 1918, also encouraged improvements to living conditions for workers. Le Corbusier's (1887–1965) well-known observation "architecture or revolution – we can avoid revolution" was particularly realistic for Finland. As noted by Kirsi Saarikangas,[52] planning and control concerning the family, the home and the interior design of dwellings defined Finnish applied arts and design until the 1960s.

Alongside the earlier predominant practice that preferred complete suites of furniture, there now emerged a desire to offer the working class and young families proper, low-priced furniture. There also arose the aim of steering mainly middle-class interior design from an aesthetic point of view. In 1923, the architect Gustaf Strengell (1878–1938), who had influenced interior design through his writings and practical work since the early 1900s, published the book *Koti taideluomana* (The Home as a Work of Art),[53] in which he demonstrated alternatives for interior design of good taste, using his own home as an example. Devoted mainly to discussion in visual terms, Strengell's work was soon matched by similar and more realistic guides by female architects, such as Salme Setälä's book *Miten sisustan asuntoni* (How to Decorate the Home)[54] from 1928. These guidebooks proceeded from the functional problems of the small apartments that had become widespread in contemporary urban development, with particular focus on their kitchens. Discussion on small apartments and their interior design became a leading theme of the following decade, and even the post-war years, with female designers and women's organizations prominently involved.

The home – along with its interior decoration and its educational role in general – was regarded as a particularly important factor maintaining the social fabric. Initially, there was emphasis on its harmonizing role, bringing the family together and shielding it against the bustle of the world and even the conflicts of society. This was soon replaced by emphasis on functional considerations of hygiene and the more prominent role of women. A middle-class focus on a family managed by housewives superseded the patriarchal-matriarchal model with hired servants. At the same time, the drawing-rooms and so-called gentlemen's rooms for receiving guests became less important, as did their furniture. Change began to be achieved in the early 1930s through modernism in its social, architectural and design aspects.

Furniture design leads the way

The closing of the eastern border and the loss of the St. Petersburg market was the death knell for many significant furniture manufacturers, especially those that had survived on orders of a public nature. The loss was made up by consumers' homes, where furniture was the main and most prominent investment in applied art. Demand for furniture was fanned by economic growth that gained pace towards the end of the 1920s and was fast even in the international context, benefiting the countryside, the rapidly growing towns and their new middle class alike. The Finnish furniture industry expanded quickly in the 1920s and developed increasingly towards mass-production methods, with the town of Lahti as its main centre. More affluent circles still had suites of furniture

▶ Poster of the 1927 Furniture Fair by Harry Röneholm. The fair was a tour de force of Finland's rapidly developing furniture design and manufacturing sectors.

Huonekalu Messut

Messut

Helsingissä
17–25. IX. 1927

◀ A chair by J. S. Sirén, the architect of Parliament House in Helsinki, from the turn of the 1930s. A combination of freely interpreted antiquity, opulence and comfort.

▶ The so-called *Barcelona* vase from 1929 was designed by Henry Ericsson, engraved by Teodor Käppi and made by the Riihimäki glassworks. It was an official gift from the City of Helsinki to the City of Barcelona at the 1929 World's Fair. A graduate of the Central School of Arts and Crafts, Ericsson was not only a versatile ornamental artist but also a visual artist in his own right. The vase is one of the few examples from the 1920s of collaboration between the Finnish glass industry and decorative artists.

made to order by manufacturers such as the Boman company of Turku, which was known for its high quality of workmanship.

The furniture industry was among the first sectors of applied art to combine domestic design, materials, manufacturing and consumption. Mass-produced textiles and ceramics, for example, did not follow this example until the 1930s. The teaching of so-called "furniture composition", which had begun at the Central School of Arts and Crafts in 1909 had produced skilled individuals who soon began to lay claim to their share of a field that had previously been dominated by architects. They included Arttu Brummer (1891–1951),[55] who had graduated in 1913 and would become a key figure in the applied arts. Towards the end of the decade he became presumably the first in Finland to call himself an "interior architect". Instead of industry, Brummer was oriented towards

unique projects such as Parliament House, while many others, such as Werner West, combined their artistic and design skills with the opportunities of contemporary manufacturing technology. An indication of the internal organization of the furniture industry and its self-esteem was Finland's first national furniture fair held in Helsinki in 1927.[56]

Improving the quality of the home and its utility objects was also the objective of the pamphlet *Vackrare vardagsvara* (Everyday Products of Greater Beauty)[57] by Gregor Paulsson (1889–1977), a leading figure of the Swedish applied art and design community. Published in 1919 in Sweden, the pamphlet was also influential in Finland. Paulsson's main consideration was the aesthetic and functional quality of serially manufactured objects such as furniture, tableware and textiles, the goal being simple, restrained form and reasonable prices, specifically improving the quality of everyday life through applied art and design. In Finland, furniture design and manufacturing pointed the way in this respect in the 1920s.

In ceramics, Arabia, Finland's largest manufacturer in the field, had begun in the late 19th century to employ consultant artists, such as the architect Jac. Ahrenberg (1847–1914)[58] and persons with applied art training as assistants. But it was not until the 1930s that it hired a trained professional to steer product design as a whole, when it employed the Swede Kurt Ekholm (1907–1975) to renew its traditional products aimed at a broad public. By this stage the goal of "everyday products of greater beauty" was already associated with modernism, aiming at simplicity of form and restrained abstract decoration. During the 1920s, the glass industry displayed signs of using domestic skill, hiring, for example, Eric O.W. Ehrström as artistic director of the Karhula glassworks in 1925. This did not yet concern the redesigning of mass-produced utility glassware but instead art glass pieces made on a unique or small-edition basis.

Many areas of applied art are divided into industrially produced utility products and artistically oriented handcrafted objects. This is the case for example, in glass and ceramics. Furniture also displays hierarchical differences based on need, but even though furniture design is referred to as an art it always involves the utility of objects. There cannot be a chair without someone to sit on it, whether a milking stool or a throne.

▶ The Finnish department at the Milan Exhibition of Applied Art in 1933. Woven textiles by Maija Kansanen, among other items, hang on the wall. The picture is of the experimental mounting carried out in Helsinki before the exhibition.

▶ An advertisement for the Pirtti crafts and home industries company from around 1920. The wooden utility objects previously offered by the company had now become souvenirs aimed at an international audience.

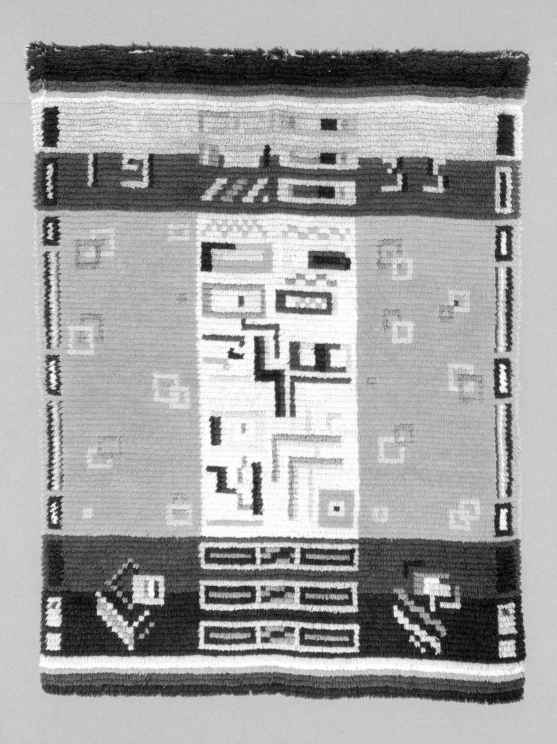

Textile art

The range of production methods and uses, however, was the widest in textiles. Before industrial manufacturing (and, later, alongside it), textiles have always been made in the home. It was noted above how the work of the Friends of Finnish Handicraft[59] to promote the utilization of motifs regarded as national marked the whole field of applied art. Then, as later, this involved handcrafted woven textiles. The Friends of Finnish Handicraft had expanded its activities by the 1920s. Its significant weavery employed professionally trained designers such as Eva Brummer (1901–2007) and Laila Karttunen (1895–1981),[60] who explicitly designed and did not execute the works, unlike in the ceramics industry. Textile designers such as Eva Anttila (1894–1993)[61] and Maija Kansanen (1889–1957)[62] also founded their own weaveries and studios, where they could control both design and execution.

Textile art hung on the wall like visual artworks was highly successful in the 1920s and 1930s and received prizes when Finnish applied art was displayed abroad. Unlike works employing material from tradition, which were often ryijy-rugs, these art textiles aimed at individual expression. It was sought through abstraction no longer informed by ethnographic heritage. Some of Maija Kansanen's works of the turn of the 1930s, for example, represented with their abstract composition modern (visual) art in a country where such art was still not accepted in the 1950s. Applied art could thus take artistic licence in matters that were still out of bounds in the official system of the arts – but this, of course, was harmless utility art "lacking content".

Handcrafted textiles thus thrived in homes, home-industries, leading weaveries and the works of individual artists. Since the mid-19th century, however, there had been significant textile mills, such as Finlayson in Tampere, Barker in Turku and the Forssa mills. Producing cotton and, later, knitted fabrics by the yard these companies mainly relied on models from abroad or patterns adapted from them. Some textile companies such as Tampereen Pellava- ja Rautateollisuus (later Tampella)[63] would occasionally consult designers when introducing products with patterns of domestic origin. Such designs could be adaptations of

the rich heritage of East Karelia, which had become topical through the Friends of Finnish Handicraft.

But as noted by Marjo Wiberg,[64] this sector did not begin to make consistent use of Finnish design professionals until the 1930s, and slowly even then. Education in textile design began at the Central School of Arts and Crafts in 1929. Finland thus had for a long while a technologically evolved and successful textile industry that did not rely on Finnish designers.

The advent of the modern

The atmosphere of the 1920s is described above mainly in terms of classicism and a vernacular heritage that was still vivid. In general, the preceding years were culturally more international and cosmopolitan

▲ The interior of the Fazer café and pastry shop in the centre of Helsinki, designed by the architect Jarl Eklund, 1930. Continental metropolitan modernism employing glass and chrome-plated metal.

▶ An advertisement for an electricals range of the Strömberg company from the turn of the 1930s. Electrical home appliances rapidly came into widespread use during the inter-war years. They represented anonymous industrial design that had great impact on everyday life.

G.S.-
SÄHKÖLIEDET y.m.
SÄHKÖLÄMPÖKOJEET

SUOMEN SÄHKÖ OSAKEYHTIÖ
GOTTFR.STRÖMBERG

I ALLA kvalitetstävlingar ha våra tillverkningar erhållit *högsta pris, guldmedalj*

MERIVAARAS MARKE GARANTERAR PRODUKTENS KVALITET

than the early 1920s. The pre-World War I Russian avant-garde was now a thing of the past and the eastern border was closed. There was no awareness of, or willingness to learn about, the radical constructivism or graphic arts of the young Soviet Union. Even in the early 1930s, the avant-garde was regarded as left-wing, Bolshevik, which, in the prevailing rurally oriented cultural scene, approached treason. Continental European futurism or Dada made no landfalls here and the same was mostly true of German expressionism of the Weimar years. Finland mostly looked to the Nordic countries, and Sweden in particular. Art Déco, which made its breakthrough at the International Exhibition of Applied Arts in Paris in 1925, appeared in the decorative arts, especially in interiors, but with some delay, becoming mixed with mainstream modernism in the 1930s.

At the same time, technological progress accelerated the spread of products and devices employing the internal combustion engine and electricity. The number of automobiles grew rapidly – the car was one of the main focal points for the romanticizing of the machine in the late

▲ The modernism of everyday life, also known as functionalism. Unknown designer, advertisement for the Merivaara company. Mid-1930s.

▶ Unknown designer, the *Pekka 300 vk* radio receiver made by the Salora (Salon radioteollisuus) company in the early 1930s. The Finnish electronics industry did not begin to employ professional designers until the 1950s.

1920s. Flight was an even more modern experience of travel. The mechanical reproducibility of culture, and entertainment in particular, was reinforced through the advent of the phonograph and motion pictures. They also introduced American popular culture, which invaded the Old World. The Finnish Broadcasting Company began its radio service, joining the country in a shared reality operating in real time.

The young generation active in Finnish culture in the late 1920s eagerly adopted this new modernity. Underscoring their urbanity, they were mostly active in Helsinki and Turku. Mainly influential in literature, visual arts and criticism, these individuals and groups, such as *Tulenkantajat* (The Torch-Bearers) resolutely looked towards the metropolises of Europe and North America, constructing identity from their impulses. Cultural modernism evolved within the framework of buildings and applied art which – like Alvar Aalto's architecture and furniture from before the late 1920s – mainly drew upon the heritage of classicism. In applied art and design, fashions reacted most quickly to pressure for change – the flappers of the late 1920s danced in their short skirts in pavilions adapted from Greek temples.

In Finland, as in the other Nordic countries, the tides of style turned from classicism to modernism around the turn of the 1930s. The Nordic context is important here, for in these countries the agenda and ideology of modernism had a distinct socially conscious and reformist tone. Marking architecture, applied art and graphic design since the early 1930s, modernism was part of the process of modernization, with "new form" serving societal, industrial and cultural change. Transformed and gaining greater structural depth, this process marked the overall development of Finland until the 1970s.

As is so often the case, change in style coincided with economic change. The economic recession of the early 1890s, for example, had hastened the emergence of new currents when the economy, building and consumption gained pace towards the middle of the decade. Economic reorganization and the end of relations with Russia through national independence created an interval during which classicizing principles gained a foothold. The economic boom of the late 1920s which spurred internationalization ended in economic collapse and an

▶ Furniture designed by the architect Pauli E. Blomstedt and made by the Merivaara company at the Finnish Furniture Fair of 1937. Blomstedt applied influences of Continental European modernism to Finnish conditions and the advanced manufacturing techniques of the Merivaara company.

▶ Alvar Aalto, in turn, adapted Continental modernism to Finnish birch and the most recent techniques of curving and laminating the material with the aid of the Korhonen furniture factory and its director Otto Korhonen. The examples shown here are from the early 1930s.

international economic depression at the turn of the 1930s. Around this time the design principles of international modernism that had been developed in Germany, France and the Netherlands began to be adopted.

When the economy started its rapid recovery in 1933, the Finnish milieu came to be designed and created largely with the means of modernism. This was also the case in the other Nordic countries, but no longer in Germany or Italy where totalitarian governments saw the avant-garde with its left-wing associations as a threat. Around the same time in the Soviet Union, Stalin ended the rich and varied experiments in art, architecture and design that had followed the October Revolution. Nordic modernism could develop on a broad front and it also became a type of expression favoured by the public sector and even the state. In Finland, this tendency was fanned by the desire to express the young republic's contemporaneity – a modern country of the Western and democratic cultural sphere. Where democracy had been framed ten years ago by themes from Antiquity, modernism, with its anti-totalitarian connotations, served the same purpose in the 1930s.

Functionalism – towards the rationalization of everyday life

In Scandinavia and Finland "functionalism" became a blanket term for modernism in architecture and applied art, literally underscoring its functional starting points as opposed to emphases on history and style, which it sought to discard through functionalist design. Functionalism was intended as a set of design principles that would profoundly steer everyday life and even society, rationally improving the quality of life in all sectors. This called for the radical reshaping of the whole environment. Everything from town plans down to tableware was to follow rational approaches and design based on unified principles. At the level of form, there had been attempts at the turn of the 20th century to create a new predominant style. The goal now was an approach drawing upon theoretical, "scientific", thinking and technological progress that was not intended to lead to any particular style – in fact style as such was to be rejected.

Despite this, functionalism became a style, particularly in furniture where specific choices of material and construction such as curved chromed steel tubing expressed the modernity of the products and their consumers. It ran parallel to the German tendency of rationalization and simplification known as *neue Sachlichkeit* or neo-objectivity, but was less declarative, emphasizing plainness and distinct, simple form.

Modernism was introduced into Finland by architects and in their work in the late 1920s, the leading names being Alvar Aalto, Erik Bryggman (1891–1955)[65] and Pauli E. Blomstedt (1900–1935). Aalto and Blomstedt were also actively interested in applied art, mainly furniture, like their international counterparts Walter Gropius (1883–1969), Ludwig Mies van der Rohe (1886–1969) and Le Corbusier. Aalto also studied the use of light in interiors, leading him to lamp design, which continued throughout his career. Among the reasons why furniture design was given emphasis was the fact that, for example, Aalto's important early modernist projects, such as the Viipuri Library (1927–1935), the Turun Sanomat newspaper building (1928–1930) and the Paimio Tuberculosis Sanatorium in particular (1929–1933) called for an extensive programme of furnishings suited to their overall design. Aalto did not wish to rely on imported products, such as the tubular steel furniture of Marcel Breuer (1902–1981). Similar reasons led Blomstedt to create furniture for the buildings of his design, such as Hotel Helsinki (1930) and the Suomalainen Säästöpankki bank building in Kotka (1934–1935). These were items employing chromed tubing in the Continental European manner. Among contemporary architects Aalto was exceptionally well versed in furniture design technically. This led to his renowned series of furniture making ingenious use of Finnish wood, which is still being made.

Although the introduction and growth of modernism should be considered a fundamental change, we must remember that many of the tendencies of the 1920s continued in changed appearance. This was particularly true of discussion and practices regarding homes, dwellings and housing in general. The social ethic of modernism merged with a design ideology emphasizing the functionality, health effects and aesthetic aspects of the home. This continued, in a new form, the reforms already launched in the early 1900s. In 1930 the so-called *Exhibition on the Rationalization of Small Apartments*[66] was held at Kunsthalle Helsinki in connection with the 1930 Finnish Exhibition of Applied Art and Design. The complete designed interiors of this exhibition showed how urban housing even in limited space could be organized to provide comfort and functionality by means of modernism, i.e. rationally. In addition to Alvar Aalto, who was the commissioner of the exhibition, it included several other younger architects, such as Aalto's wife Aino Marsio Aalto (1894–1949),[67] Blomstedt, Bryggman and Märta Blomstedt (1899–1982). Pauli E. Blomstedt wrote an analysis entitled *Vanha ja uusi taideteollisuus* (Old and New Applied Art)[68] for the exhibition booklet, presenting the small apartment as the core unit of all habitation and the "housing issue". Examples in this area were to point to solutions for housing on a larger scale.

The exhibition crystallized the comprehensive view of functionalism according to which even small elements, such as chairs, could have a broader role in a larger entity, with impact on human society as a whole and as a reflection of the latter. Well-designed furniture and other artefacts – everyday products not only of greater beauty but also more sensibly designed – were to be sold not only to the middle class but especially to less-affluent young couples setting out in life. It was thus necessary to provide replicable furniture types, in turn created through standardized mass production. The concepts of types, standards and series were among the key considerations of functionalism. While already present in the 1920s, they were now addressed more programmatically.

Also in the background was admiration of the reproducibility of modernist design and assembly-line manufacture, examples of the latter being industrial products such as automobiles. If Henry Ford could offer reasonably priced cars through standardized work and rationalized production and distribution, why couldn't the same be achieved in the building and furniture industries? Serial industrial construction methods for wood were achieved in the 1940s and, on a more general level, as late as the 1960s – production in series had been a standard aspect of applied arts at the turn of the 1930s, in furniture among other areas. There was now programmatic discussion of standards and types as part

▶ *Maamiehen ryijy* (The Farmer's Ryijy) by A. W. Raitio from the mid-1930s. Despite the breakthrough of modernism, Finland was still a predominantly agrarian society, which was reflected in prevailing values and the material culture of homes, which included handicrafts.

of modernist expression. Aalto, for example, would note "Aalto standard" against mounts and door pulls in his building designs, though this was more of an expressed aesthetic-functional wish than an actual instruction for producers.

Industry – a promise and a threat

Discussion of applied art focused increasingly on collaboration with industry, the needs of the masses and the conditions of manufacturing. How did the training in the field react to this? The concepts of the Bauhaus school and other aspects of Continental European modernism figured prominently in architecture, though not in architectural education. Shouldn't the school of applied art that had been established expressly to serve industry have trained its students to respond to the challenges of increasingly mechanized working life? Or was the artisan accepting the terms of mass production a human robot who would be crushed in the machinery, as in Charlie Chaplin's film *Modern Times*?

One of the enduring main themes of Finnish applied art and design has been the relationship between industry and training in the field. Until the 1980s the Central School of Arts and Crafts and its successors had a monopoly in higher education in this area. Unlike in countries with a more diversified training system, the Finnish situation was dominated by the views and attitudes passed on by leading figures in design education to their students. We must also consider how students, younger and reacting more acutely to their own times, may have opposed the ideologies that were offered to them. As pointed out by Marianne Aav,[69] the School changed in the mid-1920s – after the Finnish state took on responsibility for its economy and explicitly vocational subjects were transferred to other schools – finally becoming an institute of education purely devoted to applied art and design. Important steps in expanding the curriculum were in particular the launch of teaching in graphic art in 1926, and in textile art and design in 1929. Although finances were continuously strained, the faculty could be kept in their positions. The architect Rafael Blomstedt had succeeded Armas Lindgren as Artistic Director of the School in 1912, serving in this capacity for the next thirty-one years.

The most influential figure within the school and before long in the whole sector of applied art was, however, Arttu Brummer, who joined the faculty in 1919. Although Brummer had graduated as a furniture designer, he taught so-called general design, as well as furniture design from 1928 and heraldry from 1930 onwards. With his teaching in the general design courses that were compulsory for all students, he influenced the views of the whole student body. Brummer's writings and his activities on the boards of important associations in the field and exhibition juries and in many other ways made him the figurehead of Finnish applied art, especially in the 1930s but also later and until his death in 1951. In his conception of applied art, Brummer was a romantic who underlined craftsmanship and viewed with deep suspicion the opportunities of the machine culture that was now emerging unopposed and of its own accord. It had become obvious, however, since the 1920s that evolving industries rather than arts and crafts would increasingly employ graduates of the school. Export efforts aimed at the Western countries required the applied arts to reorient themselves towards principles emphasizing industry in the manner pointed out by Estlander.

The emergence of modernism, growing awareness of the principles of teaching followed by the Bauhaus and the issue of applied art as a factor for developing industry that had been raised by the depression all added to pressure to focus training with industry in mind. This, however, was not done. Although Brummer underlined the importance of objects serving the culture of the home, he did so in a completely different spirit than the above-mentioned 1930 exhibition on the design of small apartments. Brummer emphasized decoration and the artistically ennobling nature of unique, one-off, works. He felt that such objects would give homes warmth, atmosphere and beauty for their own sake in a world dominated by technological evolution and excessive rationality. At the time and even after the Second World War, arts and crafts in the role of art – the art of glass, ceramics and textiles – served the aesthetic needs of middle-class homes, while visual art as such remained expensive and less accessible. The school, however, kept to its emphasis on arts and crafts, which aroused criticism by the mid-1930s. Critical views came from representatives of practical work in applied art who emphasized the union of mechanization and modernism, rather than from within the school.

The 1930s as a whole were in fact marked in various ways by the conflicts of views and activities between Brummer, the undeniable leading figure of the field, and Alvar Aalto, who had made a breakthrough in furniture design even at the international level. It is a paradox that a school that had been specifically established to serve industry was represented by a person with a sceptical attitude towards it, while the leading contemporary figure in architecture, a field dominated by craftsmanship and low-level technology, had studied the technology and mass production of wooden products. Brummer's teaching and other activities were inspiring and selfless and they made a permanent impression on developments throughout the whole field. But the graduates of the school were in any case increasingly employed by trade and industry. They took with them a "high" conception of applied art, saturated by art and artistic skill. Already in the international exhibitions of the 1930s, and even more prominently after the war, prizes showered upon arts and crafts as unique pieces or in small editions, as emphasized by Brummer. It was only in the post-war years that the initially tentative accommodation of training to the needs of industry was achieved.

Applied art on display – culture, commerce and popular education

Up to the present day, exhibitions have been one of the most important ways for the applied arts to present themselves. Varying in scale and objective, exhibitions have been combined with export policies to enhance the cultural image of Finland abroad. Domestic exhibitions have underscored the economic aspects of the applied arts: their cultural message and function in embellishing homes and rationalizing their design. In addition there have been exhibitions held by companies utilizing applied art and design and, of course, individual and group exhibitions of arts and crafts in galleries. The following section focuses on the self-image projected abroad by the applied arts community of Finland.

Prior to gaining national independence, Finland had displayed itself with the aid of its applied arts at world's fairs, as in Paris, and in international exhibitions of applied art. At the world's fairs, applied art was more generally linked to creating an image of Finland, while at the applied art fairs the purpose was to compete with similar products from other countries. In 1925 applied art from the young republic of Finland was on show on a small scale at the international biennial held in Monza and in better-prepared fashion at a large exhibition of applied art in Paris. The latter small-scale display did not have its own pavilion and was a poor echo of the Finnish exhibit staged a quarter of a century earlier at the Paris World's Fair. This reflected uncertainty regarding the need to exhibit in general and the nature of the exhibits in particular. This is surprising, particularly since 1925 was the 50th anniversary year of the Finnish Society of Crafts and Design and was marked by a major exhibition in Helsinki. On the other hand, the young republic invested its efforts in internal development and was uncertain about its foreign orientations in matters related to the applied arts.

One of the benefits of world's fairs generally was the opportunity to erect a national pavilion, which would ideally have a distinct effect on viewers when seen together with the visual and artefactual exhibits. This required agreement between the architect of the pavilion and the commissioner of the exhibition as to the objectives of the display. This could succeed or fail, as is illustrated by international displays of Finnish applied art in the 1930s. Nonetheless, the decade included success that made Finnish achievements internationally known in a completely new way. Finnish applied art was already being exhibited at the Barcelona World's Fair of 1929 and the Antwerp International Exposition in 1930, which included Finland's own pavilion. Designed by Erik Bryggman, it was the first Finnish pavilion since the 1900 World's Fair. As the economic depression abated, Finnish participants prepared for the Milan Triennial of 1933. This exhibition was the first in a series that was to establish the international reputation of Finnish applied art after the Second World War. The displays, moved from Monza to Milan, were held in ready-made classicized venues of the early 1930s that did not permit the use of independent architectural effects, which also posed positive challenges for the design of the actual exhibition.

The Society of Crafts and Design and the Ornamo association were active from an early stage and the international exposure intended for

Milan in 1933 was prepared for with care. As pointed out by Pekka Suhonen,[70] the preparations were nonetheless marked by the ongoing disagreements of the applied arts community. They concerned the nature of the exhibited collection and the national and international aims of the exhibits. Despite this, the showing was highly successful as regards prizes and coverage in the local press. Three main prizes (*Gran Premio*) were received, for the exhibition architecture by Harry Röneholm (1892–1951), for textiles by Laila Karttunen and ceramics by Elsa Elenius (1897–1967), along with dozens of other prizes. As would be the case in the future, success abroad enhanced the domestic status of the whole field and its representatives.

The following Milan Triennial, in 1936, was to a great degree a solo exhibition by Aino and Alvar Aalto, since the extensive national displays of 1933 were not repeated for reasons of international politics. There were reactions against the totalitarianism of Mussolini. In addition, preparations were already under way for the Paris World's Fair of 1937. The competition for the pavilion in Paris was won by Alvar Aalto.

In the competition for the Finnish pavilion at the New York World's Fair of 1939, the first three prizes went to Aino and Alvar Aalto.

Aalto – types, standards and factory production in series

Alvar Aalto had definite advantages in exhibitions: he could both design the pavilion and display his own furniture, either together or individually. He was the first Finnish designer to hold solo exhibitions abroad, not in architecture but in furniture design. As early as 1933 he had an exhibition at Fortnum & Mason in London, which opened the British market to him. After having achieved professional success as an architect with the Finnish pavilion in Paris he was the subject of an exhibition dominated by furniture at the Museum of Modern Art in New York in 1938. Before the Second World War, the architect was best known internationally as a furniture designer, while also being Finland's most successful practitioner of applied art in both artistic and commercial terms. This excluded him from the favour of the gatekeepers of applied art such as Brummer or the architectural classicist J. S. Sirén, who was also influential in the applied arts, since Aalto happened to personify international modernism aiming at types, standards and serial factory production. The matter was not helped by the fact that Aalto gave this modernism an original interpretation employing Finnish wood.

The Finnish pavilion designed by Aalto for the 1937 Paris World's Fair received international praise, even being commended by Le Corbusier, the high priest of modernism. Brummer was the commissioner of the exhibited collection of applied art, which had been selected by the Finnish Society of Crafts and Design. Conflict was inevitable and the display did not become the integrated entity intended. The choice of exhibits had sought unbiased representativeness, but no positive tension or dialogue was achieved between the objects, commendable in themselves, and the dynamic interior of the pavilion. This suggests the view that architecture was at a completely different level of development than applied art.

At the New York World's Fair of 1939, Aalto had almost dictatorial authority over the design of the interior as well as the exhibits. This was facilitated by the fact that the commissioner of the exhibition was his

schoolmate William Lehtinen (1895–1975). Aalto shaped the existing box-like space in a dramatic manner with an undulating wall leaning forward, covered with enlarged photographs of Finnish nature and industries, while the exhibited objects were at floor level beneath it. The whole selection of exhibits focused on the significance of wood in Finnish nature, architecture and industries. Aalto achieved the total effect that he had sought and it received a great deal of attention. It is true that applied art was not prominently displayed, and the pavilion was rather a showcase of Finland's wood-based export industries, raised to the level of a more general experience of Finland through the means employed by Aalto.

In view of the role of world's fairs this may have been a better choice than displaying ryijy-rugs and ceramic art. In a sense, it marked a return to the late 19th-century displays that gave industry a leading role, while skills in the applied arts were associated with the quality of industrial products. The old divisions still applied. Aalto had allied himself with liberal, internationally oriented industrial circles seeking modernity. The Finnish Society of Crafts and Design and Brummer underlined arts and crafts and individual achievements. The pavilion's separate department of applied art and design also followed the line defined by Aalto. It contained three rooms with interior design by Werner West, Lisa Johansson-Pape (1907–1989) and Margaret Nordman (1898–1981) demonstrating the modern Finnish culture of the home as part of social progress with focus on the future.

It was in this manner that Finnish applied art gained international success in the 1930s, especially in Milan in 1933, but also in Paris four years later. Success at the New York World's Fair was overshadowed by the Finnish-Soviet Winter War of 1939–1940. Despite the publicity accorded to these exhibitions in the Finnish media and their electrifying effect on applied art, they did not have much impact on investments by Finnish industries in applied art and design. The invigorating effect permitted by applied art thus remained unused and the country's rapid economic growth was left to rely on exports of butter, lumber, pulp and paper. These were felt to be sufficient – an awakening would not follow until twenty years later.

Domestic exhibitions and information

While presence in the international arena was significant, domestic displays and information were of primary importance for the internal marketing and consumption of applied arts products. The field was represented in both general exhibitions and limited displays restricted to the applied arts. Industries, and the consumer goods sector in particular, had to find a new orientation in the independent republic of Finland, without the benefit of the Russian market. The first Finnish Fair, held in Helsinki in 1920, launched the custom of general exhibitions that began to be staged on a regular basis. These fairs gave domestic manufacturers an opportunity to display their products, for the purpose of encouraging consumption and to present innovations. The fairs spurred companies to modernize and develop their products and permitted commercial buyers and consumers to compare them. Towards the end of the decade there were also exhibitions of specific sectors, such as the above-mentioned furniture fair of 1927. The latter events were better suited than general fairs for evaluating the quality offered by manufacturers and how up-to-date they were in matters of style.

The applied arts were on display in their own right in the annual exhibitions of the Finnish Society of Crafts and Design. Unlike the fairs, these events were not overtly commercial, but instead cavalcades of designers and products estimated to be the best in their respective fields and intended to improve the tastes of the public. On display in these exhibitions were the art products of applied art, such as textile and ceramic art. Artisans, who had neither cause nor desire to participate in the national fairs, displayed works under their own names. A further incentive for the public to attend these exhibitions were the raffles that had already been launched in the late 19th century and in which the main prize could be a complete, and valuable, suite of furniture, the design and manufacturer of which were regarded by the Society to be of the highest possible standard.

Furniture and objects for the home were included in housing exhibitions, which in turn were associated with architecture. Thus, the dwelling – the home – was the core unit of all architecture and town planning. As is known, it was regarded as the essential setting of nuclear family life by the early 20th-century reform movements, their successors and the movements in social engineering that would soon emerge. Its functional, spatial and artefactual organization was by no means insignificant. During the interwar years, the home and family life within it were regarded as maintaining social stability. The modernization that had been implemented with an iron fist in the 1920s in the Soviet Union, Finland's eastern neighbour, had led to the collectivization of habitation and family life. Nordic and Finnish modernization, instead, was to apply modernization as a factor supporting the nuclear family.

Housing exhibitions had already been held in the 1910s, when social concerns mainly applying to workers' housing were addressed. This issue also involved the national economy, since a working class enjoying well-being and living in even moderate conditions would be more productive. To ensure the availability of labour, Finnish industries, which were dispersed into small factory communities, had to provide for their workers and clerical staff alike. The home reform movement, represented by an association of the same name founded in 1910, joined forces with modernism in architecture and applied art. The Finnish Society of Crafts and Design was also linked to a process of social reform, for which Sweden had provided a template since the 1910s. The presentation of modernism at the 1930 Stockholm Exhibition of Applied Art provided inspiration for Finns. This exhibition underscored the alliance of the built and artefactual environment as part of modernization with impact on society as a whole. The leading figure of this exhibition was Gregor Paulsson, who represented the concept of "everyday products of greater beauty" and was a long-term proponent of the joint efforts of modernization and a new kind of applied art.

The image of Finnish modernism

A housing exhibition that was staged in at the Finnish Fair Hall in Helsinki in the autumn of 1939 but was open for less than a week because of the threat of war, was a synthesis of the achievements of the past decade in housing and interior design. The commissioner of the exhibition was the architect Kaj Englund (1905–1976). The walls inside the venue were lined with "small apartments" that were as realistic as possible. In these

▶ Furniture designed by Ilmari Tapiovaara for the Asko company in 1939. These items were also intended for export. Alongside Werner West, Tapiovaara was one of Finland's first furniture designers employed by large-scale industry who internalized modernist design.

HAT-RACK N:o 607

Lengths: 31", 39", 47".
Delivered knocked down.
Designed by: Ilmari Tapiovaara.

**WRITING TABLE
N:o 435**

with linoleum top, partly painted
and in natural birch. Delivered
tops and endboards separately.
Fitted with 3 drawers and with
a fall flap.
height = 29"
top = 25" × 47"
Designed by: Ilmari Tapiovaara

ARMCHAIR N:o 21

Height 31 1/2"
Size of seat 17 1/2", 19" × 18 1/2"
Delivered partly assembled:
24 chairs in a case.
Fronts assembled other parts loose
Measurements of the case:
74" × 29" × 19" = 22 j³
Gross weight 130 kilos
Net weight 100 kilos
Designed by: Ilmari Tapiovaara

units, furniture and furnishings were arranged into functional groups without displaying the names of the designers or manufacturers, which were listed in the exhibition catalogue. The leading idea was of thematic entities in furniture, lamps, fittings and other products serving the rational design of the home by means of modernism. At the exhibition on the same theme that had been held nine years previously, modernism had still sought its place but now it had a leading role.

Unlike in Continental Europe, modernist design was realized in Finland in wooden furniture. The familiarity of the material helped in accepting a new formal idiom that was simpler than previously. Simplicity, light weight and adaptability were selling points as the young, growing middle class furnished small apartments provided by rapidly

increasing urban development, as in the Töölö section of Helsinki. A good example is a collection of furniture designed by Ilmari Tapiovaara (1914–1999)[71] for the Asko[72] company in 1939 and displayed at the housing exhibition held in the same year. The items were modern and functional but without any radical experiments of form and were made of Finnish birch left with a light-coloured finish. Restrained modernism, low-cost domestic material and the Asko company's capability for mass production converged in the collection. The elements of commercial success were present, but this was not to be the case. The manufacturer's sales organization regarded the products as too radical and simple for the clientele. The completed items were destroyed in bombings during the war.

Tapiovaara was a rising name of the 1930s, and he had an exceptionally international background. After graduating in 1937 from the Central School of Arts and Crafts he worked in the same year at Le Corbusier's

▲ Furniture suite from the Finnish Fair of 1939. Over the course of a decade modernism had been domesticated, softened and accepted.

office in Paris. Here he was employed finishing photographs of the master's works, but the experience was nonetheless of prime importance for the young Finn. On the same "grand tour" he prepared interior designs for the Finnmar company[73] in London, which marketed furniture by Aalto. Tapiovaara's career is an illustrative example of how designers with Finnish training increasingly stepped forward to realize their intentions through industry rather than craftsmanship. The housing exhibition of 1939 also featured a farmhouse interior for a smallholder with furniture designed by Tapiovaara. This interior design connected with the non-modern countryside where most of the Finnish population lived. The country was still predominantly agrarian and the modernism of applied art was mainly an urban phenomenon. Exceptions were the communities of the wood processing industry that were located near water sources and forest regions.

The Finnish countryside had adopted technologies including new agricultural equipment, radios, phonographs and automobiles. But actual habitation and life in homes were different, with traditional customs and social regulation having strong impact on the artefactual aspects of life. Here it can be asked what improvements a modernist range of products would have provided. They were, however, well suited to the emancipated middle class as part of its mentality.

Despite their comprehensive approach of combining architecture and applied art, the housing exhibitions, such as the one held in 1939, did not take over the role of the annual exhibitions of the Finnish Society of Crafts and Design. In November 1939 the Society held its exhibition at Kunsthalle Helsinki, with Tapiovaara exhibiting a total interior design for a hotel room. Times were now changing and the Society had taken note of the housing exhibition's thematically illustrative displays. The hotel-room interior was now dominated by wood in contrast to the hotel furniture of steel tubing designed by Pauli E. Blomstedt for the small apartment exhibition of 1930. Modernism/functionalism had been domesticized, its principles translated into the language of the Finnish tradition of materials and new skills developed for working in it. The decisive impulse for this course of development had been provided by Alvar Aalto some ten years earlier.

The encounter of modernism and enlightened capital

Alvar Aalto furniture, its design, manufacturing and distribution are among the most interesting, and exceptional, phenomena of applied art and design in Finland in the 1930s. This situation includes the founding in 1935 of the Artek company, which marketed Aalto furniture. Along with Aalto, this scheme included Harry Gullichsen (1902–1954) the managing director of the Ahlström company, Finland's largest privately owned industrial empire, and his wife Maire, née Ahlström (1907–1990), who was more actively involved.[74] In the early stages Artek also involved Aino Aalto and the art historian Nils-Gustav Hahl (1904–1941), who was a proponent of new applied art.

Artek is still in operation over seventy years after its founding. Its main line of products consists of Aalto furniture, which has been made without interruption since the early 1930s. This is exceptional in a world where the classics of modern design have become expensive collectibles or have been reissued. Also for this reason the role of the Korhonen[75] furniture factory and its predecessor must be emphasized, as it has had sole rights to produce Aalto furniture since it was first introduced. It is highly important for an innovative designer to find a manufacturer who trusts him on a long-term basis.

Aalto was able to interpret the technical and formal aims of Continental European modernism in an individual manner. With the aid of an entrepreneur who believed in experimentation, he combined Finnish wood with technological and production-related skills. In the 1930s, Finland was one of the world's leading producers of birch plywood. In association with the furniture manufacturer Korhonen, Aalto developed a number of lamination and curving methods for wood, for which patents were granted. These were technological patents and not the registered design models that were common in the design sector. The main problem that had to be solved was how to curve the upper part of a solid-wood upright component 90 degrees without breaking the grains of the wood. The purpose was to create a visually and structurally solid and durable support. The solution was to saw notches in the end of the strut, to place thin strips of wood in them with glue and to heat the assembly while it was curved. In varying sizes, this basic type of supporting structure has been the core element of most items of Aalto furniture, such as chairs and tables.

The chairs designed by Aalto in the early 1930s for the Paimio Tuberculosis Sanatorium belong to the canon of modern design. In these chairs, the seat and backrest consist of a single form-pressed piece of birch laminate. The support is a single curved wooden element that forms the legs and the hand-rests, and replaces the curving steel tubing familiar, for example, from chairs designed by Mies van der Rohe and Marcel Breuer. The result was technically, functionally and aesthetically convincing. The Paimio chairs made a commercial breakthrough already in 1933 in London, and around the same time in Zürich. They were the first export item of Finnish modernist applied art. The chairs were also noted at the Milan Triennials of 1933 and 1936.

In the mid-1930s, Aalto had come to know the Gullichsens when he was chosen to be the architect of the new industrial community of Sunila at the mouth of the Kymijoki River in south-east Finland. The Sunila project was headed by Harry Gullichsen. Maire Gullichsen had studied art and was a passionate proponent of the new modernism and its utilization in all possible ways. These aims coincided with the Gullichsens' deeper commitment to the modernization of industry and society, with architecture and applied art among its means. Collaboration with the Gullichsens gave Aalto exceptional opportunities to realize his own concepts. One such opportunity was the design of homes and their furnishings on a wide scale ranging from the executive couple's residence to housing for workers.

Founded in 1935 with decisive support from Maire Gullichsen, Artek was a project that was distinct from the Ahlström corporation. Artek's purpose was to market products for modern interior decoration. Already, at the time, the core items were furniture designed by Aalto and made by the Korhonen company. In addition to sales, Artek also provided interior design services for public spaces. This became the work of Aino Aalto, who also designed furniture and textiles separately from her husband. Aino Aalto headed Artek from 1941 until her death in 1949. Nils-Gustav Hahl, the first managing director, had died in the war. Hahl was a proponent of modern applied art, who alongside his work at Artek actively participated in related debate in newspapers and applied-art and design journals.

At the time and throughout the rest of his career Aalto had an exceptional opportunity, even by international standards, to have furniture designed by him manufactured and sold. This was made possible by an enlightened and loyal manufacturer, Artek as the distributing and marketing partner, and demand both in Finland and abroad. Artek naturally provided the furniture for the architectural projects designed by Alvar Aalto. Before the Second World War, however, Aalto furniture was mostly used in public space. It was quite radical for private consumption in a broader sense. For example, the non-upholstered elegance of the Paimio chairs was regarded as unadorned and barren. Exports based on foreign demand were slowed in the mid-1930s by the painstaking manufacturing process, mostly of a handcrafted nature. Although one of the reasons for establishing Artek had been the more effective marketing of Aalto furniture, manufacturing proved to be a bottleneck.

Artek's starting point was an attempt – exceptionally ambitious for the time – to spread the message of modernism in Finnish interior design. This required, however, the fortuitous synthesis of design skill, enlightened capital and modernism subscribing to an agenda – i.e. Aalto, Gullichsen and Hahl – to launch this brilliant experiment and to keep it going. The earlier, similar attempt represented by the Iris factory and its salesroom had not succeeded at the beginning of the 20th century.

Acceptance of the modern
Finnish applied art and design of the late 1930s reflect the relatively wide acceptance of modernism. This was aided by its comprehensive nature – designed artefacts were required for new public building and homes. Growing numbers of automobiles, increased mobility in the form of domestic and foreign travel, the spread of technology in everyday life and economic growth spurring consumer demand all created conditions for the adoption of a modern artefactual world. Reformist tendencies had a similar aim, steering society and the family towards the "modern". The last year of peace, 1939, has a gilded image in

▶ The anonymous modernism of everyday life that became widespread in Finnish homes was represented by, among other products, tubular-steel beds available in several models and generically known in Finnish as *heteka*. Especially in small homes they doubled as sofas in daytime. The *heteka* beds were easy to clean and being fitted with casters were also easily moved. Picture from the catalogue of the Merivaara furniture company.

DUPLO-
sohvassa
ihanin
lepo

J. Merivaara

Finnish historiography, and it was indeed the climax of the country's rapid rise to affluence and its multi-level process of modernization. The corresponding level of national income would not be achieved until the mid-1960s.

The furniture introduced on the market by the Finnish cabinet-making industry was of restrained modern character and made of domestic timber grades, and was also truly serviceable and moderately priced. It did not arouse the same kind of rejection as the "tube-functionalist furniture" that was largely felt to be intended for public space. Acceptance was abetted by the fact that this modernist design in wood was by no means uniquely light-coloured. Dark-stained surfaces of birch veneer in imitation of hardwoods together with neo-objectively simple and appropriate form gave this furniture both use value and symbolic status. The spread of the modern idiom of form also to small towns and rural communities was speeded by the shops of the cooperative movement and their interior design.

In Finland, as in the other Nordic countries, positive attitudes to modernism were aided by its connection with the modernization of society. The objective here was the welfare state, the construction of which did not properly come under way until after the Second World War. Its undeniably positive goals included emphasis on gender equality, social egalitarianism and education. Even the modernism of applied art gradually become part of the everyday lives of many people. It did not remain the sole property of the cultural and economic elite, as had been the case in England and France, among other countries. But it would be an error of perspective to maintain that the Finnish mentality and material environment would have been comprehensively modernized without the above-described success. Finland was still an agrarian country and its forest industry's plants, which were large even internationally, were at the boundaries of forests and bodies of water, and connected with the countryside.

The 1930s were also a time of cultural introversion and a farmer-spirited nationalism with its basis in the predominantly agrarian nature of the country. In such an atmosphere, heralds of modernism like Artek were an exception, not an overall image. A parallel here is the fact

▶ The ethic of Nordic modernism in particular included the idea that design of high aesthetic and functional quality should be available to a broad sector of the population. The architect Aino Aalto designed this low-priced pressed-glass tableware service for the Karhula-Iittala glassworks in 1932.

◄ The so-called *Savoy* vase designed by Alvar Aalto for the Karhula-Iittala glassworks was the winning entry of a glass design competition held by the glassworks in 1936. Still in production, it is probably the best-known example of Finnish design ever made.

▶ *Vähän vino* (Slightly askew) carafe and tumbler set of green bubble glass designed by Yrjö Rosola in 1932 for Karhula-Iittala.

that the year 1935, when Artek was founded, was also the centenary of the publication of the *Kalevala* epic, which was celebrated with due nationalist pathos. It is obvious which event was of greater cultural importance nationally. The same year saw the start of the Kalevala Koru company, still operating today, which produced items of jewellery copied from the prehistoric past of Finland. The key source of international inspiration had traditionally been Germany, whose exemplary role was now clouded by Nazism. Interest in the culture of England, Finland's most important trading partner, was maintained by Western-oriented liberal industrialist circles and a few figures prominent in cultural life, such as the Ahlströms and Aalto.

Finland in the inter-war years

How did professionalism in applied art, its utilization and related business emerge during the inter-war years? In what connections was professional skill applied and did its role essentially change during this

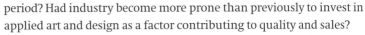

period? Had industry become more prone than previously to invest in applied art and design as a factor contributing to quality and sales?

The industrial backbone of Finland was the forestry and paper sector, which had no need for any design to embellish its bulk goods. Finland differed from Sweden, for example, which had major corporations applying design in the manufacturing of vehicles and electrical equipment. On the other hand, Finland's forestry industry, as in the case of the Ahlström and Enso-Gutzeit companies, could rely on modernist design and planning in creating their own milieux. Although the country's large textile industry had not shown interest in Finnish professionals in the applied arts, the situation changed in the 1930s. The teaching of textile art and design had been introduced at the Central School of Arts and Crafts in 1929 and these graduates were now being increasingly recruited for industrial textile design.

The glass industry, another traditional sector, also saw changes. A key role was given to competitions, through which companies in the field sought ideas for renewing their ranges of products. The competitions had two objectives: product types for mass-produced household glassware and designs for art-glass pieces. The latter were handcrafted objects made in small editions, mostly vases.

The glass design competitions led to the manufacturing of products designed by Aino and Alvar Aalto for both everyday use and interior decoration. In a competition held in 1936 by the Ahlström corporation's Karhula-Iittala glassworks, Aalto was awarded a prize for a free-form vase blown into a wooden mould. Subsequently known as the *Savoy* vase, this item would become the Finnish glass industry's most widely known product abroad. In 1934, Aino Aalto designed a set of pressed-glass plates, pourers and tumblers which the company began to manufacture. Unlike her husband's design, which was of an exclusive nature and associated with contemporary Continental European and abstract visual art, Aino Aalto's tableware represented "beauty for everyday life" created with the industrial means of modernism.

Although modernist design was adopted in Finnish applied-art products, the turn of the 1930s did not mark any fundamental change in production and technology. With the possible exception of Aalto, new form thus did not stem from any comprehensive change in the level of technology. This had been the case in the areas where the original avant-garde of Continental Europe had emerged, where the level of technologization, mass production on a large scale and related practices of rationalization were reflected directly in the ideas and work of the leading ideologues of new architecture and design. In Finland, many sectors that had been based on mass production for a long while, such as the textile, glass and furniture industries, gradually took design skills into use to a growing degree in order to respond to increasingly quality- and style-conscious demand mainly among middle-class clients. As modernism gained an established role, it became profitable at least to experiment with this new orientation – while not rejecting by any means the more traditional product types. The extremely modern symbiosis of Korhonen, Aalto and Artek was thus an exception to the rule.

Change was nonetheless present, and it also involved the Arabia factory, the leading enterprise in applied art. Arabia's output of ceramic products was significant even in international terms and its exports, all the way to South America, were of considerable scale. In 1932, the company hired Kurt Ekholm of Sweden to be its artistic director. The *Sinivalko* (Blue-White) collection, created under his direction and produced for some twenty years, was launched in 1936. It combined the Swedish concept of "beauty for everyday life" with form and simple ornament designed in the spirit of modernism, i.e. functionalism. Around the same time, the Arabia Art Department was established upon Ekholm's initiative. It served as a base for free ceramic art and also provided impulses for mass production. Arabia thus invested efforts in two areas, the reform of mass production and ceramic art. After the war the Finnish glass industry was to adopt the same strategy.

Trained ceramists thus began to find more challenging and independent tasks than decoration, initially in the 1920s but for the most part in the following decades. The so-called applied art sectors of Finnish industry, such as furniture, glass, textiles and ceramics, and professionals with training in the field approached each other during the 1930s. Architects were still prominently involved. The long-term and slowly progressing "push" of designers into industry was turning into

▶ Advertisement from the late 1930s of the Taito lamp company headed by Paavo Tynell, a pioneer of Finnish lamp design. Founded in 1918, Taito was one of the first design companies operating in the newly independent republic of Finland.

TAITO-valaisimia

Postitalon
toimistovalaisin

Oulu Oy:n
tehdasvalaisin

Helsingin Sa-
nomain kirja-
painosalien
sekavalo-
kaluste

Suomen Filmi-
teollisuuden
studio-
valonheittäjä

Kaukopään
tehdasvalaisin

K. O. P:n
johtokunnan
huoneen
kattovalaisin

Sunila Oy:n
konttori-
valaisin

Valtioneuvos-
ton halli-
valaisin

Outokumpu
Oy:n klubi-
valaisin

Ruotsalaisen
Teatterin
hallivalaisin

Rajamäen kirkon alttari-
kynttiläjalka

Mikael Agricolan kirkon kruunu

Eduskuntatalon kruunu

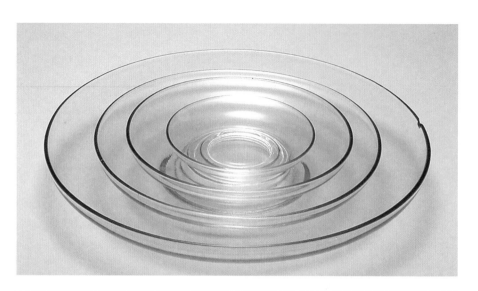

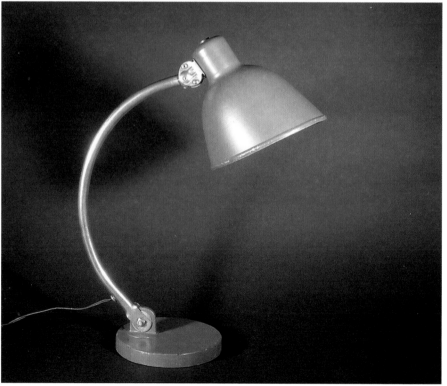

◄ Design professionals and everyday material culture: Göran Hongell's pressed-glass *Silko* collection, designed for the Karhula-Iittala glassworks in 1936 (top) and a table lamp (bottom) designed by Paavo Tynell and made by the Taito company in the 1930s.

a reciprocating "pull" by industry. Graphic designers, in turn, were being increasingly employed by the advertising industry, which had begun to grow in the 1920s. Pre-war advertising agencies such as SEK and Mainos-Taucher (founded 1940) offered their services to the business community, while large central retail organizations, such as the Elanto cooperative, established their own information and advertising departments.

How then did professionals in design engage in their own business activities? In 1907 the architect Eino Schroderus (1880–1956) had founded the Koru company, focusing in particular on lamps of his own design. Their market had expanded and uses had changed through the spread of electrification. The Taito company, established in 1918 by Eric O.W. Ehrström and Paavo Tynell (1890–1973),[76] professionals in metalwork, operated successfully into the post-war years, concentrating above all on producing lamps designed by Tynell. It was described above how in the 1920s independent weaving studios were founded in the female-dominated arena of textile art, in which the artist or designer was also an entrepreneur. In graphic design pioneering entrepreneurial efforts were made by Finland's first commercial drawing office known as De Tre (The Three), formed by Toivo Vikstedt (1891–1930), Harry Röneholm and Bruno Tuukkanen (1891–1979). It was founded in 1914, but operated for only a few years.

Even in the 1930s entrepreneurship in applied art and design was still a precarious area, and there were no offices or agencies offering design services in the present sense of these terms. Alongside all the above-described modernization and mass production there were also old professional identities of applied art underlining continuity that were still in demand. The decorative artist Bruno Tuukkanen, for example, still worked successfully in the 1930s in preparing tradition-bound briefs for the decorative painting work of major public buildings such as churches. The slow stream of tradition still continued alongside modernism declaring its message and agenda. Therefore, the image of the applied arts of the 1930s is richer than some have wanted to see it in retrospect. Traditions, their merging with the modern, and self-aware avant-gardism were all simultaneously present.

A SYMBOL OF THE YOUNG REPUBLIC

As political stability was achieved in the 1920s after independence in 1917, a new building was needed for the parliament of the young republic of Finland. The architectural competition for the project was held in 1924 and was won by the office of Borg, Sirén, Åberg. Based on designs by J. S. Sirén, Parliament House was completed in 1930. Its classicist exterior and the motifs of the interior were not only related to the trends of the 1920s but also made reference to Ancient Greece as the birthplace of democracy. Although Sirén designed part of the interior, the work included Finland's leading professionals in furniture and textile design and metalwork. The project was highly demanding and, owing to its national significance, it was generously funded. It thus helped raise the standard and visibility of applied art in Finland. The professionals of applied art who had established the Ornamo association in 1911 were now involved as designers and no longer in realizing the designs of architects.

1

1. Parliament House in Helsinki.

2. Main staircase of Parliament House.

3. Cafeteria. Furniture designed by Werner West.

4. Women's lounge. Furniture designed by Elsa Arokallio, carpet by Maija Kansanen.

4

AALTO AND ARTEK

In the late 1920s the architect Alvar Aalto began to experiment with new techniques of curving and laminating Finnish birch in collaboration with the furniture manufacturer Otto Korhonen. These experiments led to a series of chairs and other furniture designed in the spirit of international modernism. In the earliest versions, a leg part of curved steel tubing was joined to the curved wooded seat and backrest. The armchairs designed by Aalto for the Paimio Tuberculosis Sanatorium in the early 1930s marked a transition from laminated wood to curved flexible structures comprising the leg part and handrests. Aalto's collaboration with Korhonen in the 1930s resulted in a wide range of furniture in which combinations of the same techniques and parts were used to make a variety of products for both public and private interior design.

The marketing of Aalto furniture began to be managed in 1935 by the Artek company, which was founded at the time and is still in operation. A background figure of Artek was Maire Gullichsen, a leading proponent of the culture of modern art and habitation, who could rely on the funds of the Ahlström corporation. The collaboration of Aalto, Korhonen and Artek was exceptionally successful and provided Aalto's designs with not only a manufacturer but also with a domestic and international channel of distribution. Artek provided furniture for Aalto's architectural projects until the 1980s.

1. Exhibition interior of the early 1930s. Furniture from the years 1930–1933.

2. Chair combining birch laminate and curved metal tubing, 1930.

3. Chair originally designed for the Paimio Sanatorium, 1932. The metal tubing has been replaced by curved wood.

4. In its initial stages Aalto furniture was mostly made by hand, which slowed responses to international demand.

5. Aalto designed two chair types for the Paimio Sanatorium in 1932 (see fig. 3). The chair shown here is known internationally as the *Paimio* Chair.

6. View of the Artek shop in Helsinki after the mid-1930s.

1

2

3

4

5

6

THE EMERGENCE OF POSTER ART

Poster art, which had already been introduced in the 19th century and mainly employed lithographic printing technology gained significance in the early 1900s. Posters announcing cultural events and exhibitions kept their former role, but as commercial activities expanded advertisements drawing attention to businesses or their products became more common. The design of posters for tourism and fairs also expanded. Posters were designed by artists, such as Akseli Gallen-Kallela, a leading pioneer of Finnish poster art, architects, and before long by trained professionals in graphic design. Before electronic communications posters played an important role in visual information, and they had considerable visibility in the townscape.

1

REKLAAMI
MESSUT TAIDEHALLISSA
HELSINGISSÄ 21/29 HUHTIKUUTA 1928

TILGMANNIN KIVIPAINO H:KI

3

4

1. Akseli Gallen-Kallela, the 'Bil-Bol' poster for the Yrjö Weilin car dealership's department at the Stockholm Automobile Exhibition of 1907.

2. Poster for an advertising fair, Toivo Vikstedt 1928.

3. Car exhibition poster by Carolus Lindberg, 1927. Urban elegance had now replaced passion (fig. 1).

4. The Elanto cooperative's advertisement for Pommac soft drink. Aarne Eklund, 1933.

5. Advertisement by Göran Hongell for the Helsinki Fair of 1935.

SUUR-
MESSUT

HELSINGISSÄ
LOKAK. 5-13 P.

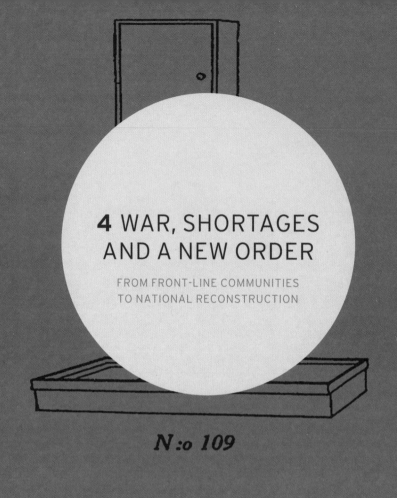

4 WAR, SHORTAGES AND A NEW ORDER

FROM FRONT-LINE COMMUNITIES
TO NATIONAL RECONSTRUCTION

N:o 109

N:o 111

N:o 112

N:o 110

N:o 103

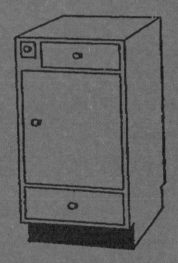

N:o 107

N:o 104

N:o 106

1939–1945	1946	1947	1948	1949
The war years	The *Nordisk Konst-hantverk* exhibition of applied art in Copenhagen	The construction and interior deco-ration of the Do-mus Academica student housing project	The magazine *Kaunis koti* (Beautiful Home) begins to appear	The *Kauneutta arkeen* (Beauty for Everyday Life) exhibition at Kunsthalle Helsinki

The period that lasted from the late autumn of 1939 to the spring of 1945 included the Finnish-Soviet Winter War and Continuation War (1939–1940; 1941–1944) and the Lapland War (1944–1945) which was fought against Germany. These conflicts and their repercussions constituted an emergency and an exceptional state of affairs, which had a major impact on opportunities in the applied arts and their realization and implementation. Industry largely focused on the war economy, exports had for practical purposes ceased, and the younger male age-groups were at the front. Despite this, the years of shortage that followed the war and the reconstruction process that came under way were, surprisingly, a period during which many sectors of applied art flourished. This mainly concerned crafts, products made on a one-off basis or in small editions, but there were also breakthroughs, for example, in furniture and glass. Under the severe conditions of the time it was possible to continue the developments of the 1930s that had been interrupted by the war, now with new and fresh actors. The period saw the emergence of a group of young designers who were to dominate the scene over the following decades. The results of the immediate postwar years and the persons involved provided Finnish applied art and design with astounding success at the Milan Triennial of 1951. This was the first international acclaim gained by the field after the war.

The terms of war and austerity

During the so-called interim peace between Finland and the Soviet Union from March 1940 until June 1941 there was some recovery of industries and applied art. For example, the housing exhibition of the previous autumn that had been suddenly closed reopened in 1940. This time, however, it addressed reconstruction – homes were needed for 400,000 evacuees from Karelia and the Hanko region now under Soviet control and for others who had suffered from the war. In this situation, the housing exhibitions of the previous decade, which had also been rich in terms of applied art and design, were given a less ornate appearance and a focus on minimum needs. Although the annual exhibitions of the Finnish Society of Crafts and Design continued through the war years, production in these fields had mostly come to a halt. A significant ex-

Jälleen-rakentamaan

ASUNTO NÄYTTELY
JA RAKENNUSMESSUT

◀ Because of the impending threat of war, the Finnish Housing Fair in the autumn of 1939 was closed soon after it had opened to the public. The fair reopened in the summer of 1940 with the new themes of reconstruction and serving the basic needs of the home. The exhibition poster was designed by the architect Jorma Suhonen.

ception, however was Arabia, which was even given special permission to expand, because its significant exports provided foreign currency needed by the country.

Two foreign exhibitions of Finnish applied art were held during the interim peace. A relatively small showing in Copenhagen in 1940 was followed by a larger event at the Nationalmuseum in Stockholm in the spring of 1941. This exhibition was enthusiastically received. While no doubt partly due to political goodwill in response to Finland's difficult position, this appreciation was also genuine. Sweden, which had always been regarded as a source of inspiration, now received something found to be different, authentic – and Finnish. It was also an entity in which crafted objects predominated. However, the ceramics of Michael Schilkin (1900–1962)[77] and Toini Muona (1904–1987)[78] and richly coloured ryijy-rugs that differed from traditional designs were noted because they stood out from the restrained elegance popular among Swedes and their rational "everyday goods". The commissioner of the exhibition, the Arabia factory's artistic director Kurt Ekholm, originally Swedish, knew how to stage a Finnish display for his compatriots.

But people lived, dwelt and consumed even during the war. In what kind of space could design and applied art exist? The shortage of materials particularly concerned textiles, but, as so often before, Finns turned to the forests, albeit indirectly. Paper now had to replace textile fibres. Industrially made utility textiles of paper were widely used as carpets and curtains, among other items, and they were also designed by well-known names such as Dora Jung (1906–1980),[79] later known for her damask work. Also "art textiles" as elements of interior decoration were made of substitute materials because of the lack of fibres. In 1942 Greta Skogster-Lehtinen (1900–1994) had wallpaper made at her weavery of birch bark, grease-proof paper and paper string.

Front-line communities – back to a subsistence economy

Because of the general shortage of materials and male labour, pre-war levels of applied art production, however, could not be maintained. This sector of the workforce was at the front, which was stuck in a three-year deadlock with no major advances or retreats. In the meantime,

the women of the home front attended to work in the homes, and in agriculture and industry. Men at the front had to be provided with an environment congenial to habitation and other activities. As fighting as such had been interrupted, activities had to be found for soldiers, as pastimes and for useful purposes. The result was a strange phenomenon consisting of temporary communities for soldiers built deep in the forests of Karelia — craft products were created there. The material for all this production was local timber.

This milieu, necessarily unadorned but specifically aiming at making life comfortable, consisted of buildings, furniture and both useful and ornamental objects. Their design and execution harked back to the world of home crafts and the subsistence economy, with knives, axes, planes and saws as tools. On the one hand it was necessary to create a setting for the everyday environment of even large bodies of troops, while on the other hand the small works of handicraft were mostly taken home, when soldiers went on leave, to be used there. This, however, was not applied art as such, even though it had parallels with the products of the so-called crafts or work cottages that operated in the Finnish countryside towards the end of the 19th century.

There were also professionals of design and applied art at the front, such as Tapio Wirkkala (1915–1985)[80] and Ilmari Tapiovaara. During the period of so-called standstill in warfare, Tapiovaara, who had already enjoyed some professional success, was responsible at his section of the front for the design of public buildings such as canteens and dug-out shelters, and finally for planning all building work. In this process he gained command of design, execution and use of labour on a large scale. At the same time, he applied the principles of modernism, including those absorbed as a trainee in Le Corbusier's office in the late 1930s. Under the exceptional front-line conditions, the results as such were of modest quality, but the scale of requirements no doubt made Tapiovaara develop to respond to the opportunities that arose after the war.

In a broader sense, practices of creating types, standardization and serial production in stages became the heritage of the war years. Although this process was most advanced in the United States, it also emerged on a smaller scale in Finland. In a way, the war was a decisive factor whereby the methods that Aalto had developed as an individual in the early 1930s were now achieved more generally. Ambitious object design combined with reproducibility, offering opportunities for production, could improve the lives of broad sectors of the population.

The rise of furniture design

The post-war years were marked on the one hand by a shortage of materials dictated by a rationed economy and on the other hand by reconstruction launched quickly and in response to necessity. Those who had lost their homes had to be provided with environments for habitation. Further pressure was created by a very high birth rate between 1945 and 1950. Responses to this were mainly wooden single-family houses and their simple furniture, reflecting the period of austerity. Hard times and limited resources produced a functioning, if ascetic, culture of interior decoration.

Pre-war tendencies for the functional rationalization of the home continued under these conditions. Particular attention was now focused on kitchens, their dimensions and ease of use. Education in this area was led by women's organizations such as the Martta Federation together with other public bodies. In the kitchens of post-war buildings, architecture, interior design, furnishings and, before long, tableware were combined as a whole. The basis of this combination was a "laboratory" of the home created through measurements and standards, in which a housewife without domestic help could attend to the well-being of her family as efficiently as possible. Standards made the products of kitchen-cabinet manufacturers compatible, and suited to the spaces created in the extensive programme of reconstruction. These externally modest spaces that were important for everyday life were among the most important achievements of applied art and design in the post-war years of shortages.

Immediately after the war a broad process began to create the functions of the welfare state and their spaces and facilities. Child care, education at all levels and health care required buildings and their furnishings alike. Also for this reason, the design and production of furniture were important areas. The situation also had positive effects on related professional practices. Relationships between manufacturing, training and professional practice in the field were consolidated.

'Interior architect' became the professional title for designers of furnishings and furniture, and this group engaged in successful and wide-ranging cooperation with architects. This was partly due to the extent of the work; architects would no longer have had the time to design the interiors of their projects as they had done before. Training also produced professionals with better capabilities who could respond to the challenges of the period. Although some architects, such as Aalto, carried out large projects down to their furnishings, the collaboration of architects and interior architects became standard practice in the 1940s. The SIO association of Finnish interior architects, founded in 1949 as a section of the Ornamo association, became Finland's first organization of design professionals in a specific field. It was the first to reflect the rise and self-awareness that was soon to mark the whole field of applied art and design. The pressures of reconstruction and industrial progress speeded by war reparations to the Soviet Union created a situation in which applied art and design could prove its usefulness. The symbiosis of industry and art envisioned by Estlander in the 1870s was becoming reality – industrial art.

Rationalization and romanticism
Ilmari Tapiovaara and the Domus project are a good example of these developments. In 1947 the Domus Academica project was launched, a major housing facility for university students who were now coming in droves to Helsinki from the countryside and smaller cities. The competition for the furnishing of the hundreds of dormitory rooms and public spaces of Domus Academica was won by Annikki (1910–1972) and Ilmari Tapiovaara. Tapiovaara's own furniture company, Keravan Puuteollisuus Oy, was now able to carry out the serial production that he had already envisioned before the war. The core item of the interior decoration brief was a wooden all-purpose chair. Known as the Domus chair, it was distributed widely, first in Finland, followed by the Nordic countries, England, Central Europe and finally in the United States through the Knoll company. This structurally simple product made of

solid wood, two pieces of plywood and a few screws was realized with limited means while successfully combining a high standard of design, mass production, distribution and universal functionality. The *Domus* chair was Finland's first significant exported post-war design product and a crystallization of Tapiovaara's pre-war hopes regarding the social role of modernism. Though unassuming in appearance, the chair made good design available to the masses.

The *Domus* chair, however, was mainly an item for public spaces and its subdued design was inappropriate for the living rooms of post-war homes. Times were hard, and comfort was sought in the home to provide a contrast, for example with fully upholstered and cushioned sofa and armchair suites, such as the *Laila* collection made by the Asko company. Suites of upholstered furniture show how two seemingly contradictory yet complementary trends were present in post-war applied art. On the one hand, standards, rationalization and types were applied to produce

▲ The *Domus* chair from 1946 was designed by Ilmari Tapiovaara and made by the Keravan Puuteollisuus company. It expresses both the austerity of the post-war years and the designer's ability to find a functioning equation of material, manufacturing and usability – without ignoring the aesthetic dimension.

▶ After the Second World War there was focus on the functionality of homes and their kitchens in particular. The spread of standardization in housing development permitted the production of kitchen cupboards in established sizes. The dish-drying rack shown here is a Finnish invention that is still in use.

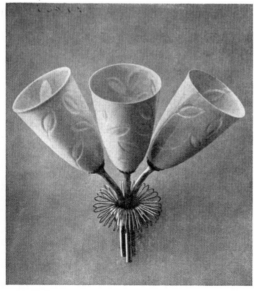

a high-quality environment quickly and to a large scale. On the other hand, the 1940s were marked by romanticizing trends emphasizing comfort and the enhancement of everyday life. In homes, these trends were evident in the nature of kitchens and living rooms respectively. One was an efficient working environment, while the other was a space for rest, comfort and the family spending time together – the function of reception and representation is a survival of the traditional drawing room. This "romanticization" had already begun to emerge before the Second World War, softening the requirements of programmatic modernism. Now the contemporary period and mentality created demand for it. The many public interiors of these years show how crafted details and fashionable shiny brass surfaces created comfort and even opulence in the austere conditions of the period. Good examples are the lamps designed by Paavo Tynell and made by the Taito company, which combined brass, opal glass, ornamental forms and details.

The polarity and coexistence of rationalization and the design of ornamental objects were also typical of glass and ceramics. Glass production involving applied art can be divided into three areas: industrially made pressed glass, blown serial objects and blown art glass in small editions or as unique, one-off pieces. In addition, glass could either be blown by machine or hand. Companies such as the Iittala and Karhula glassworks of the Ahlström group had already acquired design services through competitions held before the war. This was how everyday glassware and art glass by Aino and Alvar Aalto came to be made. In 1937 Göran Hongell (1902–1973),[81] who had been trained in design, designed the *Silko* tumbler collection, which corresponded to the *Sinivalko* (Blue-White) ceramic tableware made by the Arabia factory. In 1948, the *Aarne* glassware designed by Hongell for the Iittala glassworks was introduced. Its simplified form referred to modernism and set the stage for the future success of blown Finnish utility glassware.

In the three-tiered hierarchy of glass, pressed glass ranked lowest; next came blown utility glassware; and art glass was placed uppermost. The last-mentioned category aroused the greatest amount of attention during the war and later. It permitted companies gaining their income from household glassware and other serial products, such as Karhula-

◀ The Sokos department store in the centre of Helsinki had been designed by the architect Erkki Huttunen before the war. The department store and the Vaakuna hotel and restaurant in connection with it were opened to the public in 1949. Plywood panelling, shiny brass, indoor plants – a feeling of luxury achieved with sparse means.

▶ The *Aarne* glassware collection designed by Göran Hongell for the Iittala glassworks in 1948 continued the modernism of the previous decade and made the glass itself part of the form of expression and structure of the work.

Iittala,[82] Nuutajärvi and Riihimäen Lasi,[83] to enhance their reputation through these exclusive art pieces and their designers, who were given public exposure. Although this marketing strategy became common in the 1950s, the new status of art glass had already been created.

Versatile professional designers

The leading names to renew glass art in the 1940s were Gunnel Nyman (1909–1948)[84] and Tapio Wirkkala, both of whom had graduated from the Central School of Arts and Crafts. At the time and for a long while afterwards, professionals in the applied arts worked in several disciplines and did not rely solely on the qualifications of their personal training. Regarded as a characteristic and an asset of Finnish applied art, this has been explained by the fact that the artistic skills underscored by Arttu Brummer and joint courses in general design laid the basis for endeavour in many directions. As a result, the criticisms of the modernists of the 1930s, such as Nils-Gustav Hahl, regarding the separation of training from industry, became an asset after the war. Best known for her work in glass, Nyman had originally graduated in furniture design, and the multi-skilled Wirkkala was trained as an ornamental sculptor. Of the famed designers of later years, Timo Sarpaneva (1926–2006)[85] was originally a graphic artist, but first achieved renown in glass design. Kaj Franck (1911–1989),[86] known for his work in ceramics and glass, had graduated in furniture design, while Vuokko Nurmesniemi (1930–)[87] was a ceramist.

As early as 1941, Gunnel Nyman had designed a free-form glass piece entitled *Facett* (Facet) for an exhibition sent to Stockholm by the Finnish Society of Crafts and Design. While this shallow, irregularly shaped crystal dish could be functionally classed as an object for serving, it was above all an abstract work of art perceptively utilizing the properties of glass. This was a feature that would mark Nyman's later work as well as a major portion of all post-war art glass in Finland. Although these objects, mostly vases, were with certain restrictions bound to use and function, their main subject concerned the art of glass. The basis for this art was laid by a new understanding of the opportunities of glass and the close cooperation of designers and glassblowers.

The *Kantarelli* (Chanterelle) vase designed by Tapio Wirkkala in 1946 was in turn derived from a motif from nature, but given abstract form as a glass sculpture of small format. Made in small editions, *Kantarelli* was a jewel of the post-war glass industry in its skill and delicacy. It was at one end of an axis extending to utility glassware. The other end consisted of household glassware, jars and bottles for milk and cream, essential aspects of the everyday life of Finns until the 1960s.

Arabia: unique works alongside mass production

Finland's glassworks now began to hire designers on a permanent basis. Both Wirkkala and Kaj Franck were employed by Iittala on the basis of a competition held in 1946. Art glass was increasingly featured in exhibitions and the press but despite its exposure it was an auxiliary product in relation to the renewal and extent of the mass-produced product lines of these companies. The new homes of the reconstruction period needed not only furniture but also tableware, of both glass and ceramics. Where the kitchen was the place for household and utility glassware, the vase

▶ Art glass created by Gunnel Nyman at the Nuutajärvi glassworks in the late 1940s represented a new kind of sculptural expression based on glass as a material. The *Helminauha* (String of Pearls) vase from 1948.

◀ *Kantarelli* (Chanterelle) vase by Tapio Wirkkala, Iittala glassworks, 1946. Highly stylized from a motif from nature, this piece is on the borderlines of utility and art object.

produced by the same manufacturer for the decoration and aesthetic needs of the home was on the sideboard in the living room.

Arabia, the leading company of the Finnish ceramics industry, had already chosen the above-described double strategy before the Second World War. It had both set out to modernize its basic production under Kurt Ekholm and established its art department to serve free ceramic art. Nor was the factory restricted to the same degree by the rationing of the economy as other sectors of industry. Ceramic art was able to evolve undisturbed through the efforts of Toini Muona, Friedl Kjellberg (1905–1993), Aune Siimes (1909–1964) and Birger Kaipiainen (1915–1988),[88] and others. After the war, the factory's art department could offer the international exhibitions that now opened up a wide range of unique, one-off objects of art ceramics. The department's artist Michael Schilkin, who was a ceramic sculptor, also managed to include his work in public urban space. Schilkin's works, such as his colourful stylized naturalistic figures from 1952 on the façade of the Helsinki School of Economics building, were on the borderlines of decoration and figurative sculpture. Sakari Vapaavuori (1920–1989), also of the art department, made abstract chamotte sculptures, some of which were large, for public outdoor space near the Arabia factory. But since they were "only" ceramics and the works of professionals in applied art, they were not noted in the small art world of Finland. The works of Vapaavuori, like Maija Kansanen's textiles of earlier years and the art glass of Wirkkala and Sarpaneva in the 1950s, were non-figurative art which was still rejected by official art circles.

As a company, however, Arabia was not based on art, but instead on utility ceramics produced in large series. A class apart, and a source of income, was sanitary porcelain, i.e. washbasins and toilet seats, which were in considerable demand during the post-war years. Although they can be classed more as building supplies rather than applied art, the boundary is flexible. Vapaavuori applied his sculptor's skills to toilet seats with lids designed by Tapio Wirkkala. Down-to-earth beauty for everyday life.

With few exceptions the factory's mass-produced items were quite conservative after the Second World War. This policy was also supported by the preferences of consumers. As noted above, the mainstream during and after the war preferred security, ornamentality and comfort. The *Myrna* coffee service designed by Olga Osol (1905–1994) and introduced on the market in 1942 is a good example of the trend. To the disappointment of modernists and the joy of consumers, it remained in production for sixty years.

After the war, however, there was growing pressure to renew the basic models of tableware. This was not, however, due so much to the enlightenment of the company management, who were satisfied so long as operations were profitable regardless of the appearance of products. Criticism came from outside, because Arabia's range of products lacked "everyday wares of greater beauty" meaning items of contemporary, i.e. modernist, design. With this in mind, Kurt Ekholm had already persuaded Arabia to employ Kaj Franck as the artistic director of

◄ During the Second World War, and especially after the war, the Art Department of the Arabia factory played a key role in reinterpreting ceramic art and in expanding its scope. Vases by Toini Muona, late 1940s.

▶ Art ceramics also served as public works of art that influenced the townscape. Michael Schilkin of the Arabia Art Department made a large series of reliefs symbolizing study and world trade for the façade of the new building of the Helsinki School of Economics, built in 1952.

the applied art department, serving mass production. Franck, however, had little influence on decisions concerning production, and the company continued to make its cautiously conservative models with reference to historical examples, such as the Rococo style. After having first renewed the Iittala glassworks' range of utility glassware, Franck had already designed, in 1948, a simple multipurpose home tableware service for the Arabia factory. This, however, was regarded as too radical for the markets. This situation repeated Tapiovaara's experiences in furniture design with the Asko company in 1939.

Franck's tableware, named *Kilta*, did not come into production until 1953. By that time, however, a fundamental change had taken place in the attitudes of Finnish design as a whole and the industries that utilized it. Consumer attitudes had also changed, and companies had cause to note these signs carefully. The nostalgic romanticism of the years of shortages was now giving way to broad acceptance of modernism. This, however, did not take place overnight, or of its own accord. Success, publicity and public enlightenment about the beneficial effects of good taste were needed. Good taste was, of course, defined by the main actors of applied art, the gatekeepers of style and the educators of the public, from their elevated status, where good was synonymous with modern.

International success – the awakening of Finnish industry

The active pre-war exhibition efforts of the Finnish Society of Crafts and Design had presented the best of Finnish applied art and design to the domestic public, while also enjoying success in the international displays of the 1930s. After the inactivity of the war years – an exception being a successful showing in Stockholm in 1941 – the best achievements of the field were again taken to Stockholm, now to be part of a joint Nordic exhibition of applied art in 1946. The commissioner was once again Kurt Ekholm of Arabia, who had also become an agent of the Finnish Society of Crafts and Design. His duty was to make the new design and applied art known in industry and among the Finnish and international public alike. The exhibits, now including, among other items, new glass design by Gunnel Nyman and Tapio Wirkkala, and lamps by Paavo Tynell and Lisa Johannson-Pape, were positively received. A note of discord, however, were comments expressing surprise over the absence of modern everyday items and wares. This, as well as subsequent comments on international showings, aroused discussion in the Finnish applied art and design community. The situation of Finland in these years of austerity was, of course, completely different from that of neutral Sweden, which had been able to develop in peace. The elites who dictated tastes in Finland, however, gained from this criticism further support for their concern over the prevailing quality of the applied-arts products.

▲ Abstract public work of sculpture in chamotte from 1955 by Sakari Vapaavuori, who designed, among other products, sanitary porcelain for the Arabia factory.

Discussion in professional circles led in 1949 in to the exhibition *Beauty for Everyday Life*, organized by the Ornamo design association. Planned on a triennial basis, it was meant to lead the public to good applied art and design. The problem that arose was that basic Finnish design and applied arts products that would be of sufficient quality from the organizers' point of view would not be available for many years, and therefore only a single exhibition was held. The future success of Finnish design, especially in the international arena, would still be achieved through unique or small-edition works.

The Milan triennials had been resumed in 1947, but Finland did not participate at the time. It was decided that the country would take part in the next triennial, in 1951, and Tapio Wirkkala was chosen to be the commissioner of the exhibition. Around the same time, the Kunstgewerbemuseum of Zürich stated that it wanted to stage an exhibition of new Finnish applied art. The schedule and tour were both suitable, and it was decided to take the collection via Zürich to Milan. The showing in Zürich would be a dress rehearsal for the much more important event in Milan. Financing proved to be a problem, as this was an expensive undertaking. The Finnish Ministry of Education, which had previously funded exhibitions of this kind, now felt that it could cover only part of the costs. Herman Olof Gummerus (1909–1996),[89] who would become a leading figure in promoting Finnish design in the decades to come, now came on the scene. Gummerus was Arabia's chief information officer. He had lived in Italy as a child, spoke Italian and was in many other respects an appropriate ambassador of Finnish industrial design. He managed to convince industrial circles of the importance of the venture. When funding had been secured, the collection, its display equipment and Wirkkala and his wife Rut Bryk (1916–1999),[90] Gummerus and the carpenter Martti Lindqvist (1945–2004) set out to take Finnish design and applied art abroad, with consequences that could hardly have been anticipated.

Gummerus's role in this connection and his later work, from 1952, as the first managing director of the Finnish Society of Crafts and Design, cannot be emphasized too much. Since he did not come from applied art circles, he did not have the affiliations that marked this small and poorly funded sector and often impeded cooperation. He could thus concentrate on obtaining funds, providing information and public relations, an area in which Finns were somewhat deficient at the international level, with the possible exception of Aalto.

The Finnish department at the 1951 Triennial employed limited effects, but was impressive in its simplicity. Wirkkala's concept of using low display tables presented the sparsely placed objects well. The selection mostly contained crafted pieces, and serially produced items were represented by Tapiovaara's Domus chair, Aalto's three-legged stools and lamps by Johansson-Pape, which were placed along the walls. The Finnish department was immensely successful among critics and in terms of prizes and publicity. While Italian newspapers and magazines presented the exhibition and the Finnish department, the international

press was also present. Generally speaking, modern applied art and design were now featured in the media at a completely different level than before the war. As the standard of living had risen in the West, they had become the object of a new kind of consumption of explicit awareness and cultural distinction. The American magazine *House Beautiful*, for example, chose Wirkkala's vase of aeroplane plywood which had been on show as the "the most beautiful object of 1951".

It is almost impossible for people in today's stream of media to imagine what this sudden international publicity meant, especially for design and applied art in a country in the north-east margins of Europe that was still poor and isolated. And now, unlike after the success in Milan in 1933, this could be put to use both nationally and internationally. Under Gummerus, the Finnish Society of Crafts and Design continued its exhibition and publication work with great success. Finnish industries, in turn, had a late but effective awakening regarding the importance of design quality.

International acclaim – domestic success

The years of shortage and austerity began to end in 1952, Finland's "annus mirabilis", when the last war-reparations train left for Moscow, Helsinki hosted the Olympic Games and Armi Kuusela was crowned Miss Universe. As economic rationing eased, a large range of materials now became available to the applied arts. The ensuing Korean War boom speeded manufacturing and applied art and design were positioned well to respond to its requirements. The field no longer had to offer its services on its own – it was now being actively included and involved in developments.

Finland's modernist applied art and design sector had got off to a good start in the late 1930s, survived the war years at a slow pace, and emerged in the post-war period of shortages to continue what exceptional circumstances had postponed. This, however, was broadly the case for arts and crafts, where exoticism, national motifs and allegories of nature also replaced the abstraction of the 1930s. In mass production, the leading manufacturers kept to tradition, partly for reasons of ease and partly because they assumed the "people" wanted it. And this was also true, since consumers who were tired of the war and oppressed by shortages wanted security and comfort.

Refined asceticism and aesthetic minimalism are usually the interests of the elite, who feel it is their calling to "enlighten" the common people about the benefits of self-denial. This almost Calvinist attitude shunning comfort and ornament, has marked Finnish design-related thinking for many years. For the average consumer, popular education in the functional modernization of society and the home, for example, was quite welcome. A well designed kitchen no doubt made everyday life easier. At the aesthetic level, however, tableware services regarded as beautiful and prestigious were replaced only slowly with products such as *Kilta*, which were felt to be unadorned while simultaneously regarded as paragons of good design by the elite.

After the war, public and some private construction and development were the domain of architectural design. In this connection, this generally modernist environment of reconstruction was received as something given, not to be influenced by private individuals or families. On the other hand, acquisitions for the homes that were within the modernist framework were a private matter. It is here that we come to the problem of steering consumer habits. If modern artefacts were desired for the home, this required not only wide availability of these products and suitable pricing but also assurances for consumers that they were better. Large numbers of consumers and the housewives who mainly decided on these purchases were to be converted to modernism in design and applied art. Success in making modernism accepted over the following decades made Finland a wonderland of environmental and object design that the international press often wished to present. This took place especially in interaction with the international context. Success and prizes in foreign exhibitions, such as the triennials of the 1950s, gave the new applied art a positive aura. This phenomenon was similar to developments in Finnish sports. When the country's athletes were successful in international arenas, they fanned significant interest in sports, and at the same time domestic forms of supporting sports evolved, making Finland an even more important sporting nation.

keittiöön

5 THE GREAT RISE

SUCCESS IN EXHIBITIONS AND
OBJECTS FOR EVERYDAY LIFE

Hyvin muoto

vetaa avio

kei

Muotoilija tajuaa

kuluttajan tarpeen jo ennen

sen syntymistä

Hyvä muotoilu alentaa
tuotantokustannuksia ja lisää
markkinoita

talouskone

ehenkin

ön

Koneen muotoiltu vaippa ei saa
olla itsetarkoitus — sen on kuvastettava
teknillisesti tutkittua sis

1951	1952	1954	1957	1960
The Ninth Milan Triennial	Last war reparation train leaves for Moscow.	The Tenth Milan Triennial	The exhibition *Teollinen muoto* (Industrial Form) at Kunsthalle Helsinki	The Eleventh Milan Triennial
The founding of the Marimekko company	The Helsinki Olympic Games			

Finland's design sector began to change in a fundamental way in the early 1950s, with major developments in both quantity and quality. There were changes in the professional field, industry and consumption. Coinciding with this, the breakthrough of the Milan Triennial of 1951 was continued by international success that lasted until the end of the following decade. Exhibitions and the media spurred both domestic and international demand. The corporate and business sector showed interest and began to increasingly employ design professionals produced by a system of training undergoing modernization. These positive developments created by several simultaneous factors reinforced design and applied art in many ways.

The diversification of the field necessarily makes its description fragmented. Even the developments of the preceding decades can hardly be included in a single account. The phase that began in the mid-1950s calls for an even more dispersed narrative and a more limited range of examples. The terminology also becomes more varied as the concepts of product design and design in general now began to appear alongside applied art.

The outline of the narrative also changes. With the possible exception of the recession of the early 1990s, the post-war era and its applied art and design are not clearly divided into stages by any major and sudden events at the national level, such as independence and war. Instead, changes overlap and occasionally coincide in only some sectors. Factors in change included internationalization, technological progress, professional image and, before long, the phenomenon that later came to be known as design policy. This term refers to comprehensive efforts to bind elements of the overall framework of education and training, design, manufacturing and export. This approach was by no means new – Estlander already had similar aims. Consolidation now took place in a different reality, however. The same was to be repeated in the early 2000s, as described in the closing chapter.

Design education meets industry

The Central School of Arts and Crafts, which operated at a minimum level during the war, received a large influx of students in 1945. Training

took place under the conditions of austerity that marked the whole post-war period. Arttu Brummer became the school's artistic director in 1944, replacing Rafael Blomstedt, who now became its rector. Brummer could influence the atmosphere of the whole school even more than before. He was not, however, able to witness the success of the Milan Triennial, as he died in 1951 just before this event. Tapio Wirkkala, the hero of Milan, was immediately given Brummer's post, where he remained for four years until industrial commissions began to occupy his time. Even by 1949, however, the status and structures of the school had been changed by reorganizing it as the Institute of Industrial Art.

The essential aspect was that design education now clearly approached industry. Mandatory workplace training was introduced after the war for students in furniture design, followed by interior architecture. Also, the importance of taking industrial and related technological

▲ An example of good interior decoration in the magazine *Kaunis koti* (Beautiful Home) from 1953.

▶ Redware teapot from 1953 made by the designer Marita Lybeck's Emmel company. Although Arabia dominated the ceramics industry there were also products on the market made by smaller firms, such as Emmel and Kupittaan Savi.

progress into account in training, which had already been debated in the 1930s, became apparent. War reparations to the Soviet Union had forced Finland to renew its industrial infrastructure and as exports to the West now opened up, issues of quality became prominent. As shortages abated, increasing domestic consumer demand and an expanding range of products had the same effect. Products from a growing numbers of manufacturers were now available, and consumer choices were no longer dictated by price alone. Home appliances began to include electric ranges, refrigerators, washing machines and electronic equipment, of which television sets would radically alter the interiors of traditional living rooms in the late 1950s

Training and curricula based on conventional professional identities were, however, poorly matched to the design requirements of an increasingly technological world. This did not concern sectors such as ceramics or furniture design, in which the technical requirements of products were limited and the materials were mostly traditional. However, even in these areas, as also in industrial textile design, the development of manufacturing techniques called for a dialogue with manufacturers and technological experts. On the other hand, the design of products of new industries, such technical devices, automobiles and home appliances required broader qualifications.

International impulses for education

Ilmari Tapiovaara, who became head teacher of furniture design at the Institute of Industrial Art in 1951, was a proponent of joining training with industrial culture. He received a first-hand introduction to training in product design, i.e. the general design of industrial products, in 1952–1953 as a visiting professor at the Institute of Design of the Illinois Institute of Technology in Chicago. Developed mass production and the overall level of technology in the United States provided a model that Tapiovaara sought to apply at the Institute of Industrial Art upon returning to Finland. Like Wirkkala, he resigned in 1956 because of other work.

During the "design boom" of these years, Finland's leading designers had neither the time nor the economic need to remain in the education sector. This is a perennial problem of training in the arts, architecture and design. Individuals at the peak of their careers would have a great deal to offer – but the effort of maintaining a career leaves no time to pass experiences on to students in need of them. A later exception to this rule was Kaj Franck, who served as the artistic director of the Institute from 1960 to 1967.

The Institute of Design in Chicago, where Tapiovaara had been a visiting professor, was the "New Bauhaus", founded by Laszlo Moholy-Nagy (1895–1946) who had fled from Nazi Germany. Bauhaus principles with an American technological accent thus came indirectly to Finland after the war – during the period of the original Bauhaus its principles had hardly any influence on Finnish design education. This American Bauhausian orientation at the Institute of Industrial Art was reinforced further by the fact that Kaj Franck, of its faculty, had familiarized himself in 1956 with the curriculum of the Rhode Island School of Design, which also followed the principles of the Bauhaus. In 1954 Tapio Wirkkala worked in the office of Raymond Loewy (1893–1986) in New York and was able to experience how a large design agency serving mass production operated, and came to know the leeway of the designer in such a context. Fortunately for Finnish design, Tapiovaara and Wirkkala did not remain in America, despite opportunities to do so. Like Alvar Aalto, who had been there in the 1940s, they found the primacy of

▶ An artefact collection on the borderline of utility and art typical of post-war glass manufacturing in Finland. Glassware designed by Timo Sarpaneva for Iittala, mid-1950s.

economic parameters and the resulting hectic pace of work to be oppressive.

▶ Timo Sarpaneva, *Orkidea* (Orchid) vase/glass sculpture, Iittala, 1954.

Training in general product design addressing the terms and limitations laid down by industry was not implemented until the introduction of product design as a subject in 1961 at the Institute's department of metal art. This marked the beginning of training in industrial design.

As a whole, design education in the 1960s began to evolve increasingly towards cooperation with industry. The next reform came when the Institute of Industrial Art was taken over by the state and a four-year curriculum was introduced in 1965. Finally, after operating for over a century, the Institute was made part of Finland's system of tertiary education in 1973, when the University of Industrial Arts Helsinki (present-day University of Art and Design Helsinki) began its work after the deliberation of many official committees, and even disputes. For many years, it was the only university-level institution for the teaching of design and applied art in Finland and the Nordic countries. When the University gained the right in the 1980s to grant licentiate and doctoral degrees, Finnish design education had achieved full rights to everything that university status could provide. The full utilization of this situation began slowly, but hardly even Estlander, who had been a founder of the Craft School, could have imagined the future role of design education. It should be remembered that in 1871 the Craft School was in the same city as the country's only tertiary institute of learning, the Imperial Alexander University of Helsinki.

Professional practice

Trained professionals initially worked independently in arts and crafts, such as textiles, and gradually began to gain a position in industry in the pre-war years. The large amount of work for furniture designers after the Second World War brought them closer to industry while bolstering their self-esteem as a distinct professional group, as shown by the founding of the SIO association of interior architects within the Ornamo organization in 1949. Professional specialization proceeded apace with demand for individual areas of skill and expertise. The TEXO association of textile artists and designers was established in 1956, followed

by the MTO fashion designers' association in 1965, and the TKO product designers association in 1966. The increasingly industrial orientation of the field as a whole was also reflected by renaming the Association of Ornamental Artists Ornamo the Industrial Art Association Ornamo in 1966 (present-day Finnish Association of Designers Ornamo). The overall number of design professionals grew, although the groups of various sectors still remained relatively small.

Although professionalization progressed, reflected in associations for specific sectors, this did not imply distinct professions or professional identities in the traditional sense as among physicians, lawyers or civil engineers. Even the identity and organization of architects, the sector nearest to the design community, were more distinct. There were several reasons for this. Firstly, the number of active professionals in design and applied art was small in the 1950s and 1960s. Many of them worked in several areas, often quite different from their original training. Although this enriched contemporary design and no doubt generated ideas within the field, it failed to create distinct professional identities in any broader context. This was not regarded as an impediment as such, as there was growing demand for skills nonetheless. Interior designers, for example, collaborated with architects in building projects in a sector that was highly regulated with various conditions and requirements. This led to awareness of the requirements and contractual procedures within one's own field. There was no similar contractual regulation of design work, for example, in the glass or textile industry.

Individual designers, however, were very well known, especially in the 1950s and 1960s. Names such as Franck, Wirkkala, Jung or Sarpaneva were even familiar to the masses because of the prizes won by them and many others in international exhibitions and from resulting publicity. The companies using their services naturally utilized this aura of fame in advertising. This meant that while the designers themselves were featured prominently, their actual work was known to a lesser degree, a situation that survived into the 1990s and is even partly true today. Designers enjoyed an aura of mystique, and they were given the role of shamans of creativity who only needed to touch worthless raw material to convert it into brilliant design objects. Few people con-

▶ *Neljä väriä* (Four Colours),
ryijy-rug by Uhra-Beata
Simberg-Ehrström, 1958.
Abstract visual art with the
means of traditional weaving
technique.

sidered the fact that art glass by Wirkkala or Sarpaneva did not spring
from their own hands but instead required skilled people experienced
in glasshouse work with a sensitive yet assured approach. For the designers, it was fortunate that since the early 1950s the business world
had wanted to see more and more of this Midas touch. The ability of
designers to respond to the challenge at the levels of fame and cash
flow alike reinforced the positive developments mentioned above, in
which success fostered new success and fuelled demand for design in
new areas of industry.

Design becomes business

After the war, companies began to hire growing numbers of designers for permanent employment or collaboration. Franck worked for Arabia; textile designer Dora Jung had cooperated with the Tampella company since 1936; Wirkkala designed for the Ahlström group; and Tapiovaara had his own furniture company. This was a state of affairs that had been dreamed of in the 1930s, in which industry in the process of modernization would employ modernist designers to improve the quality of everyday objects.

Internationally, however, there were independent design offices and agencies offering a wide range of services to the corporate sector. There were no such firms in Finland, partly because of small scale. In

▲ As the standard of living and consumption rose in the 1950s, the need for business premises also grew, leading in turn to work for interior architects. Ilmari Tapiovaara designed the interior and corporate graphics, including neon signs for ten businesses, for the Kaivotalo building designed by the architect Pauli Salomaa and built in 1956.

the 1950s industries employing designers still represented only a small part of overall industrial output, which was mainly in the forest industry and the emerging heavy metal industry. Neither sector had any great need for design to improve the processed value of their products.

Nonetheless, there were signs of design becoming a distinct business sector. Ilmari and Annikka Tapiovaara, for example, left their Keravan Puuteollisuus company in 1951 to establish a separate furniture and interior design office. Through his practice, Tapiovaara provided consulting services simultaneously to several leading furniture makers, such as Asko, Merivaara and the Laukaan Puu company. As construction for the private business sector increased in the mid-1950s, growing numbers of large-scale interior design projects were commissioned by companies.

They would often include a graphic design programme and signs for the company. Eero Aarnio (1932–),[91] who had left Tapiovaara's office for Asko, made a similar independent move in the 1960s. He resigned from the Asko company to achieve an independent role and went on to sell his services to his former employer. Antti Nurmesniemi (1927–2003),[92] who had gained his professional reputation in the interior design of the Industries Palace building and its Hotel Palace, built next to the South Harbour of Helsinki in 1952 – the year of the Helsinki Olympics – established his own design office in 1954.

Interior architects were thus the first to set up their own businesses, but also designers permanently employed elsewhere could be consultants. Tapio Wirkkala, for example, who was the artistic and design manager of the Ahlström group in the A-Studio company from 1957–1965, also designed on a freelance basis for Rosenthal of Germany.

Independent business activities based on design and production on a large scale were still rare. Marimekko[93] developed into an important exception. At the turn of the 1950s, the Printex company owned by Viljo Ratia (1911–) began to print cotton fabrics with the assistance the owner's wife, Armi Ratia (1912–1979),[94] who had attended the Central School of Arts and Crafts. Under her artistic direction and with the aid of hired designers, fabric printing developed, followed before long by ready-made clothing. Marimekko launched its first collection in 1951. It explicitly focused on printed patterns of graphic clarity and collections differing from the ideology of haute couture. Marimekko's best period was in the 1960s, when it was an integral part of the Finnish textile, clothing and lifestyle scene.

Technology permeates design

Until the 1960s professionals abreast of their times could keep up with the technical requirements of design and related manufacturing technology. Chairs, tumblers, printed fabrics or dinner services could be redesigned and technical improvements made on a continuous basis. The same was true of some innovations in ceramic art. New dyeing and glazing methods were developed without interruption, while the classes of products remained traditional. The situation began to change in

▶ The development of vehicle and machinery manufacturing led to a need for design expertise in these sectors. Since there were no professionally trained industrial designers at the time, the manufacturers of these products relied on designers in other fields. In the upper picture is a Valmet tractor from the 1960s, with exterior parts by the graphic designer Jukka Pellinen. Below is the Solifer moped from 1960, exterior design by the ceramist Richard Lindh.

the mid-1950s. The Finnish metal industry proceeded towards manufacturing devices and equipment, soon followed by home electronics. The motor vehicle industry also had to decide on the external appearance of its products – overall form had to be given to mechanical equipment. This meant that design skills had to be increasingly applied in projects mainly based on engineering. Accordingly, the work of designers was increasingly defined by technological development and its commercial applications, often combining the technology of materials, electronics and mechanical engineering.

By this stage, design's reputation for improving both the sales and quality of manufactured products was well known throughout industry. The domestic manufacturers of kitchen ranges, refrigerators, motor vehicles and, before long, television sets approached designers. The latter, in turn, were not accustomed, either through training or professional experience, to design technical products – or more precisely their external appearance. Accordingly, the industrial product design that Tapiovaara had already called for was carried on by designers, though not by industrial designers. The ceramist Richard Lindh (1929–) designed the Solifer moped in 1960, the graphic artist Eero Rislakki designed an AGA-brand television set in 1961, and his colleague Jukka Pellinen (1925–) the Valmet 361 D tractor in 1960 and the Terhi outboard engine in 1963.

Tapio Wirkkala's wide-ranging achievements are a good example of the expansion of the work of designers. Post-war art glass was paralleled by projects for utility glassware, and later by furniture, commercial art and household ceramics, among other works. In the design of technological products he worked, for example, on refrigerators, plastic light switches and incandescent lamps. As the winner of an international competition, Wirkkala designed a "city of the future" for the Brussels World's Fair of 1958. This project was realized as a large-scale model and rooms in full scale. Wirkkala's work ranged from coffee cups to town planning. Previously, only architects had opportunities to shape environments in such a comprehensive manner – now this was being done by a designer originally trained as an ornamental sculptor.

▲ ▶ Originally an ornamental sculptor, Tapio Wirkkala went on to an extensive and wide-ranging oeuvre clearly demonstrating the variety of tasks addressed by post-war Finnish designers. The upper picture is a plastic ketchup bottle from the 1960s. Below is a light switch designed for the Strömberg company in 1949. On the facing page is a toilet seat designed by Sakari Vapaavuori for Arabia with a lid designed by Tapio Wirkkala, 1965.

The traditional metal industry also provided work for designers as it renewed its range of products. This led to the redesigning of a few old product categories of anonymous design and adding the designer's "signature" to them. In this way, Antti Nurmesniemi created a coffee pot for modern homes and Timo Sarpaneva did the same for cast-iron cooking pots. The new form was combined with monochrome enamelling, associating these products with other, also modernist, household items, such as Arabia's *Kilta* service or the colourful tumblers designed by Saara Hopea (1925–1984).[95]

The evolution of the applied-art professional – the designer – had proceeded from ornament-oriented work of the late 19th century to independent work and public appreciation, and even fame, at the turn of the 1960s. There was now considerably more confidence in the skill of the designer than previously, and professional organisations formalized the status of designers in specific sectors. The variety and requirements of the tasks entrusted to them would expand even further through industrial design. Although progress had already begun before the war, the 1950s marked a turning point in the mutual interaction of industry and designers. At the same time, the applied arts maintained their

▲ ▶ The metal industry utilized design skills in renewing the most traditional product groups. Enamelled coffee pots designed by Antti Nurmesniemi for the Wärtsilä company, 1958; right, cast iron pot by Timo Sarpaneva, Rosenlew company, ca. 1960.

former role in arts and crafts, through which international acclaim was initially achieved. When design work developed into a separate profession, business activity and even design-based entrepreneurship the whole field had achieved a state of maturity. Its manner of operation would not significantly change until the 1990s.

The Milan Triennials – elegance and images of Finland

Success at the Milan Triennial in 1951 was a gateway from the old to the new. It was a culmination of the changes in applied art that began in the late 1930s and gained new impetus during the war and the years of shortages. Its modernity lay in the creation of forms that approached abstract art, fantasy and sculpture. Acclaim opened the way for new and similarly successful displays. Mass production also gained a foothold in the ensuing exhibitions as Finnish industries managed to develop products meeting international critical standards with the aid of design. Exceptional success in exhibitions that continued until the mid-1960s also laid the basis for exports of design. In the background were the Finnish Society of Crafts and Design and its leading figure H. O. Gummerus with regard to exhibitions and general promotion, and the Finnish Foreign Trade Association along with individual companies in connection with specific export efforts.

Continued international exposure was provided by the Milan Triennials, in which Finland participated with success until 1964. In 1954 Wirkkala was again invited to design the Finnish section for the Triennial. Encouraged by previous success, the Finnish organizers invested more than before in the display, the result being a combination of abstract elegance, a rich array of objects and artefacts and imagery of Finland in the form of a large wall of photographs of a lake panorama. An astounding number of prizes were received on behalf of Finland, a total of thirty-two by the thirty-three participating designers. In the Grand Prix class, 20% of all the prizes went to the Finnish participants. Wirkkala also received a Grand Prix for his exhibition design.

Although the 1968 Milan Triennial was assembled, the Finnish department designed by Yrjö Kukkapuro (1933–)[96] was never properly displayed, nor the whole exhibition for that matter, as it was closed be-

▲ Cover of the magazine *Kaunis koti* (Beautiful Home) from 1958. This magazine was the leading arbiter of taste in design.

cause of student unrest on its opening day. When the Triennials were resumed in 1973, both the period and design were different from ten years previously.

The international press again featured the success of the Finnish designers prominently and magazine *Domus International* of Milan became a permanent showcase of Finnish design. Gio Ponti (1891–1979), the editor-in-chief of the internationally read and influential publication, became a personal friend of Tapio Wirkkala, among others. *Domus* repeatedly featured double-page spreads of new Finnish design. Publicity in Italy was important because Italian design of the 1950s was internationally regarded as first-class. It was generally held that anything given attention by the gatekeepers of Italian design must therefore be exceptional and trail-blazing.

Success was repeated in 1957, now with exhibition design by Timo Sarpaneva, who also received a Grand Prix while Finland was awarded a quarter of all the prizes. This time, Sarpaneva's exclusively elegant design was balanced by the Finnish contributions to an adjacent exhibition of housing. Designed by Olavi Hänninen (1920–),[97] it contained new Finnish furniture in functional groups and not just as isolated objects in showcases insulated from the visitors. The Finnish departments at the 1960 and 1964 Triennials were designed by Antti Nurmesniemi, who received a Grand Prix on both occasions. The displays created by him tended towards even greater abstraction. Their sparsely placed objects, partly floating in the air, like a hunting rifle made by the Sako company, were accents, allusions to Finnish design that was already famous.

Fame and growing export revenue as goals

Alongside the Milan Triennials, Finnish design and applied art were exported through international exhibitions at an ever faster pace. Gummerus felt that expanding exhibition activity abroad would pay its way through international renown and export revenue. Not everyone shared his view of the primacy of internationalization, but dissenting voices were easily drowned by a shower of gold medals. In architecture, the Finnish Association of Architects assisted by the Museum of Finnish Architecture, followed precisely the same policy. The ambitious and

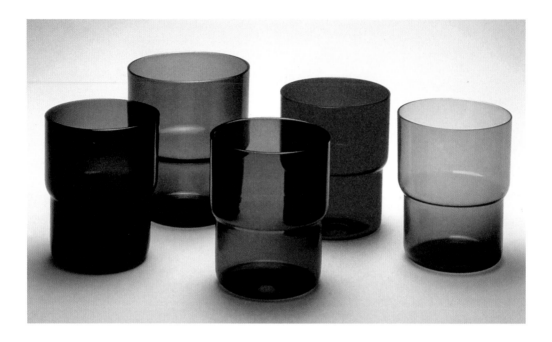

polished international touring exhibitions of these two levels of Finnish culture of the human environment, architecture and applied art, largely created the image that the international public had of Finland as an Eldorado of modern architecture and design.

▲ Saara Hopea, stackable glasses designed for the Nuutajärvi Glassworks, 1951.

The exhibitions did not always feature Finland alone. The Nordic countries also collaborated in exhibiting their applied art and design. The first and most important of these showings was *Design in Scandinavia*, launched in 1954 to tour the United States and Canada for three and a half years. These efforts were based on the important aspects of Nordic cooperation and shared identity which had already emerged before the Second World War. In the post-war international political climate, it was considered of prime importance to associate Finland with the democratic, liberal image of Scandinavian countries.

The idea for the exhibition came from the journalist Elisabeth Gordon (1906–2000) of the magazine *House Beautiful*, who had been to the 1951 Milan Triennial. The leading Nordic actors and organizations of the field were gradually included in the exhibition projects, and the result was a truly joint Nordic effort in concrete terms. The touring exhibition was a great success among the public and the media and laid the basis for the concept of 'scandinavian design' that is still used. The fact that Finland does not technically belong to the Scandinavia archipelago was brushed over. The important thing during these years of the Cold War was to signal Finland's Western orientation and modernity with the means of design. In this sense, 1954 was a milestone for international exposure of Finnish design along the Milan–US axis.

Critiques of elitism

This undeniably excellent international exhibition activity also generated controversy in Finland. The generally positive Swedish reviews of the 1946 Stockholm exhibition, with its emphasis on arts and crafts, as discussed above, noted the absence of well-designed everyday objects and products. As was seen, this was reflected, however, in the Finnish discussion without any immediate visible results in manufacturing. The H-55 exhibition held approximately ten years later in Helsingborg in Sweden again inspired debate in Finland. Sarpaneva's elegant minimalist exhibition design inspired almost elated praise, but again questions arose about the state of designing everyday objects in Finland. Elitism could well have been called for in foreign arenas, but items and displays of a different kind were needed for domestic manufacturing and consumption. The discussions returned to the arguments of the 1930s on the right of everyone to the fruits of modernist design. Towards the end of the 1950s such objects had already become widely available in all the traditional and new sectors of design work.

The annual exhibitions of the Society of Crafts and Design, which led domestic efforts to educate the public, took note of this discussion. For example, the exhibition *Teollinen muoto* (Industrial Form) held in 1957 at Kunsthalle Helsinki emphasized the way in which a symbiosis of industrial and design culture could shape the everyday environment in terms of both function and aesthetics. But criticism was once again aroused, quite heatedly, by an exhibition for display abroad. As commissioner of the Finnish section of the joint Nordic design department

◄ *Pirkka* furniture (1955) designed by Ilmari Tapiovaara for the Laukaan Puu company was suitably dimensioned for the restricted space of post-war apartments.

at Expo 67 in Montreal, Timo Sarpaneva chose five large (9 × 4.5 metres) works, one of which was by the sculptor Laila Pullinen (1933–) and from outside the domain of design proper. This no doubt stunning ensemble of applied art led, however, to domestic reactions that underscored the democratic role of art and design and belied a budding cultural radicalism. The cultural tide was definitely turning – with design as part of it.

In the 1950s and 1960s Finnish design received more exposure than ever before, not only abroad but also within the country. There was discussion, not only in design publications, such as *Kaunis Koti*, but also at a more general level in, among others, the *Kotiliesi* magazine, as part of an agenda of popular education for homes. Aesthetics and reason appeared to merge in the various forms and manifestations of applied art. Arts and crafts, their textiles, ceramic art and glass, ennobled everyday

life, while serial products like the *Kilta* service made practical life in the home proceed more fluidly.

Not only the objects and products but also the designers themselves were featured. It was mainly success at the Triennials but also other international exposure that gave the stars of Finnish design their aura of heroism. As noted by Harri Kalha in his research on the publicity of Finnish design in the 1950s, this was a cultural mechanism with which a nation recovering from war and years of shortages healed its wounds.[98] This called for successful figures, with whom the public could identify. In the national gallery of heroes, Paavo Nurmi (1897–1973), Jean Sibelius and Alvar Aalto were now accompanied by demiurges of design, such as Wirkkala, Sarpaneva, Franck, and many other successful figures who seemed to have sprung from nowhere. The companies that utilized the contributions of designers signed their products with the names of the latter. In this manner, mass-produced objects also became a part of "authorized" design. The magic associated with a renowned designer became attached to them.

By the turn of the 1960s modern design had become a natural part of the everyday life of Finns, the standard of living had risen, and national self-esteem had improved. The need to personify design and for the publicity generated in this way decreased. The world now appeared to be larger and broader through the influence of television alone, which had spread rapidly. In terms of marketing, companies – and magazines – still benefited from the idea of star designers instilled in the minds of consumers. By the 1960s, however, the continuous public exposure of a select cadre of designers who had established their reputation in the 1950s became counter-productive. Young professionals setting out on their careers regarded the giants of the 1950s, who were still at the peak of their powers, to be unbeatable. On the other hand, the post-war baby-boom generation that was reaching adulthood in the 1960s did not want to be part of the "establishment" but instead desired an end to the status quo and an era of new rules.

The breakthrough of modern design

The flourishing of design and applied art in the 1950s, described above in broad terms, was the result of several coinciding and mutually reinforcing factors. The Milan Triennial of 1951 opened a window of opportunity, and the field in Finland was now ready to utilize the situation, which was not the case after success at the 1933 Triennial. The economic and political situation forced the immediate utilization of the opportunities for internationalization and export that now appeared. Despite its glamour, the international market was only one side of the story. Towards the end of the decade, domestic industries rapidly adopted design in the spirit of modernism. It can well be said that by the turn of the 1960s modernism had become the predominant way of thinking and mode of perception in the culture of most private and public environments in Finland. It was no longer necessary to steer the choices of consumers in the manner of the 1940s, because the products that were available mostly followed the rules of modernism, at least in an adapted way.

▶ There was considerable building activity, both public and private, in the decades after the war, which raised the standards of the Finnish furniture industry and design. The *Nana* all-purpose chair by Ilmari Tapiovaara from 1956, made by Merivaara; below, the *Mademoiselle* chair, also by Tapiovaara and made by the Asko company, 1958.

◄ Lisa Johansson-Pape was one of the leading lamp designers of her time. The lamps on the facing page are from the 1950s and were made by the Orno company. The lower picture shows the *Maija Mehiläinen* lamp by Ilmari Tapiovaara from 1956 made by the Hienoteräs company for Asko. This lamp employed the tube-light technology that had recently come into widespread use.

This would not have been possible without the support of corporate management circles that relied on design and invested in it. Arabia was part of the Wärtsilä group of companies, the management of which gave its full support for the experiments and the factory's art department, and for reforms in mass production. The Iittala and Karhula glassworks belonged to the Ahlström group, where Maire Gullichsen was an influential figure – a leader in efforts to promote the modern culture of art and the environment. The management of Tampella, in turn, understood the importance of Dora Jung as a figurehead of the company's textiles. There are many examples of this sympathetic corporate culture.

The new applied art and design would not have made a breakthrough if its message had not been spread and promoted. The role of H.O. Gummerus in the process of internationalization was described above, while domestic consumption benefited from work in popular education and information that combined design, manufacturing and the home as an entity. Despite their popularity, the annual exhibitions staged in Helsinki by the Finnish Society of Crafts and Design concerned a relatively small public. Contemporary magazines, especially *Kaunis Koti* and *Kotiliesi*, had a broader audience, including readers in the countryside. Women's organizations, such as the Martha Federation, held popular education events in different parts of the country, discussing, among other subjects, the benefits of rational objects and furnishings for the home, i.e. modernity. Individual firms and the central retail organizations published their own magazines. As a result, the message of new applied art and design was spread simultaneously by several parties, which in turn reinforced its universal applicability.

Everything, however, ultimately derives from the products themselves. International fame, exports or popularity among domestic consumers could not have been achieved if the designed objects had not been of functional and aesthetic quality and of a trailblazing nature. The concept of *Finnish Design* that was constructed at the time could then, and later, be of interest only through the products subsumed under the umbrella concept. Without this basis and the contribution of those who shaped and designed, no cultural or commercial sales pitch would have had credibility.

INTERNATIONAL SUCCESS IN EXHIBITIONS

While applied art from Finland was already successful at the Milan Triennial of 1933, it was the 1951 Triennial that launched a period of almost two decades of international fame for Finnish design. Held at three-year intervals, these exhibitions in Milan reaped a large number of prizes and awards. They were important for visibility in the international press, as the Finnish displays also implemented a cultural policy of presenting Finland abroad as a progressive Western nation.

The material for the Finnish departments at Milan originally focused on arts and crafts, but before long they began to include serially manufactured and industrial products. Alongside the exhibits, their display and the exhibition architecture were important aspects. The designers of the Finnish departments, such as Tapio Wirkkala, Timo Sarpaneva and Antti Nurmesniemi, created environs of disciplined elegance and employed the imagery of Finnish nature, which is still used for marketing Finnish design. The "victories" prominently featured in the Finnish media had great impact on the reputation of the designers, which in turn was applied in marketing by the companies that used their skills.

1. The Milan Triennial of 1951. Exhibition design by Tapio Wirkkala.

2. The Milan Triennial of 1954. Exhibition design by Tapio Wirkkala.

3

4

5

3. The Finnish department of a housing exhibition held in connection with the Milan Triennial of 1957. Designed by Olavi Hänninen.

4. The Milan Triennial of 1964. The extremely restrained and clear-cut exhibition design was by Antti Nurmesniemi.

5. The Finnish department at Expo 67 in Montreal. Exhibition design by Timo Sarpaneva. In the foreground is *Sea of Violets*, a ceramic wall piece by Birger Kaipiainen. In the background is *Sun in the Fells* in bronze by sculptor Laila Pullinen.

FINLANDIA – MODERN FINNISH DESIGN

This was the title of an exhibition of Finnish design held at the Victoria & Albert Museum in London from November 1961 to January 1962. It was curated by Timo Sarpaneva, who also designed its catalogue. The name "Finlandia" – not Finland, the international name of the country – is associated with Jean Sibelius's famous patriotic symphonic poem from the turn of the 20th century, a time when Finnish applied art made its international breakthrough at the Paris World's Fair of 1900. The exhibition involved cultural diplomacy at a high level and was organized "under the gracious patronage of H. R. H. The Duke of Edinburgh and H. E. Dr U. K. Kekkonen, President of Finland".

The exhibits consisted of unique, one-off pieces of a crafted nature, objects issued in small series and mass-produced items in much the same way as in the recent Milan Triennials, in which Finland had been successful. This aspect in particular, the mixing and coexistence of these different areas of applied art and design in Finland and the professional involvement of designers in one-off production and industry alike, aroused the interest and appreciation of the organizers of the exhibition. In England, as is known, so-called studio pottery and industrially made ceramics were quite distinct areas, while in Finland both thrived within the Arabia factory in Helsinki. The museum's Keeper of the Department of Circulation Hugh Wakefield, who wrote the introduction to the catalogue, observed: "Instead of two separate exhibitions, of arts and crafts on the one hand and industrial design on the other, we find a continuous merging of handwork, which proves to be the product of many hands, with factory products which express almost to the point of eccentricity the personality of their designer."

1. Light fittings (designed c. 1960) by Tapio Wirkkala for Idman, Helsinki.

2. Glass bird *Lehtokurppa* ("Woodcock", in production 1953-1968) by Kaj Franck for Wärtsilä-Notsjö, Helsinki.

3. Table service *Ruska* (in production 1960–1999) by Ulla Procope for Wärtsilä-Arabia, Helsinki.

4. Laminated wood stacking chairs *Wilhelmina* (designed c. 1959) by Ilmari Tapiovaara for Schauman, Jyväskylä.

1

2

3

4

ADVERTISING AND POSTERS

Poster art, which had flourished before the Second World War, was a significant medium for advertising. Its importance began to wane in the 1960s, when television offered a more efficient channel of corporate and commercial information for reaching larger numbers of people. Until then, Finland's large retail chains had their own "commercial art offices", and the high-standard advertisements of the foodstuffs and refreshments industry, in particular, were real applied art that was present in everyday life. In the late 1960s, poster art found new subjects, such as presenting the problems of the environment to a broader public.

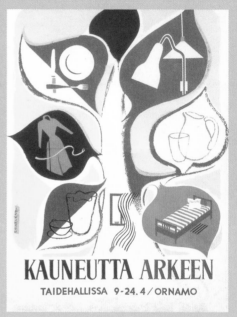

1

1. Poster for the *Everyday Beauty* exhibition of applied art and design by Holger Erkelenz 1949.

2. Erik Bruun, advertising poster for Jaffa soft drink, 1960.

2

3

4

3. A crispbread advertisement for the Elanto cooperative, Pertti Pohjola 1960.

4. Poster by Jukka Veistola protesting the use of DDT pesticide, 1969.

5. Oiva Toikka, exhibition poster of the Nuutajärvi glassworks, 1971.

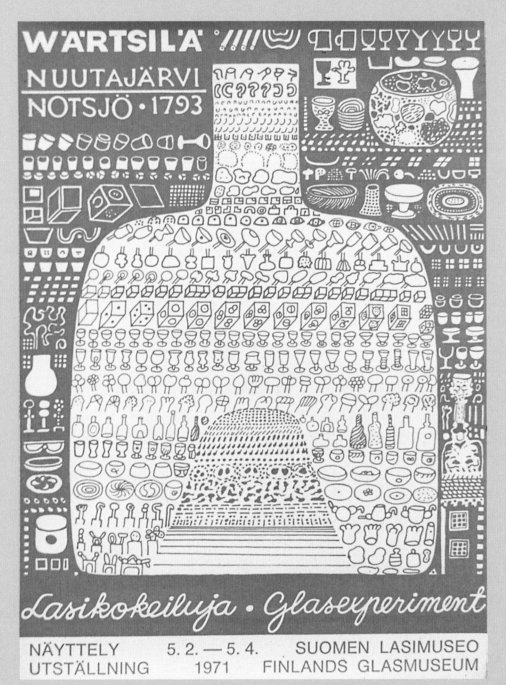

6 DESIGN IN A SOCIETY OF ABUNDANCE

INDUSTRY, COMMERCE, URBANIZATION

1961	1965	1973	1975	1979
Finland joins the European Free Trade Association	The Institute of Industrial Art taken over by the state	The founding of the University of Art and Design Helsinki	The centenary exhibition of the Finnish Society of Crafts and Design at the Ateneum Art Museum	The reopening of the Museum of Applied Arts

Post-war design production in Finland is mainly outlined by economic factors. The early 1950s were fanned by the so-called Korean War boom. Finland's agreement with the European Free Trade Association (EFTA) in 1961 removed most of the tariffs that had let Finnish industries develop without any major competition from foreign products. Less restricted Western trade and international competition led to greater awareness of quality and thus to a broader use of design skills. Trade with the Soviet Union which grew radically in these years also created affluence which could promote the establishment of the welfare society that had already been envisioned before the war.

In the mid-1960s Finland finally achieved its pre-war levels of consumption. It was becoming an affluent Western country and it rapidly adopted an international orientation. This coincided with urbanization at an unprecedented pace. The process of reconstruction transformed Finland from an agrarian nation into an industrialized society. It meant, among other things, extensive development of suburban housing areas The exceptionally large young generation now became consumers. In the 1960s this young generation changed cultural practices, and the whole atmosphere of cultural policy by the end of the decade.

Design reacted strongly to these factors that were changing the whole country. It was now a self-evident part of both industry and ever-growing consumption in everyday life. In 1959 the design-based sector's proportion of Finnish exports was around one percent; by 1965 it had grown to five; and by 1970 to seven percent. The progress seen in this booming decade ended in the international oil crisis of 1973 and the ensuing economic recession. At the same time, design as part of culture and its mainstream became markedly politicized. Under these conditions, industrial design in particular developed significantly.

Teamwork replacing the individual

During the 1960s, Finnish design culture evolved from emphasizing the visibility of the individual designer, to become less personified and to stress activities based on teamwork. The reasons for this were two-fold. On one hand, the personification of design by a few famous names that started in the 1950s was now outmoded. On the other hand, rapidly

Niva. Design Tapio Wirkkala.

emerging industrial design was no longer based on individual effort but instead on the achievements of a group or team.

There was also growing awareness during the decade of both national and worldwide problems to which designers, too, sought solutions. These issues of society and environment could not be solved by individual designers, or through the design of objects. The problems involved systems of a cultural, political and technological nature. Towards the end of the decade technological progress, which had previously been seen as a blessing, and the capitalist market economy that maintained it both came under criticism. Paradoxically, technology-based industrial design managed to reinforce its position amidst this turmoil, as a result of its problem-oriented mode of operation that avoided the "signature" of its authors. Multidisciplinary projects combining design and hospital technology, for example, were identified in terms of the manufacturer and not the individual designers.

The domestic and international success of Finnish design continued unbroken into the 1960s. Consumer demand spurred by a rising standard of living, an ever wider range of products offered by industries and the expanding utilization of design created a knock-on effect, serving all parties. The main focus of design was still on consumer products for the home, such as furniture, tableware and lamps. Expanding construction in the public sector and the growth of business environments fanned by the economic boom of the 1960s also created solid demand for interior design and decoration. The flagship products of the design sector, such as art glass and more expensive furniture, were still marketed under the name of the designer. This was called for insofar as in these products the choices of material and techniques were mainly under the command of a single skilled person. In such cases there could be grounds for personalizing the result. This was also profitable for manufacturers and marketing, because it distinguished products in a competitive marketplace by reference to noted designers, e.g. "Sarpaneva glass" or "a Tapiovaara chair".

Over time, however, it became increasingly difficult to market products with the name of the designer. There were growing numbers of manufacturers of consumer goods, and the range of available products also expanded. There were not enough famous names to go around as designers or marketing ploys. Distinction was now claimed with terms such as "Finnish design" or "design product". Their excessive use, however, diluted the meaning and importance of design skills as such and led to purely image-based marketing. The rapidly developing and expanding training system introduced young designers lacking the fame of those who had established their reputation in the previous decade and still dominated the public image of design. A generation shift was approaching and the field was evolving towards technological devices and equipment made by a diversifying industrial sector. Discussion of the presence of the designer in the final product and its publicity value was instigated, however, by Kaj Franck, one of the designer heroes of the 1950s.

In 1966, Franck published an article in Finnish entitled 'Anonymiteetti' (Anonymity) in the magazine *Keramiikka ja lasi* (Ceramics and Glass), in which he underscored the role of product design in serving the public.[99] This was only natural for him in view of the collections of glassware and tableware services that he had designed for everyday use since the late 1940s. Franck did not criticize the visibility of designer-artists in small-editions or one-off products, for their author or auteur was prominently involved in conceptualizing and making the pieces. It should be remembered that Franck, the designer of the renowned *Kilta* tableware, also made a great deal of experimental art glass in small series. He opposed, however, the use of the signatures of specific designers in mass-produced items and their marketing.

Franck's comments on anonymity in design aroused heated debate but were especially echoed by the young generation. There was discussion along completely similar lines in contemporary Finnish architecture in the shadow of the almost overwhelming reputation of Alvar Aalto. Young designers in both disciplines were beginning to regard their work increasingly in terms of developing, in an industrial manner, the infrastructure and services required by work, habitation and the lives of people. This was a collective and multidisciplinary field in which the public exposure of specific professionals was of secondary importance.

From art to product development

The rise of industrial design in Finland was in part a reaction to the development of Finnish industries and their export prospects, while also part of the international evolution of this sector. In this sense, industrial design was developed, also in Finland, into an area of training and professional activity in quite a different manner than the so-called traditional disciplines of applied art and design. As specific sectors, ceramics, glass and textiles were long-established, and furniture-making also had roots extending far back in time. While these fields had been updated in terms of materials, form and production, the function of the products remained tradition-bound.

In the early 1960s, the expansion of industrial manufacturing led to consideration of how the interests of design and industry could be combined in the best ways. The reforms of design education that had been envisioned by Tapiovaara in the mid-1950s but not realized now became topical again. Professionally active designers, in turn, awoke to view their work in terms of technological and industrial requirements that were being renewed and becoming more complex. The potential for design to raise the quality of manufacturing and export products was becoming evident. As early as 1961, an organization known as the Research Foundation for Efficient Production proposed increased technological expertise in design. In Finnish industry in general, the production of machinery and equipment was gaining ground alongside the traditional forest sector and the heavy industries. Although there was sound training in the design of utility objects in the traditional sector, there was hardly any education for designing products involving technological expertise. In the same year, the teaching of industrial design was launched at the Institute of Industrial Art.

As the first graduates in this discipline entered working life, the Finnish Society of Crafts and Design also realized that obvious changes had taken place, and carried out a survey in 1967 and 1968 on the degree of utilization of industrial design in Finnish industries. This area was regarded as separate from the "mature" fields of ceramics and furniture, considered as "artistic design". Utilitarian objectives emerged in this connection as defined by the business sector of design and exports, and

◀ ▶ The varying dimensions of the textile artist's work. In the picture on the left are the *Finnair* table mats designed in 1969 by Dora Jung to serve air travel to America, which was still an exclusive domain at the time (the glassware is of Wirkkala's *Ultima Thule* collection). Jung's tapestry *Biafra*, is a political statement in textile art from 1970.

also the desire to exclude art as a factor irrelevant to industry. It became the designer's task to change from an artist into a product developer.

Proceeding as it did from a purely business-oriented profit principle, the technocratic-economic model of the survey aroused criticism. As applied art and industrial design in particular were given the role of serving industrial productivity and exports, opposition arose from within the field. Criticism and reactions among the applied art and design community were also fuelled by a more general radicalization of the ideological and cultural climate, political orientations and before long party-political affiliations. This was in turn linked to world-wide activism in which a young emerging generation sought alternatives to a world which they regarded as dominated by technology, commerce and materialism.

Industrial design becomes a separate field.

The 1960s witnessed more systematic and goal-oriented efforts to bring industry and design closer to each other. These involved, among others, the Ornamo association, the Finnish Foreign Trade Association, the Ministry of Trade and Industry and the corporate sector. In 1972, Sitra the Finnish Innovation Fund, with Ornamo as a background actor, published an extensive report on the role, tasks and responsibilities of industrial design. This report went beyond the earlier considerations underlining efficiency and market value. Technological suitability was matched by the relationship of people and products, issues of safety and comfort in working life, and improvements to the quality of the environment.

By the 1970s, industrial design had thus become an umbrella concept, while some ten years previously it had been understood in much more limited and product-related terms. This was partly due to the introduction of ergonomics in product and environmental design. It was an area of expertise applied perhaps most prominently in industrial design but also in furniture and the working environment. It was influential in the 1970s and still in the 1980s. Based on "science" and measurement, it was politically value-free, serving everyone on an equal basis. It was thus excellently suited to the emphasis on democracy and equality that was typical of thinking in this period.

Industrial design, which became a separate field in the 1960s, thus interested the applied art and design sector and its organizations, industry and many public bodies. Discussion within the field sought to systematize and methodologically define this area and give it a scientific basis. At the same time, at the turn of the 1970s, the applied art and design community saw the emergence of a new generation trained in industrial design. The industrial designer Heikki Metsä-Ketelä (1942–) had studied at the Hochschule für Gestaltung Ulm, an institution that had gone on to develop the legacy of the Bauhaus, bringing from there the requirement for a methodical and a scientific attitude to training and practical work. Jussi Ahola (1940–),[100] also an industrial designer, un-

► Industrial design was also taken into use in the Finnish motor industry. Sisu truck, design by Antti Siltavuori, 1980.

derscored a comprehensive analytical approach in which the designer as an anonymous specialist would be consulted by various expert groups, providing his or her special skills to add value to the work as a whole. There was similar discussion concerning society in the "scientific-technological revolution" and design education. This was a period of so-called "planning optimism", in which industrial design was seen as having a role in organizing industry and human life in a rational and analytical way that would benefit everyone. The word 'art' was rarely used any more.

While the integration of industrial design with industry was proceeding at least at the level of objects, the concepts of social and ecological responsibility began to appear in discussion. The aim of generalizing industrial design method also implied the reduced personal visibility of the author, i.e. the designer. This was sought and it was also part of a reaction in which the young generation of the late 1960s began to take over positions from the leading echelons of design, now defined as elitist and individualist. While this aim conformed well to the requirement of anonymous design expressed by Franck in 1966, it was also related to broader international debate on industry and society. A new era of global awareness and activity was dawning. The information flows of

Marshall McLuhan's global village had been speeded by the television, which was now a common household item. People quickly became aware of the problems of the Third World, and of the environmental damage caused by industrialization and the spread of automobiles.

There was also internationalization at the level of individuals. Victor Papanek (1927–1999), a visible proponent of the social responsibility of design, visited Finland on several occasions. A seminar entitled 'Industry, Environment, Product Design' featured Papanek and speakers including R. Buckminster Fuller (1895–1983) and Christopher Alexander (1936–). The organizers of this and many similar events included Yrjö Sotamaa (1942–), a student of interior architecture at the time. Sotamaa would become one of the main figures in the whole field in Finland, especially after becoming rector of the University of Art and Design Helsinki in 1986, a position in which he served until 2008.

During the 1960s design professionals and their organizations increasingly managed to convince Finnish industry of the significance of design. The industrial sector and its organizations, in turn, regarded design as serving profit. Many of the main actors at the national level had arrived at consensus regarding the need for special measures especially for industrial design. The goal here was the technological-aesthetic modernization of both industry and design that served it. Once all the parts of this machinery were installed, it would – as part of a rationally steered society – churn out an environment and objects of quality and provide export revenue. With its post-war aura, however, design was still a permanent and prominent aspect of cultural life in Finland. The turbulence that it experienced in the 1970s did not steer it to the harbour of a Protestant work ethic guarded by technology, but to the political storms of the open sea. And finally to almost being shipwrecked.

The 1960s – the establishment and the critical gaze

During the 1960s and 1970s, design and applied art in Finland underwent rapid change that shook Finnish society as a whole. In particular, the Institute of Industrial Art (renamed the University of Industrial Arts Helsinki in 1973) was affected by currents of an ideological and general political nature. It could be said that where opening up to influences in the 1960s reflected abundance and more alternatives from a palette of choices, the following decade reduced the choice to black and white. The reasons for this were by no means generated within the field. The design community was quickly drawn into the criticism of the values and leading figures of past decades that had begun as cultural radicalism in the mid-1960s and had soon taken on a leftist tone. The internal radicalization of the field was evident in the questioning of both design education and practices. This was associated more broadly with active debate on the role of design in Finnish culture and society. The focus of publicity on the traditional areas of glass, ceramics and textiles both domestically and especially in international exhibitions, or displays of

◀ Applied art thrived alongside industrial design. Work in
this area could vary considerably in scale. In the upper picture is *Sea of Violets* (detail) a
nine-metre-wide ceramic mu-
ral work designed by Birger
Kaipiainen for Expo 67 in
Montreal. The lower picture
is of a piece from the 1960s
by Kyllikki Salmenhaara that
was inspired by Japanese
ceramics.

design as art as at Expo 67 in Montreal, were regarded as too narrow. In particular, emphasis on individuals was felt to be an obsolete feature of past decades, and the new generation wanted to commit cultural patricide as regards its prominent representatives.

The corporate sector that utilized design was, however, aware that a new, large generation with more purchasing power than ever before was now entering a market of consumption that appeared to be growing limitlessly. At same time, however, voices were heard that increasingly questioned the whole course of development in design during the post-war era. Accusations were particularly levelled against its base of values, which was felt to be shallow in its emphasis on manufacturing, marketing and exports. Aestheticization was regarded as a gloss over the failings of the field. The new generation with its political arguments sought influence and aimed criticism at the focus on objects, form and designers that had been prominent especially in Finland. All this came to the fore just when it appeared that the new covenant of industry and design that had been under construction since the mid-1950s was on the brink of being realized.

Design was thus reassessed as part of a deepening process of political debate and activism. Although the importance of technological and scientific progress and industry utilizing its results was still emphasized, the value base and objectives of work in design had changed. There was no longer a desire to regard the designer in narrow terms as someone who revises and refines the product lines of industry. Instead, attention turned from the products to the system that generated them, and to its ramifications for people and the environment. The effects of exceptionally rapid and extensive migration both within the country and abroad, the position of minorities, an urban environment suffering from uncontrolled growth and increasing motor traffic, and the quality of working environments became central issues. It was asked on whose terms and through which systems of power these problems arose. The generation that had gained its position after the war was felt to have instigated this unsatisfactory state of affairs. For many people, this generation represented an outmoded world of values and commitments in all sectors,

including design. Overturning its hegemony called for political activity and alliances beyond design.

In this situation, radicalism of a general humanistic orientation and unspecified criticism of the "establishment" were no longer enough. The trend led to the rise of parties of the political left and partly to extreme leftist positions after the turn of the 1960s and 1970s. At the same time, there were major reforms in design education. Dating from the previous

▲ During the 1960s political awareness began to gain emphasis in training provided by the Institute of Industrial Art. Temporary dwelling at Jätkäsaari in Helsinki, final project in the basic course in general design supervised by Kaj Franck, 1966.

decade, these efforts fell into a framework of turmoil in cultural and industrial policy that was marked by oppositions. The new University of Industrial Arts Helsinki (present-day University of Art and Design Helsinki) did not become the provider of design skills desired by industry, as it had been prepared to do.

Politicized education

The Institute of Industrial Art had already found itself in an internal and administrative crisis at the turn of the 1960s and 1970s, and over the following years political conflicts markedly eroded its own culture of activities and work. The institute's new status as a university and reforms to both the structures and content of teaching clearly activated training, but its ideological orientation shifted from industry to social and environmental issues. There was also a great deal of pure idealism. In 1973, when the University of Industrial Arts was selecting its students for the first time, it stated as its goals increased economic and regional equality, the efficient and non-harmful use of industry for the good of society, and the expansion of democracy. The considerations of technology, industrial culture or the economy, which had figured during the previous decade and had fuelled the reorganization of the institute as a university, were no longer important.

On the one hand, changes concerned the ideology of training, while on the other hand they were related to changed values of industrial design, environmental planning and design in general. Earlier considerations of global perspective, equality and ecology had evolved into political argument. But if the purpose of the basic scheme of education was nonetheless to train designers, what work would they have if service to the capitalist "system of exploitation" was ideologically excluded? If Finland's only higher-level school of design did not train professionals aware of the terms under which industry operated, where would the product designers of the future be found? These issues among others, and internal unrest at the University of Industrial Arts which was widely noted in the media, led to a sharp drop in confidence in the university among political decision-makers and industry. At the time radicalization and political partisanship of course permeated Finnish society as a whole with regard to decisions and control of cultural capital. Applied art and design were of considerable symbolic value especially because of their international success in the post-war years.

Political decision-makers had themselves to blame for the crisis of the University of Industrial Arts. Its facilities in the Ateneum building in the centre of Helsinki were cramped and in extremely poor condition. In the mid-1970s, the university operated in four locations. New premises were promised from time to time, but without any concrete results. In 1971 a site was reserved for a new building in Helsinki's Itä-Pasila section and plans were prepared, but this project was terminated in 1985 after various phases. By this stage, the university had moved out of the Ateneum which was being renovated to serve solely as an art museum. Continuous relocation, which seriously impeded training, finally ended in 1986, when the University of Industrial Arts moved into renovated premises vacated by the Arabia factory. The Ateneum was the last building expressly designed for it.

A broader description of training and its politicization is called for, because the university and its predecessors have had a uniquely central role in applied art and design in Finland. Generally speaking, the field was not yet in crisis in the early 1970s. Economic trends were positive and none of structural factors that were important for it had significantly deteriorated since the end of the 1960s. But the field was also small and clannish. One school of design, and a single organization, Ornamo, formed a circle within which many of its actors also influenced the Institute and later University either as faculty or members of governing bodies. Political affiliations naturally divided the membership of Ornamo and this did not improve the already frought collaboration among the institutions of the field.

Debate and nostalgia

Positive economic growth that had maintained industry, commerce and design in Finland ended in the mid-1970s in a recession following in the wake of the international oil crisis. Around the same time and in connection with the above, the design sector underwent structural change described as "the crisis of Finnish applied art and design". The

▶ Political awareness addressing the issues of society and the environment was particularly evident in various areas of design at the turn of the 1960s and 1970s. Poster by Kyösti Varis from 1970.

Pallo on nyt meillä

Pian se on lapsillamme.
Toivottavasti elinkelpoisena.
Sillä ilmaan ei mahdu loputtomasti myrkkyä.
Eikä maahan. Eikä veteen.

economic recession brought on a crisis of profitability in industries that had traditionally employed designers, such as ceramics, glass, textiles and furniture. Export to Western nations decreased and growing trade with the Soviet Union did not require the added value of design, because goods were sold through bilateral arrangements to a market without any competition.

There was broad debate on the state of design especially in 1977 and 1978, with particular concern over the fate of so-called traditional applied art, while new strengths were seen in the expanding areas of product and environmental design. Their products – hospital equipment, vehicles and public facilities for social services – were not works to be displayed on an equal basis and isolated into exhibitions like the products of the consumer goods industry. Design by the younger generation of professionals took as its starting point the relationship of man, tools and the environment; consumer-based design; and a multidisciplinary process of product development. While the press debated, among other issues, the reorganization of the Arabia factory and its reduced range of products or the economic problems of the Marimekko company, industrial design came into increasing use. Because this took place in investment goods and not in consumer products, these developments were not evident to the public. Increasing demand for these services also led to growth in the number of agencies and offices in this sector and their volume of work.

The economic recession that affected output in traditional applied art and job prospects after studies led to the growth of arts-and-crafts work in small editions, especially in ceramics and textiles. Small-scale production was in keeping with the critical attitudes underlined in training regarding capital-intensive industry. While the recession had generally negative effects on design, it also laid the basis for the significant quantitative and qualitative rise of arts and crafts in the 1980s.

Design was also influenced by the anti-urban trend of the mid- and late 1970s with its recycling of the national and agrarian cultural heritage. At the same time there was a distancing from the attitudes of the 1960s that had emphasized technology, urbanism and an international Western orientation. The traditional countryside and its material culture had been lost in the restructuring of Finnish society, and they were now veiled in nostalgia. Selectively rehabilitated and sentimentalized "folk culture" offered inspiration regardless of political affiliation. The mental and ideological framework posed by a consumer in peasant clothing amidst neo-vernacular furniture in a prefabricated apartment building in an urban housing area was different than that of a decade ago. This was naturally noticed by manufacturers and their marketing apparatuses. In both interiors and fashions, adaptations of motifs regarded as popular or folkish became common.

At the same time, however, many of the leading figures of the design community, such as Tapio Wirkkala and Ilmari Tapiovaara were engaged in serious work to maintain and revive the crafts traditions of the Finnish countryside. Despite these efforts, it became the fate of rural home industries mainly to serve tourism and the souvenir industry fuelled by it. On the other hand, the alliance of art and industry that Estlander had dreamt of a century earlier in a crafts-dominated agrarian Finland had been realized. In urban and industrialized Finland arts and crafts were now practised by persons who had been trained in the applied arts. This sector would have an important role in crafted production in small editions and especially in individual works approaching the context of art. The world of everyday material items from the simplest utility objects to more complex equipment and means of transport and communication was, instead, produced industrially.

Towards the boom of the 1980s
Applied art and design in Finland have been spurred by economic parameters at various times. The founding stage in the 1870s was a response not only to industrialization but also to the national catastrophe of famine that followed crop failures in the late 1860s. The depression of the early 1930s aroused industry to renew its product range, which also opened doors for modernist design. In the years of austerity after the war, arts and crafts and their international success fuelled the whole field of design. Now in the late 1970s, the representatives of industry and design began to approach each other once again. Industry noted the role of design as a resource that was needed to revive the economy,

while designers gradually responded to this invitation. The arguments were largely the same as in the 1960s (or even in the 1870s!) but the conception of professional responsibility and skill had both expanded and deepened. This meant that the boom of the following decade was entered with new resources at hand.

The new empowerment of design was also reflected by the fact that the collection of the Museum of Applied Arts (present-day Design Museum),[101] which had been moving from one location to another for decades and had finally been left in storage crates saw daylight in 1979, when the museum reopened in new premises in a former private school in the centre of Helsinki. Design education had been accorded the university status that was of primary importance for its future development. The museum permitted the display of Finland's design heritage and international touring exhibitions. Design education and the museum of design could once again collaborate. This meant that after having operated for a century the two original pillars of Finnish applied art and design were, in a sense, re-established in the 1970s.

The new spirit of cooperation in the Finnish design community was reflected by the international attention that it received around the turn of the 1970s and 1980s. This did not concern designed objects but instead professional and ideologically oriented activities in organizations. The International Council of Societies of Industrial Design (ICSID) was established in 1957 and those who were involved in developing design in Finland followed the definitions of the role and message of industrial design expressed by, among others, Tomás Maldonado (1922–), who had also been influential at the Ulm school. Ornamo of Finland joined the Council in 1969. In the late 1970s, when preparations began for the first joint world congress of ICSID, the IFI interior and furniture designers' federation and the ICOGRADA organization of graphic designers that was to be held in 1981, Helsinki was chosen as the venue. Designer Antti Nurmesniemi was appointed chairman of the congress. This congress was a major event that was featured prominently in the media, and it marked recognition of the international importance of Finnish design. It also led to locating the permanent office of ICSID in Helsinki, where it operated until 2005.

▲ The introduction of plastics into design and manufacturing that began in the late 1950s gave designers completely new opportunities. The *Karuselli* chair, which was created by Yrjö Kukkapuro for the Haimi company and introduced in 1964, is a good example, with the contiguous form and construction of the seat, backrest and handrests achieved with the aid of plastic.

Design in plastic

Until the turn of the 1960s designers worked with mostly traditional materials and techniques when having to provide external appearance for products such as television sets or mopeds. Although furniture design, for example, developed various techniques of lamination, curving and gluing, wood was still the material in question. The introduction of plastic – or plastics – that began in the late 1950s changed this situation markedly. Not bound to any particular product category, plastics were instead adopted at a fast pace in a highly diverse array of objects in terms of function and scale. The technology of plastics developed quickly, offering in turn a wide range of applications from objects for

the home to components of investment goods, such as heavy transport machinery. For designers, the adoption of plastic was a liberating experience because of its adaptability. At the same time it was challenging as a new, synthetic material. Before long, plastic was also regarded as "artificial", something of less value than traditional manufacturing materials. It was largely the task of designers to demonstrate the possibilities of plastic alongside traditional materials and also where it was superior to the latter.

The introduction of plastics was first evident in furniture, mainly chairs. It was heralded by an acrylic bar stool designed by Olavi Hänninen for the café of the Industries Palace building, which was completed for the 1952 Helsinki Olympics. Designers were not able to utilize plastics to any broader degree until the end of the decade and the spread of mould-cast polystyrene and fibreglass, also cast in moulds but made by layering. Fibreglass in particular initially required a great deal of work by hand, which slowed production and raised the price of products. Because of this, one of the most widely known objects of Finnish design, Yrjö Kukkapuro's (1933–) *Karuselli* armchair was originally conceived in the late 1950s, but not put into mass production until 1964 when the production properties of plastics had developed. Large-scale production was not achieved until elastic polypropene made it possible to replace the former all-purpose chairs of steel tubing and laminated wood with plastic products. Finnish designers finally had access to the same technology that was already used by foreign examples such as Charles Eames (1907–1978) and Eero Saarinen (1910–1961) over a decade earlier in the United States.

Plastic were adopted at an early stage in other classes of objects. In particular, lamps designed by Yki Nummi (1925–1984)[102] for the Orno company, such as *Modern Art* from 1955 and *Lokki* (Seagull) from 1960, showed how acrylic could achieve the same light properties as opal glass but with less restricted form and with resistance to shock. The properties and low cost of plastics led to a flood of plastic products, in which the designer played only a minor role. Despite this, the Finnish plastics industry used the skills of Tapio Wirkkala in the design of light switches, airline tableware and ketchup bottles. This realized in concrete terms the service concept of Nordic modernism – good design belongs to everyone.

Plastics proved to be particularly useful for industrial design in the housings of home electronics devices and other products such as juicers. They also replaced metal in traditional utility objects of the home – the most famous example being Fiskars scissors, millions of which have been made since the mid-1960s. In these products plastic was used to achieve ergonomically optimum cutting power and precision. The rapid technological development of plastics and composite materials in general spread their use in components in the heavy metal industry, for example in the operator's and passengers' areas of means of transport, one of the most visible examples being the bright orange benches of the Helsinki Metro carriages. Plastics had come to stay, but in the furniture industry their success story was interrupted by the sharp rise of oil prices in 1973. For example, Yrjö Kukkapuro and his manufacturer, Haimi, had just launched serial production in hardened ABS plastic, which, however, ended with the risen price of the raw material.

In addition to the price of the material the use of plastics was also reduced by growing awareness of its impact on the environment. The fossil base of plastics and the problems caused by discarded products were noted. The later recycling of plastic would eradicate most of these negative effects. But in the 1970s the design of plastic products was not regarded as ethical by the young generation. Instead, it was associated with international exploitative capitalism and a non-ecological attitude. In this situation it was interesting that towards the end of the decade Franck designed *Pitopöytä* (Feast Table) a *"Kilta"*-type tableware service in plastic, all the items of which, from the serving dishes to cutlery were of light, durable and bright-coloured melamine. Despite the obvious high quality of the tableware it did not replace ceramics in plates and bowls or metal for cutlery. The reasons for this were not rational but instead related to convention and psychological resistance. Plastics could not be allowed to dominate the shared meal, possibly the most important rite of the home.

New design products – machinery, equipment, electronics
The scope of designers began to expand in the late 1950s along with the diversification of Finnish industries. Both the masters of the older gen-

eration, such as Wirkkala, who were only middle-aged at the time, and their younger colleagues, who had been trained in industrial design, such as Ahola, designed electric ranges, sauna stoves, washing machines and other products mainly for homes. Nonetheless, few companies used the services of designers when making equipment and devices for industry. An early exception to this rule was Strömberg, which in 1959 hired Börje Rajalin, a recently graduated silversmith, to design electric motors. Rajalin became the first teacher of industrial design at the Institute of Industrial Art. When the City of Helsinki began to consider a metro system of public transport in the late 1960s, Rajalin and Antti Nurmesniemi were hired to head the design sector of the project. Lasting from 1967 to 1979, this major scheme employed and trained several young designers to have command of design for a technological and logistic context of large scale. The work involved the carriages, their space for the operators and passengers, and the stations. It was important to understand the whole as a system and design as part of it.

▼ In the 1980s, industrial design gained a foothold in areas such as equipment for public health care. Jussi Ahola, *Opera* operating table, Merivaara/Instrumentarium Oy, 1989.

▶ Manufacturers of home electronics began to utilize the skills of designers in the early 1960s. The ASA-brand television set from the late 1960s shown here demonstrates the possibilities of plastics in the design and manufacturing of housings and cabinets for equipment and appliances.

Another example of the comprehensive use of design for public transport was the GTS Finnjet from 1977. Powered by gas turbines, this flagship of Finnish technology and design expertise was the fastest passenger ship and car ferry in the Baltic. The appearance of the ship was created by designer Heikki Sorvali. The ship's information systems for passengers, various spaces, textiles and uniforms for the crew were designed by a multidisciplinary team that included Antti and Vuokko Nurmesniemi, Pekka Perjo (1936–) and Arto Kukkasniemi (1943–2005). Finnish car ferries serving German ports had already been saturated with the achievements of design, such as Birger Kaipiainen's ceramic reliefs and Eero Aarnio's impressive chairs, but the Finnjet was exceptional because designers had been given free rein from the hull of the vessel down to the details of its interior.

In the 1960s, and even in the following decade, the structure of the Finnish economy was predominantly defined by the forest and heavy industries. The situation differed from Sweden, the nearest comparison, with its output of telephones, home electronics and electrical equipment of even international significance, not to mention its large automobile industry. Finnish designers had a smaller field in which to operate. The situation began to change, however, in the early 1970s. Change was speeded by progress in electronic technology and its adoption in devices and equipment for measuring, processing and transferring data. This was largely due to the needs of the public sector rather than to consumer goods and therefore it was initially not evident in everyday life and homes but instead at workplaces and the health services of the public sector. Makers of equipment for health care now employed designers to help create ergonomically demanding equipment utilizing a great deal of electronic measurement capacity, i.e. information technology. At the same time, towards the close of the 1970s, the need for various electronic surveillance and information control systems grew, and designers were involved in designing the related workstations and equipment. Telephones also began to be made, though not yet at the consumer level. There were instead intercoms for communication in workspaces and designers were immediately consulted for developing them.

▶ Design serving everyday life – multipurpose faucet designed by Jorma Vennola and made by Oras, turn of the 1980s.

The Finnish home electronics industry gained pace in the 1970s mainly through the manufacturing of television sets. This would have long-reaching effects on the future direction of design. Traditionally designers and their still few offices were concentrated in the Helsinki region. Many providers of design services were individual designers and thus self-employed persons rather than design offices or agencies in the international manner. On the other hand, there were established design entrepreneurs providing services in various sectors, such as Studio Antti Nurmesniemi (founded 1954) and Design Tapio Wirkkala (founded 1966). In the 1970s design offices were being established by industrial designers, but the new firms were no longer multidisciplinary practices based on a single designer name and its professional renown, but specifically businesses serving the industrial production of equipment and often the internal needs of the corporate world or the public sector. Nor were their names any longer associated with certain individuals, which would not even have been possible, because the tasks were bound to teamwork.

There were young industrial designers in the field for whom the Helsinki region was too small an area in which to operate. In this situation television manufacturers in Salo (Salora Oy), Lohja (Finlux Oy) and Turku (ASA Oy) recognized the benefits of industrial design in steepening competition and began to employ designers for product development. The result was clusters of industrial design skills outside the capital, which had previously dominated the field unilaterally. Turku in particular was to become a significant centre of entrepreneurship in industrial design. When the electronics industry began to shift its focus from television sets to wireless communication, the course was marked that would ultimately lead to making mobile phones. Designers played a decisive role in these developments from the outset.

▶ In the 1960s and 1970s, the Finnish cotton industry was still a prominent actor employing the services of designers and a sector that was also important in terms of exports.

Consumer society and its arrays of goods

The relationship of design with technology and its involvement with the economy and politics discussed above were macro-level factors providing the overall framework for design in the 1960s and 1970s. Design, however, concerned the everyday lives of people in concrete terms through objects, images and the environments composed of them. The rise in standard of living and consumer demand until the middle of the 1970s permitted an unprecedented abundance of goods. Because of migration from the countryside into the cities and within cities into suburbs, housing development was at its peak from the mid-1960s to the early years of the following decade. This fuelled demand for products of the traditional applied art and design sector, such as furniture, textiles, ceramics and glass. Domestic products still dominated the market, and the furniture industry in particular increased its volume considerably.

Design skills were, of course, not evident in all products, but the idea of design as an element of quality and a competitive asset which had been expanded and actively marketed since the early 1950s had served its purpose. There was also greater consumer awareness and businesses now competed in a situation of greater supply in which choices were no longer steered by austerity. Building and construction by the public sector also expanded further in education, administration and health care, along with private development for the business sector.

FENNO-SPORT

019

OTK
FENNO-SPORT
Finland
Postbox 10120 Helsinki 10 Telex 12 - 454
Cable: **Osuustukku**

030

039

018

138

033

261

025

Agent Vertreter

Brusman B. V.
Fashion House
Kon. Wilhelminaplein 8
Amsterdam
Tel. 020-176 365

Eduard Eckrodt
Textilbüro
Bismarckstrasse 104
Düsseldorf
BRD

Herbert Neumann
Himmelreichstrasse 18
7860 Schopfheim/Baden
Tel. (07622) 489
BRD

Robert Scheuch
Ackersteinstr. 201
8049 Zürich Tel. 051/569 682
Schweiz

Finn Fashion
Robert Hammer
Graben 11 (Dorotheergasse 2)
1010 Wien Tel. 527 881
Österreich

Rolf Nielsen & Co
Grönland 4
Oslo 1 Tel. 683 616
Norge

Inkeri Inc.
131 N. State Street
Lake Oswego,
Oregon 97034
USA

While the design sector suffered no significant structural disruptions in terms of production and consumption from the early 1960s to the second half of the 1970s, the world of objects, forms and colours changed radically. The subdued, stylized modernism that dominated the early 1960s changed to experimental, boldly coloured interior design inspired by international pop culture and op art. The contemporary spirit of seeking alternatives and experimentation also led young couples furnishing their first homes to seek different kinds of artefactual identity than their parents. Informality, the overturning of (modernist) authority and impulses provided by a new internationalization not only from centres such as London but also from the cultures of South America, Africa and India influenced interior design and dress in particular.

▲ Also in design, subdued modernist simplicity began to give way in the late 1960s to pronounced colourism and ornamentality. *Paratiisi* (Paradise) tableware designed by Birger Kaipiainen for the Arabia factory, 1970.

Also history, previously banned, made a comeback, first in graphic design and fashions, but before long in objects for the home. Ornament had never been completely eradicated, for example from the Arabia factory's ceramic products, and now it made an impressive return in Birger Kaipiainen's *Paratiisi* (Paradise) tableware service in 1970. In highly general terms it could be said that the marked experimentation, daring and openness of the 1960s were followed by the much heavier forms of the 1970s and a dark, broken colour scale. The colours of interior decoration shifted from the modernist lightness and natural materials of the 1960s to the pyrotechnics of the turn of the decade and from there to spaces dominated by green, red, orange and brown in the 1970s.

The period and its design trends can perhaps best be read in furniture and textile design and the interior decoration in which they were applied. The 1960s in particular was a flourishing period of experimental furniture design, during which plastics provided new opportunities. Eero Aarnio's chairs *Pallo* (Ball) from 1966 and *Pastilli* (Pastille) from 1968 reflect the way in which design in these years rejected the rules of established modernism and subscribed to the futuristic and op-art influenced tendencies of the period. For the Asko company, which produced these chairs, they were a symbol of corporate broad-mindedness and they promoted the sales of other products as had been the case in the glass industry for many years. The message of these and Yrjö Kukkapuro's plastic chairs with their focus on the ergonomic properties of seating was highly international and they could not be associated with the established nature-oriented imagery of Finland. Instead, they pointed to the contemporary nature of design in Finland. Aarnio's *Pallo* chair soon achieved iconic status, even internationally, as a symbol of contemporary lifestyle, a repeatedly depicted metaphor of 1960s liberation.

The informal trends of the end of the decade were evident in a rejection of the "bourgeois" conventions of the previous generation – even chairs could imply hierarchy, and it was thus preferable to sit on cushions on the floor. The radicalism of the new generation now claiming its power in both consumption and politics was evident in homes and ideological discourse alike. The furniture industry reacted to this by introducing reasonably priced products suited to the spirit of the times,

◀ ▶ The rising standard of living throughout the 1960s, consumer habits introduced by the young generation and a quest for alternatives in design were also reflected in the renewed product ranges of furniture manufacturers. On the left is the fibreglass *Pallo* (Ball) chair designed by Eero Aarnio for the Asko company in 1966. Shown on this page is the *Kameleontti* (Chameleon) sofa designed in the late 1960s by Torsten Laakso for the Skanno firm.

such as Skanno's popular *Kameleontti* (Chameleon) sofa of the 1960s, designed by Torsten Laakso (1930–).

A response to the requirements of flexibility and adaptability in interior design was also offered by highly popular shelving and chests of drawers made of modular elements. Unlike sculptural luxury items such as Aarnio's *Pallo* chair, these products were related to the constructivist systemic thinking that dominated contemporary architecture. Changes in manufacturing technology in the furniture industry also steered developments in this direction. Chipboard became a common material around the turn of the decade, rapidly replacing structures of solid wood and blockboard. The traditional dovetail and groove joints were replaced by dowel and angle bar joints. This made it possible to assemble modular furniture at the retailer or at home, thus lowering prices. The ease of working with chipboard and its wide range of linings made it a highly popular material and also led design towards the use of sheet structures. A drawback was the fragility of the material, and it never gained popularity among designers, being used instead for low-priced mass-produced products.

Living-rooms taken over by sofa suites

The broad success of post-war design in Finland was implemented through a uniform national culture and an elite that guided its tastes. The examples provided by leading designers and the modernism adopted even by large furniture manufacturers were still a kind of norm in the 1960s. A change in the consumer habits of broad sections of the population took place around the turn of the decade, with strong support from the furniture industry. As analysed by researcher Minna Sarantola-Weiss, this turning point was most clearly evident in the changes undergone by so-called sofa suites – a set of two armchairs and a sofa which had become widespread through the introduction of television.[103] Their popularity, size and amount of upholstery continued to grow around the turn of 1970s. Design professionals and critics roundly condemned these "clumpy sofas", without the slightest effect on their popularity. Criticism, however, stopped professionals from designing them. As result, some of the most popular models were designed by factory technicians, managing directors and marketing managers.

Among the "people" the flagship products of the furniture industry, the sofa suites that were significant investments for the home, gained almost unanimous popularity but were condemned by the design community. The modernist project of educating the public had run out of steam and lost its legitimacy. Consumers made their choices independently for reasons of price, opulence and, most importantly, comfort. The sofa suites also reintroduced history into Finnish living rooms, after it had already been banished by modernism. This time, however, it did not concern the collecting of Finnish folk heritage, which was something for the elite, but instead reflected the Victorian environment familiar from British television series. International entertainment offered by the media outranked "real" design. From now on, the contribution of furniture designers would be more visible in quantitative terms in contexts other than the home.

Any description of Finnish design culture of the period would definitely be incomplete without the Marimekko phenomenon. The 1960s and early 1970s were the golden age of this company, which had already been founded in 1950. Marimekko's cotton prints, accessories and

► In the early 1970s the sofa suite became the most important and most valuable element of home interiors. In the upper picture are the Isku company's *Kastanja* corner sofa and the *Vohveli* bookcase, which, together with the coffee table, was made of assembled boards without traditional corner joints. In the lower picture is a solid pine sofa suite also made by Isku. Modernist lightness had now given way to heaviness, large size – and comfort.

striped tricot products found a considerably large audience of consumers, especially among younger age-groups. Led by Armi Ratia, Marimekko managed to employ open-minded and talented young designers such as Vuokko Nurmesniemi, Maija Isola (1927–2001)[104] and Annika Rimala (1936–).[105] The company was already able to reach out internationally and enter the US market by the early 1960s. Fashions by Annika Rimala were on the pages of leading international fashion magazines and her striped collections served in a democratic spirit both sexes in all classes of society. Maija Isola's printed fabrics with their prominent large designs marked interiors through use as curtains and tablecloths. Perhaps more than any other company involved in design, Marimekko also expressed a lifestyle of overall formal youthfulness, which was excellently suited to the optimistic atmosphere fuelled by economic growth in the 1960s.

From handicraft to the art of materials

Applied art and design in Finland and the Nordic countries in general are characterized by the marked presence of handicraft not only historically but also in recent decades. In Finland, for example, Design Forum Finland, a design promotion centre maintained by the Finnish Society of Crafts and Design, has displayed not only design aimed at industry but also arts and crafts. Artisans have traditionally had a prominent role in the Ornamo association. This situation differs, for example, from Great Britain, which has a Design Council to promote design and a separate Craft Council. The craft sector is not discussed in detail in the histories of design of countries that had undergone industrialization earlier and to a greater extent than Finland. The specific nature of the history of applied art and design in Finland, however, gives good cause also to consider crafts as part of the developments of the past decades.

Arts and crafts had lived on and had a definite presence throughout the whole period described above, when the use of design grew significantly in industry. The rise of industrial design did not undermine the position of crafts, since these were respectively extremes of the field of applied art and design in terms of both professional activity and expression. They were carried out by different persons in different contexts. There was, however, change in the sense that the younger generation

no longer included multi-skilled persons – industrial designers rarely created art glass any more.

However, art textiles of various kinds, especially ryijys, were successfully displayed in both domestic and foreign exhibitions of the Finnish Society of Crafts and Design in the 1960s. On the other hand, handicraft sought new opportunities alongside these unique, one-off, works, starting its quest at the grassroots level. This was spurred by the need for alternatives to the "design for exhibitions" that was felt to be outmoded and in more concrete terms by poor employment opportunities in the traditional sectors of applied art especially in the 1970s. The ideological climate of the period also led to a quest for opportunities for professional practice in other contexts than the leading manufacturers of ceramics, textiles and glass.

Ceramic studios often concentrated on one-off works or small editions by an individual ceramist. This mostly concerned utility wares and not ceramic art as such. The larger shared workshops, such as the pioneering Pot Viapori (founded in 1971) at the historic Suomenlinna for-

tress off Helsinki also made small series of utility objects. While the ceramists were involved in the whole scale of the work, from ceramic art via unique utility objects to products in small editions, workshops generally aimed to complement or serve as an alternative to the products of the Arabia factory and imported wares. Cooperatives covering several areas of crafts were organized to sell the products, an example being the Helsinki Craftspersons Cooperative founded in 1974 with its Artisaani shop.[106] This involved the desire to control the process from concept via production to distribution without any outside commercial intermediaries. This "ownership of one's own work" reflected an idealized return to the procedures of the early capitalist economy. On the other hand, the time was now ripe for the reintroduction of handicraft. Amidst the abundance of industrially made goods, more affluent and "more aware" consumers bought products underscoring materials and the skills of the artisan to enrich their private environments.

In ceramics, the search for alternatives in design and production was also associated with regional changes. Internal migration from the countryside to the cities had provided a great deal of low-cost space, such as former cowsheds, for the use of artisans. A ceramics workshop established in 1971 by Anu Pentik (former Pentikäinen, 1942–)[107] at Posio in North Finland grew under the Pentik name to become a significant and successfully international company. A chapter apart in the history of arts and crafts over the past few decades is the community that has grown since the 1980s in the historic ironworks location of Fiskars. Since 1996, it has operated as a cooperative of artists, artisans and designers. Such an entity of work, residence and exhibitions is rare even internationally, especially since it has managed to combine idealism with forms of long-term collaboration.

The founding of individual ceramics studios was not technically difficult, because a kiln for ceramics could be made with relatively simple means. The situation was similar though more demanding for glass, because of the need to achieve a temperature of 1,200 degrees Celsius. The studio glass movement, basing work on one's own melting furnace, design and production, arrived in Finland in the early 1970s. Although ceramics had been taught in the applied arts since 1902, similar educa-

◄ Björn Weckström, *Planetary Valleys* necklace designed in 1969 for Lapponia Jewelry. Weckström's works broke with the traditions of jewellery design and achieved international fame and exposure, such as this necklace which was prominently featured in the closing scene of the film *Star Wars*.

tion in glass making was not launched until the 1970s. It became established in the following decade as an area of specialization in industrial design and was later included with training in ceramics. Unlike ceramics, studio glass work with one's own furnace could not be based on the production of utility objects in small series. It would have been impossible to compete with the Finnish glass industry.

On the other hand, both the Iittala and Nuutajärvi glassworks had made experimental art glass for a long while. For example, Kaj Franck and Oiva Toikka (1931–),[108] originally trained as a ceramist, designed multicoloured crafted glass objects alongside mass-produced items. But unlike in hand-crafted ceramics, the designer and the maker were not the same person. The mouth-blowing of glass is highly demanding, and the celebrated glass art of the whole post-war era was in fact the result of glasshouse or chair work carried out in Finland's glassworks. In this context, a master glassblower would execute the aims of a designer. The

▲ The Arabia factory renewed its product range by hiring designers of the young generation. Tapio Yli-Viikari's oven-proof *Kokki* series from 1978 was highly popular and in production for a long while.

training that began in the 1970s changed the situation – students could now be given the means to make the pieces themselves. Craftsmanship in glass which particularly emerged in the 1980s and pure glass art were realized alongside each other in independent workshops and with the assistance of master glassblowers at glassworks.

Towards the context of art

The textile sector clearly demonstrates the course of development followed by handicraft and related art since the 1960s. In the development of applied art in the late 19th century a central role was played by woven textiles, such as ryijys, which had received international praise ever since the Finnish Pavilion at the Paris World's Fair of 1900. After the Second World War and especially in the 1950s and 1960s these art textiles of ancient technique but displaying abstract designs and patterns were visual art in content but applied art, handicraft, in their genre and

their hierarchical classification. They were non-figurative art executed
via applied art in the same manner as contemporary art glass was free-
form sculpture. At the same time the system and canon of "real" art still
opposed abstract expression. It was by no means surprising that Uhra-
Beata Simberg-Ehrström (1914–1979), who was famous for her ryijy designs, was originally trained as a textile artist.

Studio work also emerged in textiles in the 1970s. This time, however, it concerned individual printed fabrics rather than weaving. At
the Institute of Industrial Art, Kirsti Rantanen (1930–)[109] had developed
teaching concerning industrially made printed fabrics in the 1960s. Now
many of her former students, such as Päikki Priha (1948–) applied these
impulses in simple small-scale fabric printing in basement studios. Of
the traditional design sectors, industrial textile production in particular
found itself in difficulties in the 1970s, when it could not provide work
by any means for all who were skilled in it. Accordingly, the status of a
self-employed artisan was not only a voluntary choice.

Another route was that of textiles as an independent art form. There
was an unprecedented rise and acceptance of textile art in the 1980s.
This, however, did not concern ryijys but instead public textile works
made in various techniques and explicitly meant for the art context.
The economic boom of the decade resulted in a large number of public
buildings for which large art textile works were commissioned. The spacious lobbies of cultural facilities let these works grow to monumental
proportions. In this manner textile art gained a status and visibility that
was achieved only exceptionally by glass or ceramic art.

Beginning in the 1970s, arts and crafts moved towards the art context
on a broad front. Not just the above-mentioned ceramic, glass and textile
art but also jewellery design was displayed in group exhibitions and galleries as art, separated from its designed function. These works could now
be placed within the discourse of the art world to be evaluated. But since
the starting point of these works was nonetheless based on materials,
they fell in between crafts and fine art in the system of the arts. This was
not an issue of quality but instead of convention and hierarchy. The distinction between the higher and lower arts that had been made when the
Craft School had been established a century earlier had not disappeared.

MARIMEKKO

Marimekko grew from a family business of the early 1950s into a textile and fashion company that marked the lifestyle of the 1960s in many different ways, especially through its design-based business operations. From the outset, its director Armi Ratia hired young designers willing to experiment, such as Vuokko Nurmesniemi, Maija Isola and Annika Rimala (later Piha). Marimekko initially concentrated on printed cotton fabrics and fashions made from them. Tricot garments were introduced in the 1960s and of these products, the *Tasaraita* collection made the most definite mark on Finnish dress in the late 1960s. During Maija Isola's period printed fabrics of bold design with references to pop and op art were used as elements of interior decoration. They became applied art bought by the metre.

Marimekko was successful in becoming international and was also able to enter the American market. The company's lifestyle marketing concept also considered prefabricated houses, and the experimental Marikylä village was planned with this in mind for a location near Porvoo, east of Helsinki. Marimekko's prominence began to decline in the late 1970s through changes of ownership, but the company experienced a new rise in the 1990s, leading to success that is still continuing.

1. Fashion show at the Kalastajatorppa restaurant in Helsinki, 1951.

2. The *Jokapoika* shirt designed by Vuokko Nurmesniemi in 1956 is still in production.

1

2

3

4

3. The cotton tricot unisex *Tasaraita* collection by Annika Rimala was highly popular in Finland around the turn of the 1960s and 1970s.

4. Advertisement from the turn of the 1970s.

5. Dress designed by Annika Rimala from the *Linssi* printed fabric by Kaarina Kellomäki, 1966.

6. Printed fabrics designed by Maija Isola: *Lokki*, 1961; *Silkkikuikka*, 1961; *Mansikkavuoret*, 1971; *Joonas*, 1961.

5

PLASTICS IN DESIGN

Until the 1950s professional designers employed traditional materials and techniques in both handcrafted and industrially manufactured works. This situation changed as Finnish industries diversified and especially when a new material, plastic, was adopted in its many different forms in consumer goods and machinery. While the opportunities of plastic were a challenge for mass production, the material also opened up completely new freedom with regard to form, light weight and shockproof qualities.

Although plastics were experimentally introduced into the furniture industry in the early 1950s, they did not come into wider use until the end of the decade. Plastic furniture gained more exposure as manufacturing techniques developed and production costs went down. The material was used in both experimental furniture that gained prizes and international renown and the low-cost all-purpose chairs of school auditoria and service station cafeterias. Plastics were also put to a wider range of uses in lamps and before long in the housings of electrical devices, and they came into common use in kitchenware. Despite high-standard design, plastics never made a breakthrough in tableware. The use of plastics was reduced especially in furniture because of the rising prices caused by the oil crisis of the mid-1970s.

1

1. This stool designed by Olavi Hänninen in 1952 for the café of the Hotel Palace was the first plastic chair made in Finland.

2. Yki Nummi, *Modern Art* acrylic lamp from 1955. Made by the Orno company.

3. Eero Aarnio, *Polaris* all-purpose chair, 1966. Made by the Asko company.

4. Eero Aarnio, *Pastille* chair from 1968, made by the Asko company. Aarnio was commissioned by Asko to design furniture in plastic to suit various price groups and uses.

5. Coffee thermos jug designed by Heikki Metsä-Ketelä for the Airam company, 1984.

6. Kaj Franck designed the *Pitopöytä* tableware service for Sarvis in 1979.

7. This Fiskars-brand juicer from 1965 was designed by Olof Bäckström, who also designed the scissors in the foreground, which were introduced in 1967 and are still being made.

3

4

5

6

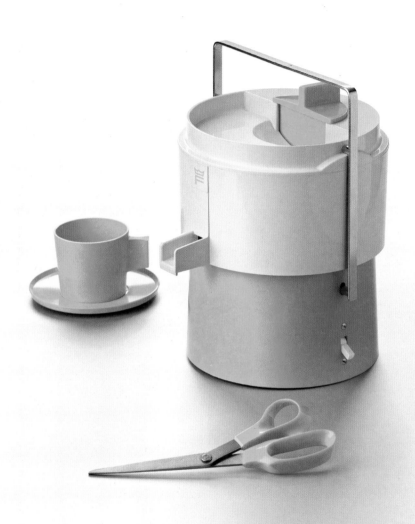

7 RISE AND FALL

DESIGN AND THE GOOD
TIMES OF THE 1980S

icsid

1980	1985	1987	1992	1995

The first Best of the Year Prize in graphic design

The magazines *Muoto* and *Form Function Finland* are launched

The secretariat of the International Council of Societies of Industrial Design is relocated in Helsinki.

The *Metaxis – Young Form* exhibition at the Museum of Applied Arts in Helsinki

The first Kaj Franck Design Prize

The founding of the Media Lab of the University of Art and Design Helsinki

The 120th anniversary of the Finnish Society of Crafts and Design

Finland joins the European Union

I n the preceding chapters, major changes in design have been linked to turning-points in the political, economic and cultural history of Finland. In the 1980s politics played a lesser role, while the economy, and culture maintained by it, were of primary importance. Design was influenced by both in very different ways. On one hand, design especially for industry sought alliances of a new kind with the corporate sector. On the other hand, applied art and design and their cultural and artistic aspects, were strengthened and gained a great deal of publicity. As a result, industrial design committed to manufacturing and technological progress and the more experimental arts and crafts and applied art grew in tandem. The economic boom that began in the late 1970s and led to an overheated economy at the end of the following decade was terminated by a recession that deteriorated rapidly in the early 1990s.

On the same timeline, the collectivism of the 1970s turned to individualism, the personal choices of individual consumers. The term "consumer feast", which appeared in Finnish parlance especially towards the end of the decade, is very apt. It was served by design, which in turn was empowered by it. Professionals and design education again turned to the realities of manufacturing, marketing and consumption. The previous decade's mission to collectively change the world was replaced by product development and design as individual achievement.

The modern project – a thing of the past?

As in the other Nordic countries, modernism in Finnish architecture and design was initially allied closely with the modernization of society and the economy. This duty was still being performed, especially in the sphere of industrial design. The formal means of modernism, however, were regarded as too limited for the design of people's immediate environment and public and private space. Systematic thinking and design rationalism, with their emphasis on restrained form, came under growing criticism in the United States and Italy, among other countries. It was specifically from these countries that new, diverse influences arose, questioning the canon of modernism and emerging into international consciousness. Under the generic name of 'postmodernism', these new movements reflected the argument, put forward in the social sciences and in cultural studies at the time, that the Western welfare states had moved on from the modern project and into a postmodern condition.

Instead of a style, postmodernism was a design orientation employing varied means, such as historicist and classicist references and forms that rejected the "rationality" of modernism. In design, it was especially present in furniture, but also in other utility items of the home that had now been "culturized". Through such products, postmodernism was launched prominently in the exhibition held by the Italian Memphis group in Milan in 1981. There was a desire to raise architecture and design to prominence once again and for them to be seen to have definite, cultural impact. The era of unseen, anonymous service to society was now in the past. Objects could be laden with cultural messages and made to communicate with users and each other alike.

The tradition of Finnish modernism, however, proved to be highly resilient, especially in the face of the tendencies of postmodernism that employed historical references. Change was more evident in colour schemes and formal departures from convention. In furniture design, for example, Yrjö Kukkapuro introduced his *Experiment* collection in 1982, employing colourful free-form elements as parts of his otherwise constructivist chairs. Although this gesture surprised the public, it did not alter the basic constructivist, i.e. modernist, orientation of his chairs. Among the younger generation of furniture designers, Simo Heikkilä (1943–)[110] proceeded towards the minimalist use of materials, underscoring structurality rather than the exaggerated abundance of international postmodernism.

The constructivist constituent of modernism led the majority of designers to develop its heritage instead of rejecting it. But this was by no means the whole picture for design in the period, which now offered many more alternatives than previously. Furniture design also sought to distance itself from the formerly predominant doctrine of ergonomics and to make chairs that were visually and emotionally communicative. This meant that cultural meanings were explicitly assigned to de-

▶ Yrjö Kukkapuro's *Experiment* series from 1982 was made by Avarte. This chair design represents Kukkapuro's postmodern rejection of his earlier unadorned design, without compromising ergonomic and structural properties.

◀ In contrast to the matter-
of-fact, functionally oriented tradition of modernism,
postmodernism underscored
a playful spirit and the narrative, semantic properties
of objects. Stefan Lindfors,
Wamba, prototype of a water
kettle for Alessi of Italy, 1992.

signed products instead of their being the unintentional by-products of
function. Communicativeness now became an explicit aim.

These few examples describe the leading edge of furniture design
in the period and its experimental aspects with their quest for innovation. The furniture in question was mainly for public space and its production was fuelled by active public building and development in the
late 1980s. At the same time, the overheated housing market also increased demand for furniture. The Finnish furniture industry could no
longer respond adequately to the situation, and by the end of the decade
importation of furniture exceeded exports for the first time in Finnish
history. This became a permanent state of affairs and continued the developments that had already begun in the 1970s, in which domestic furniture design with its ambitious goals increasingly served the public sector while furniture for homes consisted of lower-priced imports. Also in
this sense Finland had entered the postmodern era, as the popular edu-

cation project of Finnish modernism and related product design had specifically proceeded from the needs of the home.

Postmodernism, however, was a catalyst for the new internationalization especially sought by the younger designer generation after the introverted attitudes and eastern orientation of the previous years. As in the 1960s, there was once again a desire to be urban and oriented towards the West – and even American impulses were again welcomed. Design was to be part of new cultural openness and public exposure. This new publicity was supported by several different simultaneous influences. In 1980 two new design publications began to appear, *Muoto* issued by Ornamo and *Form Function Finland*, published in English by Design Forum Finland.[111] Free of any commercial pressure, these journals could concentrate on design and related discussion, while also presenting young and lesser-known designers.

Criticism of Finnish identity

The Museum of Applied Arts (now the Design Museum), which was in a sense re-established in 1979, also achieved an active role in new experimental design through the work of Kaj Kalin (1958 –), the museum's curator, was involved in the avant-garde cultural magazine *Image*, which linked design by the young generation to the overall field of culture. These young people, many of whom were still students, began to organize their own exhibitions and to export both themselves and their work abroad. These efforts were supported by the University of Industrial Arts (present-day University of Art and Design Helsinki)[112] which was recovering and launching its long-term project of internationalization. The four basic actors of the Finnish design world, the Ornamo association, the Museum, the University and the Society of Crafts and Design had resumed cooperation, now with new potential.

As before, exhibitions were the main medium for presenting design. *Metaxis – Young Hands* (Museum of Applied Arts, 1987) was the most important of the many solo and joint exhibitions in which the young generation sought not only to present themselves but also to mark a distinction from the socio-technocratic anonymity of the preceding decade. This joint showing exploring the interstices of design, art and cultural

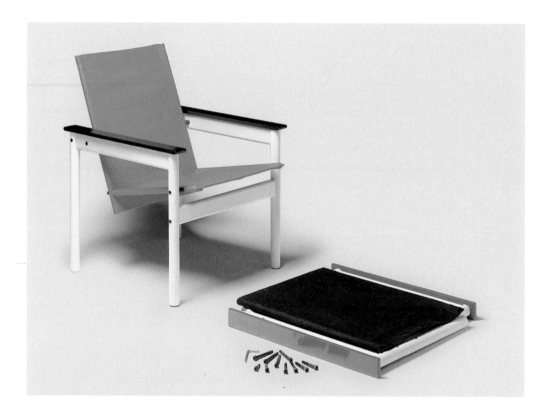

criticism largely defined the intellectual landscape in which design of the coming years would operate in its experimental, small-edition and artisanal forms. The individualistic tone of the period created in turn demand for designer-artists basking in the publicity provided by the media. Stefan Lindfors (1962–),[113] who had also been prominently featured in the Metaxis exhibition, personified both multidisciplinary skills and the importance of the artist's signature. Initially educated as an interior architect, Lindfors worked in a wide range of disciplines, from industrial product design, furniture and interiors to sculpture purely in the domain of art. He also gained an international foothold at an early stage, when his graduate-project lamp design was included in the product line of the Ingo Maurer company of Germany.

▲ Simo Heikkilä, *Markiisi* chair from 1986, made by Artzan. Heikkilä is a good example of how Finnish designers continued to interpret the heritage of modernism in the years of international postmodernism. In this chair, design also sought to conserve material and packaging.

▶ Tapani Aartomaa, exhibition poster *Neljäs vempula*, silkscreen print, 1988. Finnish art posters enjoyed international success in the 1980s.

NELJÄS VEMPULA

LAHDEN TAIDEMUSEO VESIJÄRVENKATU 11

The new premises of the Museum of Applied Arts also permitted the revived annual exhibitions of the Society of Crafts and Design, beginning in 1979 under the title *Finland Designs*. A dedicated Finnish design panel was established to select the exhibits. The aims of the panel regarding exhibitions were largely the same as before the war: to display the best contemporary works of design and to promote good taste. This, however, led to a crisis in the Finland Designs exhibitions towards the end of the decade. As analysed by Vuokko Takala-Schreib,[114] it became more and more difficult to define the "quality" and "Finnishness" of design in the increasingly international setting of the 1980s, especially since these concepts were still often regarded as commensurate (Takala-Schreib 2000). Criticism of the Design Panel also arose. Consisting of representatives of the small design community of a small country, this body was no longer regarded as having any authority to define quality in design. The above-mentioned Metaxis exhibition operated on its own terms and was a comment by the young generation on the Finland Designs institution.

Although the increasing speed of internationalization of the 1980s was in many ways desired, it once again shed light on a perennial subject of the design debate: the tension between "national" uniqueness and international currents, the latter often being regarded as a threat. The estimates of the panels of the Finland Designs exhibitions often contained descriptions that incorrectly branded submitted objects as international – i.e. being of foreign origin. Postmodern experimentation was seen as a threat to the national tradition of modernism, which was readily understood as a continuation of the simplicity and functionality of vernacular material culture. Finland had already succeeded with these means at the Paris World's Fair of 1900. Times changed but the arguments remained the same – only in different guises.

Design in decision-making

The deepening cooperation of industry and design ran alongside the new public exposure and impulses of design, though with less visibility. It was manifested not only through products but also as an explicit effort to have design included in corporate decision-making. The reasons

▶ Stefan Lindfors, *Scaragoo* table lamp from 1988. Lindfors was the most prominent representative of Finland's young generation of designers and he was also able to follow an international career. Lindfors's work ranges from industrial design to visual art.

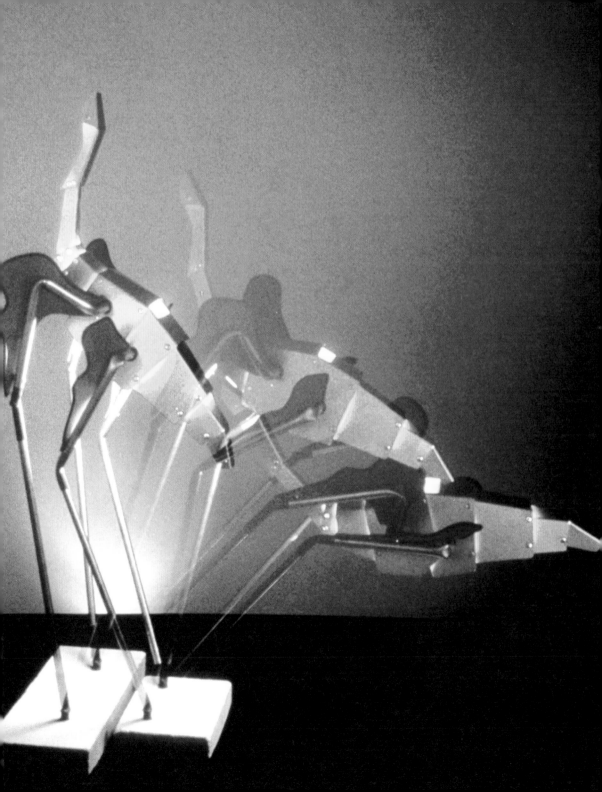

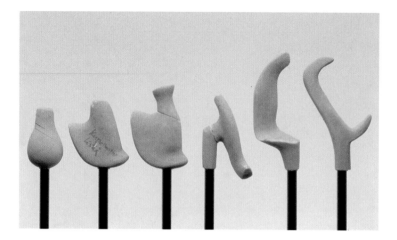

◄ ▶ A traditional Finnish object – a ski pole – reinterpreted through industrial design and new manufacturing technology. On the left is a series of prototypes from the design process and on the right is the Exel company's final carbon-fibre version. Pasi Järvinen, Crea-Design Oy, 1987.

cited for this were the clearly increased economic significance of design in the domestic market and especially for exports. By now, equipment and systems featuring design input had become a notable component of foreign trade. The same was true of consumer electronics products, such as television sets. Two decades of training industrial designers had expanded the ranks of these professionals and diversified the age structure of the field, permitting younger designers to learn from more experienced colleagues and to be recruited by their offices and agencies.

While commissions for industrial design still came from the electronics industry, the health-care sector and for kitchen appliances, there were significant changes during the decade in the objects to be designed and in the actual design work. In the motor vehicle industry, the Sisu[115] company began to use the services of Antti Siltavuori (1942–) for designing heavy transport vehicles. He also designed earth-moving equipment for the Valmet company.[116] Towards the end of the decade, industrial designers were involved in developing combine harvesters, tractors and even papermaking machines. Although the main focus was on the ergonomic aspects of work and safety, appearance was also considered in the design of vehicles. It was of primary importance for the credibility of the profession that successful work in the design teams of complex and expensive machinery and equipment for major corporations would con-

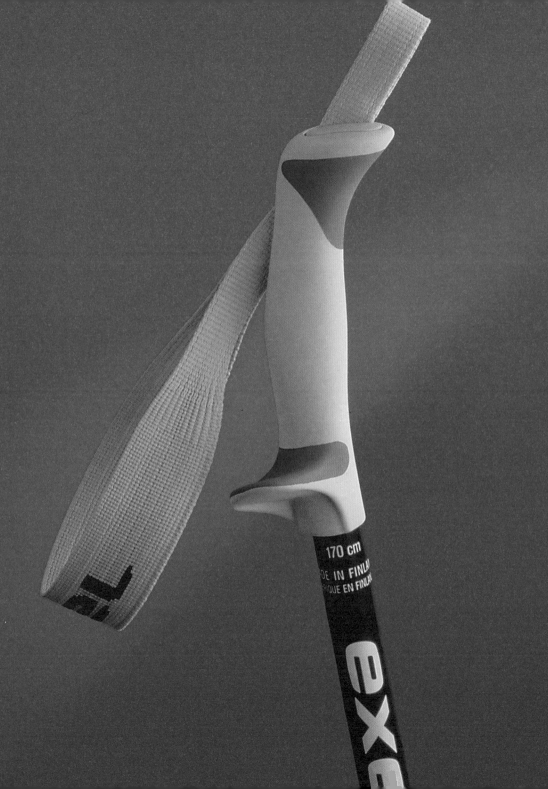

vince industry of the economic significance of design. This would eradicate the entrenched preconceptions of the corporate sector regarding design, an area that was still considered slightly peripheral.

Electronics was to play a decisive role in design entrepreneurship and the nature of work that came to be commissioned from self-employed designers and their offices. Television manufacturing, which had actively recruited industrial designers, and corporate acquisitions in this field led to the Nokia conglomerate becoming an owner of the Salora company. In one of Nokia's main areas of production, cables for data communication, there was also interest in a wireless telephone network that was being developed at the time. This led industrial designers such as Heikki Kiiski (1943–), Jouko Tattari (1957–) and Jorma Pitkonen (1945–) to begin designing mobile phones in the mid-1980s at the company's factory in Salo. The first fully developed mobile phone models were introduced in 1987. Nokia's mobile phone production which began in this manner and the design skills that were integrated with it from the very begin-

▲ Hannu Kähönen and Juhani Salovaara, Ergonomiadesign Oy, the SLO Intercom phone, 1977–79. In the 1970s data communications and various electronic control systems and their work stations began to provide an increasing amount of work for industrial designers.

ning would became the most important individual factor of Finnish industry and the visibility of design.

The professional activities of industrial designers in the electronics industry also brought them together, leading indirectly to the founding of Finland's largest design office in Turku in 1990. This office, Muotoilu-toimisto E&D (presently known as ED-Design),[117] was a merger of two local offices, Destem founded by Tapani Hyvönen (1947–) in 1976 and Juhani Salovaara's (1943–) Ergonomiadesign, established in 1973. Designers Hannu Kähönen (1948–) and Eljas Perheentupa (1951–), who had worked for this office, went on to set up the Creadesign[118] and LinjaDesign[119] offices in Helsinki. In her research on change and development in the industrial designer's profession, Anna Valtonen has observed how the in-house designers of companies thus became independent entrepreneurs who continued to provide services for their former employers through their own practices.[120] Industrial design had markedly expanded and diversified by the turn of the decade. Now, almost without exception, design offices comprising several individuals and the in-house designers of companies formed a mutually complementary corps of expert professionals.

Information technology revolutionizes design

The processes of change that took place in design in the 1980s cannot be considered globally or with reference to Finland without taking into account the revolution of information technology, the introduction of computers and the working processes facilitated by them. While the era of the Internet and virtual Web-based reality was to dawn in the following decade, even now work involving computers became a part of industrial design. Even more important were the programs of three-dimensional simulation and modelling permitted by this technology – CAD (Computer Aided Design) followed by CAM (Computer Aided Modelling). They introduced a revolution in the ways and means of designing, sharing and transferring information and for communicating with other professionals in industry. Where all visualization and presentation imagery had been done by hand until the late 1980s, CAD now became the tool for this purpose. It made design work more efficient and precise,

◀ Tapani Hyvönen, Destem Oy, the *Finlux Vario* television set from 1987. At the time Finland still had a significant television receiver industry, which benefited from the expansion of skills in industrial design offices, in turn furthered by the emergence of digitized design.

▼ The manufacturing of mobile phones was under way in the late 1980s, using the services of industrial designers in product development from the very beginning. The *Mobira Cityman* mobile phone from 1986 was designed by Matti Makkonen and made by Salora.

and rapidly developing software introduced data systems that were compatible with those of manufacturers. Changes had also taken place in the professional organization of designers in 1983, when the TAIKO Association of Artists and Designers was founded as a chapter of the Ornamo Association of Designers to serve artisans involved in the applied arts. Within Ornamo, the TKO association now remained to further the interests of only industrial designers. This professional group was now better equipped than before to operate under the pressures of a world that was becoming digitized.

The growing importance of industrial design in relation to other sectors of the design community was not ignored even by the Finnish Society of Crafts and Design. In 1987, Tapio Periäinen (1929–), who came to lead the Society after H. O. Gummerus retired in 1975, established Design Forum as a means of displaying industrial design. A few years later the Society organized all its promotional activities under the auspices of Design Forum Finland. Replacing the former Finnish name with an English one was typical insofar as the pressure to conform brought upon by internationalization led more widely to the adoption of Anglo-American terminology. This was also true of design education, in which the University of Art and Design Helsinki launched its international Design Leadership programme in 1991. It was a result of introducing the concepts of design management into the design and corporate sectors in Finland. The University staged its first international Design Management Conference in 1989, and went on to have leading international names as its evaluators and consultants. The objective was to obtain from the design community initiatives to serve a corporate world run by engineers and business-school graduates and to convince this sector of the usefulness of design as a means of strategic management. A person trained as a designer could be more than just a consultant or product designer.

The years from the turn of the 1970s and 1980s to the early 1990s had in many respects been a good period for design. The rise of the economy and its ultimate overheating had promoted private consumption, and consequently improved the profitability of traditional design sectors, such as furniture. Artisanship flourished alongside the progress of industrial design. Internationalization and the emergence of new generations of designers had diversified the field and expanded its value base. At the same time, structural changes were under way that would lead to a serious crisis of profitability in the textile, clothing and furniture sectors, among others, and resulting unemployment for their designers.

When the international economic crisis reached Finland in 1991, it led to a deep economic recession. The halting of public building projects, for example, was a severe blow to interior architects and also to furniture designers, because space requiring new furniture was simply not built. While the depression did not stop Finnish design, it slowed the pace of things. When progress was resumed around the middle of the decade, there was no longer any broad front of achievement in design. Not all the sectors of design could avoid permanent damage from the recession.

THE ART OF CRAFT

Although the role of handicraft gradually diminished in everyday life during the 20th century, it became a rich field of work involving textiles, ceramics and glass. Works made in small editions or as unique, one-off pieces, such as the renowned art glass of the 1950s, were in between utility objects and artworks purely for the purpose of aesthetic pleasure. As applied art and its products became industrial and technological, arts and crafts gained importance as a personal counterweight expressing the mark of its makers. As industrial design expanded in the 1970s, arts and crafts emerged in areas such as ceramics made in small series in studios. Before long, arts and crafts began to approach the field of the arts, their organization and procedures of display. Glass art was exhibited in galleries and textile art flourished in large works made for the public spaces of cultural edifices. Especially since the 1980s the range and public image of the work of professionals in design have regained the emphases on art that were typical of the years that immediately followed the Second World War.

1

1. Markku Salo, bottle designed in 1994 for the Iittala glassworks.

2. Eila Hiltunen, *The Tsarina's Collar* necklace, 1996.

3. Stefan Lindfors, a work from the exhibition *Reges Insectorum* from 1991.

2

4

5

4. *Nature as Source*, a work of textile art by Maija Lavonen for the annex of the Council of State building in Helsinki, 1981.

5. Oiva Toikka, Glass Cubes, Nuutajärvi glassworks, turn of the 1980s.

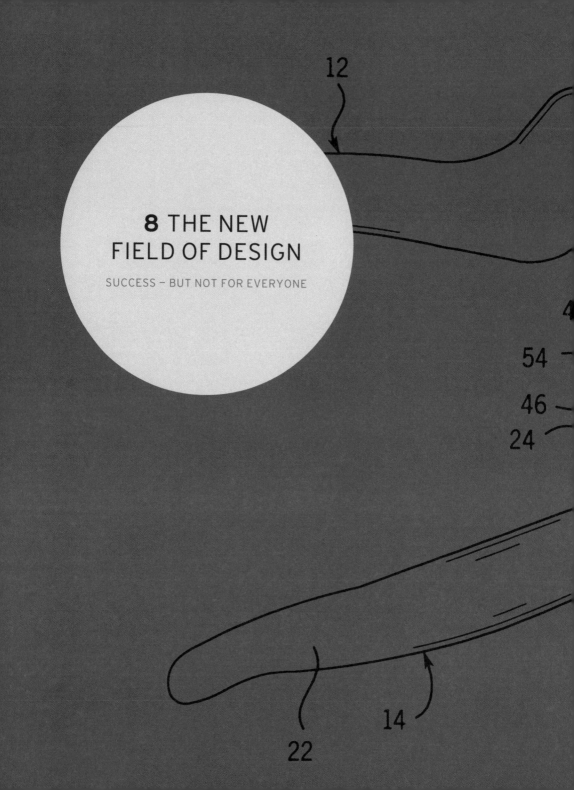

12

8 THE NEW
FIELD OF DESIGN

SUCCESS – BUT NOT FOR EVERYONE

54

46

24

14

22

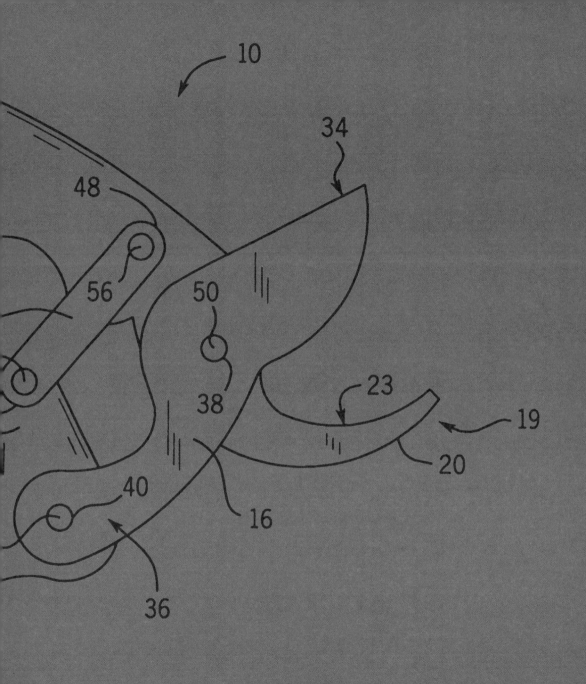

1996	2000	2002	2009	2012
The first *Young Forum* exhibition at Design Forum Finland IKEA launched in Finland	Finland's Council of State officially adopts the Design 2005! programme for developing the design sector	The launching of the Muoto 2002 pro-gramme of applied design research of Tekes – the Finnish Funding Agency for Technology and Innovation The basic research programme in design of the Academy of Finland 2003–2006	Finland's new University Act permits the launching of Aalto University in 2010, with the former University of Art and Design Helsinki as part of it	World Design Capital Helsinki 2012

B y the time the lowest point of the economic recession of the early 1990s had been reached and Finnish industries had regained their pace around the middle of the decade, the operating environment of design had fundamentally changed. The era of the global economy had begun in earnest, spurring on a flow of capital and goods with ever fewer restrictions that increased need for design as a competitive asset in the midst of a growing struggle over markets between companies, countries and whole continents. For major corporations, the planning and design of products and services and their production and marketing were no longer bound to any specific geographical place.

In the European context, a decisive step for Finland was gaining membership in the European Union in 1995. While mostly positive in effect, this also significantly increased competition. A small country like Finland had to achieve high quality in products if it was to export something other than its forestry products or machinery made by heavy industries. In this situation, both businesses and the providers of design services awoke to a joint need, something that had not been spurred by trade with the now-defunct Soviet Union. The global and EU markets could be entered only with first-class products in terms of technology, use properties and design.

Over a period of approximately a decade, Finland rose from the trough of the recession to become one of the world's most competitive economies. The economic growth that continued without any major fluctuations has only ended with a severe world-wide economic crisis. This period significantly reinforced the economic position of design. It did not, however, apply to all sectors, but primarily to the use of design in business strategy. Encompassing several areas, such as industrial, graphic and media design, this multidisciplinary use of design was more precise and explicit than previously. At the same time, the whole domain of manufacturing, marketing and consumption – in fact society as a whole – underwent digitization. In this revolution of technology and information, the practices, applications and consumption of design changed irretrievably. The introduction of computers, which had already proceeded rapidly in the 1980s, has led to a boundless universe

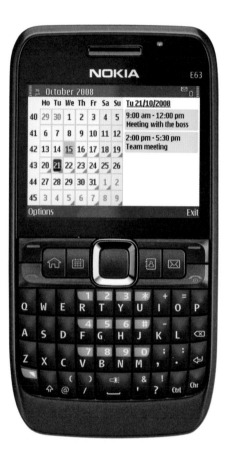

of information accessible everywhere through the pages of the Internet since the early 1990s. Work in design also changed to become networked activity that is geographically dispersed.

Coinciding with this, the near-universal availability of mobile communications broke down former restrictions of place and time. It was highly fortunate for the Finnish economy, and Finnish design, that Nokia, the leading corporation of the new mobile technology, had been able to develop in Finland since the early 1990s. As Nokia grew, it absorbed a growing amount of design expertise, the skilful application of which was also a reason for its overwhelming success.

Something old, something new

The immense expansion of digitization and the ICT (Information and Communication Technologies) sector did not do away with traditional areas of design production. People still needed tableware, furniture and textiles. The recession, however, dictated changes that weakened these sectors and the role of those who were professionally active in them. Membership in the European Union led to increasing pressure from imports. Coinciding with this, the East European countries that had emerged from under the domination of the Soviet Union were now reforming their industrial base. The glass, textile and furniture industries of these countries operated at considerably lower cost than their counterparts in Finland, which was evident in pricing. In addition, low-cost imports from the Far East eroded demand for Finnish products. The arrival of the Swedish – or, more precisely, global – IKEA furniture corporation in Finland in 1996 had the same effect.

The recession spelt the end for many traditional furniture manufacturers, such as Muurame,[121] which was known for the high quality of its products. The sudden halt of building and development by the public sector in the early 1990s and the later dissolving of the National Board of Public Building, a significant employer of interior architects, also caused problems. On the other hand, the flagship companies of Finnish design, such as Arabia, Artek and Marimekko, survived and continued their work. Profitability was sought not only in design but also through reorganization and cost efficiency. Arabia, for example, which

◀ ▼ Traditional product design is still needed even in a digitized world. On the left, *Koko* tableware by Kristina Riska and Kati Tuominen-Niittylä, Arabia/Iittala, 2006; on this page are *Ote* tumblers designed by Aleksi Perälä for Iittala, 2006.

belonged to the Hackman group,[122] carried out mergers with the Nuutajärvi and Iittala glassworks, the Sorsakoski cutlery production works and the ALU company, a long-term manufacturer of kitchenware. It also acquired Nordic companies in the field, such as time-honoured Rörstrand of Sweden, the same company of which Arabia itself was a subsidiary when it was launched in 1874. Finally, in 2003, the Arabia name was taken out of use and all of its products began to be marketed under the Iittala brand. Five years later, the Hackman conglomerate was sold to Italy, from where its Iittala section was bought back into Finnish ownership, becoming, finally, part of the Fiskars group of companies.

Since the mid-1990s, the company historically known as Arabia, which has operated throughout the history of applied art and design in Finland has used the services of recognized international designers to renew its product range, while "classics" of the 1950s and 1960s, especially in glass, have been reintroduced. Thus, the company, currently under the name of Iittala, has been able to continue in the extremely competitive market for designer products for the home.

Fiskars, one of Finland's oldest companies still in operation, is an example of how completely new functional solutions and integrated design in products can be achieved in a traditional low-technology sector such as gardening tools. The products developed under the direction of Fiskars' head designer Olavi Lindén (1946–) show how age-old yet perennially necessary tools, such as axes, can be updated through technical ingenuity, developed technologies of materials and design to respond to present-day markets and consumer preferences.

A third example of solutions followed by traditional design-sector companies under the pressures of profitability, globalization and extreme competition is provided by Marimekko. Led by Armi Ratia to international success, this company changed owners in the 1970s and 1980s, to the detriment of profitability and its creative and innovative reputation. It was bought in 1991 by Kirsti Paakkanen (1929–), a successful advertising executive and entrepreneur. She was able to raise Marimekko not only to its feet but also to its former status of an international brand. This scenario was somewhat similar to the case of Arabia/Iittala. Firstly, the company focused on new collections that were marketed with the names of their designers. Alongside this, it began to make use of its print-ed fabric collections from the 1960s, especially the works of Maija Isola. Patterns and motifs that had originally been intended mainly for cur-tains and tablecloths were now used in clothing, rubber boots and tele-vision sets. Marimekko also produced variants of its classic ready-to-wear items, such as the *Tasaraita* t-shirt and the *Jokapoika* shirt. In 2007, Marimekko opened a shop in Tokyo. Whereas the United States had been the promised land of design, along with consumption and modernity, in the 1960s, the Far East now became a hub in the 2000s.

The retro alternative

Both Arabia/Iittala and Marimekko are examples of brands that have ben-efited from the popularity of retro design, which has been supporting traditional sectors of design since the 1980s. Mostly utilizing the post-war history of modern design in a retrospective manner, this trend has two mutually complementary starting points. Already in the 1980s, the prices of Finnish art glass pieces of the 1950s had risen rapidly among international collectors and in auctions. In the next decade collections of so-called "modern classics" grew, as did Internet-based internation-al trade in them. This was also reflected in Finland where business in this sector began to emerge. Younger generations began to appreciate objects, especially furniture, of the 1950s, soon to be followed by the 1960s and early '70s. These products represented, partly nostalgia, and partly the iconized cultural capital of modernism as a means of main-taining peer status.

Companies that still possessed collections from past decades – and the rights to them – could reintroduce the same classic products that were being collected as originals. This gave consumers choices from several chronological levels; for instance, forty years after their original launches, the opportunity to arose again to combine Iittala's glassware of the sixties with contemporary Marimekko patterns. The production of furniture by some of the leading designers of the past, such as Ilmari Tapiovaara, was also resumed. And Artek continued to sell Aalto's clas-sics, which have been produced on a continuous basis for over seventy years. Artek products, however, are not classed as retro, as they offer in

▲ Ever since the Paris World's Fair of 1900 displays of Finnish design have included references to Finnish nature, and the lake landscapes of Finland in particular. Promotional material of Paola Suhonen's Ivana Helsinki company, 2007.

a sense a self-contained, permanent and unchanging range of interior design products. The recycling of recent history under the heading of retro is an essential aspect of design culture that has been manifested in various media over the past decades and in recent years. It offers yet another alternative in a seemingly endless market of individually profiled consumption.

The reintroduction of the best works of design of past decades presented problems for young designers. Just as the young generation of the sixties had found the overwhelming presence of the great masters

to be a limitation, their counterparts of the new millennium once again had to compete with the same names and products. Since Wirkkala's Tapio glassware collection is always an assured mark of "good taste" for consumers, why take risks with unknown products? As a result, the main strategies adopted by the new generation were international in scope, offering wider opportunities in work and resulting visibility also in Finland.

A group of young Finnish designers and architects known as *Snow-crash* aroused interest at the Milan Furniture Fair in 1997. Their experimental chairs and lamps once again turned international attention to Finland after a long interval. Of this group, Ilkka Suppanen (1968–)[123] was able to have his works produced and distributed internationally. Furniture designers who made their breakthrough in the late 1990s

▲ Harri Koskinen, *Block* lamp, 1997. This lamp is one of the most internationally widespread products of Finnish design – marketed by a Swedish company.

▶ Ilkka Suppanen, *Nomad* chair, felt and steel. Prototype from 1994. This widely noted design finally found a manufacturer in Italy.

◄ ▼ The applications of industrial design expanded into large-scale machinery and automation in aid of everyday life. The upper picture shows the Optiform papermaking machine made by Metso in the early 2000s. Its design involved the 5D design team collaborating with Risto Väätänen, head of design at the company. In the lower picture is a bottle refund machine from 1997 made by the Halton company. The design work for this machine was carried out by the Creadesign agency.

included Sari Anttonen (1966–), one of the few to emphasize ecological values. The internationally important Green Design movement had not yet had any major impact in Finland. There was also room for all-round designers, of whom Harri Koskinen (1970–)[124] is the most prominent example. Working internationally, Koskinen has designed glass, furniture, audio equipment and watches, among other products. He carries on the tradition of individual style in post-war design in Finland, in which it is possible to operate within a broad range of products without claiming any specific niche.

Emphasis on usability

The structures and policies of the industries that shook off the recession in the mid-1990s became ever more favourable to industrial design. Moreover, the practices, toolkits and skills of this sector of design were better prepared than ever before. CAD, the opportunities of the Internet for data communications and the rapid development of information networks opened up new dimensions for both design agencies and in-house designers within companies. New areas also emerged in which industrial design could prove its usefulness.

One of the main new areas was interface design, from which, via user-based design, 'usability' – a concept used broadly in the 2000s – evolved, along with an overall emphasis on the experiences of users as a core property of products. Underlying this was the ergonomic thinking of the 1970s, but design now had completely new focuses. Mobile devices, such as cellular phones and the cameras and other features that were soon added to them required communicative design. The products were to indicate their functions as clearly as possible, and the hierarchy of these functions. In addition to the form of the actual device and its technical use properties, it was also necessary to design its display and its various levels of information. This area was developed by Nokia, which also established its own design unit followed by a design organization that soon became global. Nokia's astoundingly quick rise to the status of a global player also encouraged the deeper awareness of design in general. The reasons for this included the fact that the company acknowledged that design was one of its main competitive assets.

From design management to brands

In the mid-1990s, Finnish businesses increasingly began to recognize the possibilities of design as a strategic tool. But in order to make full use of such opportunities, executives at the highest levels had to be made responsible for decisions concerning design. It was also necessary to prepare long-term programmes lasting several years to integrate design in operations. This could be carried out within the company by employing a designer in its organization, as was done by Valmet (now Metso Paper), a manufacturer of paper-making machines, or through the cooperation of the company's own designers with outside consultants. This policy was followed, for example, by the Suunto[125] company and the Linja-Design office. Known for its faucets, Oras, which has focussed on design for many years under the direction of Jorma Vennola (1943–), began to co-operate with the world-famous Alessi company to create integrated collections of bathroom products.

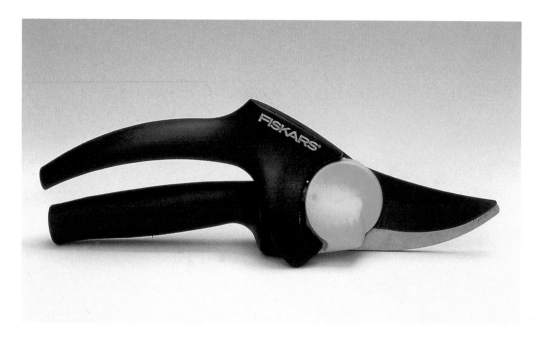

As the applications and economic significance of design grew, the question of how to direct and manage it in companies that were growing and rapidly becoming international emerged. The mainly Anglo-American theories of design management expanded in the 1990s into so-called brand management. Brands, branding and related thinking became the leading concepts of design in the early 2000s. This involved command of the compound value of the company, its product/s and information on them through varied applications of design. An integrated brand extends from products, their packaging and commercial graphics to the premises of the company and through its webpages to world-wide exposure. The concept of brand soon suffered from inflation, as not only businesses but also a wide range of public organizations and even rural municipalities began to brand themselves – i.e. to manage their public image. This, and brand awareness in general, were closely associated with digital communications, the spread of computers and the growing use of the Internet for disseminating and acquiring information.

▲ The quality of even the most traditional tools can be improved by combining design with new mechanical solutions. Long-term product development headed by Olavi Linden has ensured an international market for the garden products of Fiskars, Finland's oldest industrial firm. Fiskars pruner, 1996.

▶ Design emphasizing use properties and safety earned the Rocla Humanic warehouse truck the Fennia Prize design award in 2007. The design team consisted of Petteri Masalin, Kero Uusitalo and Piritta Winqvist.

Webpages soon became one of the largest areas of work in design. They combined the command of software with industrial and graphic design. In the early 1990s, new media and media design evolved to become a new, multidisciplinary design practice. In this area, computer technology and software, which were making enormous progress, were soon matched by the cultural and artistic appropriation of the new media, whereby it was possible to shape and communicate cultural heritage and to create a completely new artistic channel of expression of unprecedented means and scope.

As analysed by Anna Valtonen in her doctoral thesis, the practice and scope of industrial design had clearly changed, expanded and deepened by the early 2000s.[126] Having been mainly a product designer in the 1980s, the designer now also became a coordinator, innovator, manager and esteemed expert in multidisciplinary teams alongside civil engineers and MBAS. Designers themselves had actively responded to the challenges of the new technology and the global economy. At first, a few leading, trailblazing companies had invested in design, in its potential for improving usability, appearance and commercial value of the product. Success had led to growing demand for design skills. Now, a new era repeated in a deeper fashion the developments that had led in the 1950s to the first wave of expanding applications in design. Along with the cooperation of designers and businesses, the new developments were promoted by the public sector through action such as broader discussion on design as a national resource and by reforms in design education.

A national policy in aid of design

As part of the process of post-recession national reconstruction and re-thinking on almost all fronts design was recognized as a fundamental building block in the economy, thus acting for the good of society as a whole. Sitra, the Finnish Innovation Fund,[127] came to the aid of an official committee that addressed these issues in 1997. Sitra chose to carry on the committee's work with an expanded group of representatives of business and the public sector and to prepare a report on the current state of Finnish design and the challenges of the future. The report, en-

▲ New uses of wood, the traditional material of Finland, still interest manufacturers and designers alike. *Octo* lamps by Seppo Koho from the early 2000s.

titled *Muotoiltu etu* (The Designed Advantage),[128] was made public in the autumn of 1998 and it aroused surprisingly lively discussion. It placed design within the national innovation system that was being envisioned at the time along with plans for developing its various sectors. Government bodies also began to prepare a national design policy programme through the Ministry of Education. This programme was prepared by mostly the same actors as the Sitra report, and its conclusions were along the same lines. An important aspect of the programme was that it did not approach design solely in terms of its cultural dimensions, but also from the perspectives of industry and the economy. The five-year design policy programme was officially approved by the government in 2000 and its background bodies were the Ministry of Education and the Ministry of Trade and Industry.

◀ Samuli Naamanka, *Clash* chair, Martela Oy, early 2000s. The possibilities of wood for the all-purpose chair, the archetypal object of Finnish design, have not yet been exhausted.

▶ Arts and crafts facilitated by new technologies. The *Lehti* (Leaf) dish by Maria Jauhiainen, 2004. Photo-etched and plastic-coated brass.

In the meantime, a new politicization of design had been achieved in the official programme of Prime Minister Paavo Lipponen's second cabinet in 1999. This programme identified design as a central factor of change for the future economy and cultural life of Finland. When, in 2001, therefore, the leading actors of industry and the economy lent their names, together with governmental bodies, to a joint manifesto for promoting design, the field of design was now placed solidly on the economic and political map. It had support and proponents in more quarters than before. Tekes, the Finnish Funding Agency for Technology and Innovation,[129] operating in product development and applied research and the Academy of Finland with its own programme of basic-level research were included in the implementation of the national programme. The Designium Centre for Innovation in Design was established at the University of Art and Design Helsinki to develop and coordinate innovation efforts. The wide-ranging work of developing design via the national programme ended with Design Year 2005, which sought to increase the visibility of design and raise public awareness of its opportunities to promote individual well-being and the common good.

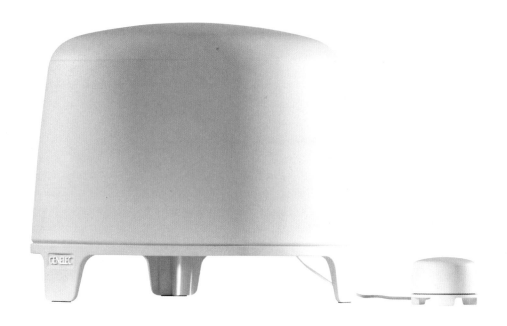

The aforementioned process of approximately a decade was a significant effort, even in an international context, of committing the private
sector of business and the public sector of the state and its various actors
to the work of developing design on a broad basis. It is difficult to esti-
mate the direct impact of the measures that arose from the design policy programme, because design always needs the private sector, the business community, to be realized. Nonetheless, it is obvious that including design in the strategies of national innovation policies gave it a foothold at levels of decision-making where it previously had no voice. This
model – combining design, industry, official policies, culture and education – has aroused considerable international interest. Finland's capacity for renewal and development after the economic recession and the
role of design in this context have been followed with interest in countries where change is required in the structures of industry and the
economy. In this respect, Finland is exporting its design skills and ex-

▲ Harri Koskinen, the *Genel-
ec 5040A* subwoofer from
2008.

pertise, though not this time as products or services but instead in the form of immaterial systemic concepts.

The University of Art and Design Helsinki was an important actor throughout the above course of events. During Yrjö Sotamaa's term as its rector, the University began to significantly develop, expand and gain an international role in the early 1990s. The need for training and development in new media resulted in the founding of the University's Media Lab[130] in 1993, and the growing overall significance of the audiovisual sector and media led in 2000 to the opening of Media Centre Lume,[131] expressly constructed for research and development in this sector. New multidisciplinary curricula and programmes were of importance for design. The Design Leadership programme, which had already been launched in 1991, merged design, management and economic elements. Based on the experiences of this programme, the University of Art and Design Helsinki, the Helsinki University of Technology and the Helsinki School of Economics instituted their joint master's-level International Design Business Management programme[132] in 1995. This multidisciplinary programme has provided the design sector both in Finland and abroad with professionals that are implementing the goals of the design policy programme for the cooperation and integration of different areas of expertise. The University of Art and Design was one of the main parties that took the initiative for achieving the Sitra report and in preparing the design policy programme, defining and ultimately implementing its content.

Design education in Finland has also expanded beyond the University of Art and Design Helsinki, which had a monopoly status since the end of the 19th century. The University of Lapland[133] began to train industrial designers in the early 1990s, when originally polytechnic-level design training at Rovaniemi was included in its Faculty of Arts. Finland came to have two university-level institutions of design education and research. In addition, the founding and rapid expansion of Finland's network of polytechnics or universities of applied science in the 1990s provided a great deal of new training in design. The Lahti Institute of Design,[134] for example, quickly became a high-standard institution that is appreciated and valued by industry. This meant that industry and

design agencies had access to considerably more trained designers than previously. While the rapid expansion of design education led to excess training, it also fostered competition over students, raising the standards of design schools.

Finnish design in 2009

Where design was considered part of the cultural industries and the process of constructing the information society, activities for innovation became the chief theme of discussions concerning development in the following decade. Design became a natural aspect of technological, social and cultural innovation. It must be remembered, however, that there is a long way to go from invention – individual advances in design – to comprehensive innovation requiring the contribution of several disciplines. Design can introduce into this context problem-solving capacities that differ from the technological way of proceeding. Accordingly, the creative characteristics of design are given emphasis. In recent years design has thus been associated with the creative industries.

The growing significance of these creative industries, both globally and in local economies, has also placed expectations on design that are linked to both the economy and the cultural domain. In all its variety, design together with architecture and reproducible cultural artefacts, such as new media and film, is regarded as a means of creating and maintaining affluence. This is important in a situation in which China and India have risen to become the new giants of the global economy and manufacturing. By the same token, Finland must use all available means to maintain South Finland, the Helsinki metropolitan region and a few other leading cities as areas that will attract international skill, or at any rate keep local talent from moving elsewhere.

The above also involves the notion that we are living in the era of the experience society. Design, too, must create experiences for products and services that will generate an emotional bond. In a period of mutually similar technological solutions the asset of design is precisely its ability to create distinctions for personal profiling in an increasingly individualistic society. In investment commodities, such as warehouse trucks or catering kitchens, design, however, still has its user-based service role integrated with the performance of the product as a whole.

The economic significance of design has clearly grown both locally and internationally. Design as business has given way to the design economy, in which not only Nokia mobile phones but also traditional products of the heavy metal industry, such as Kone lifts, gain competitive advantages through design and the cultural messages that they generate. The capital of cultural competence achieved with design has shifted from the traditional sectors of the field to industrial design and the new media. Within the culture of design, the individual's needs for experiences are now being met by a broad range of products, from mobile phones to laptop computers, from media design to MP3 players, and from fashions to interior design and the Facebook communities of social media.

Only a small portion of the above artefacts and services are designed and produced in Finland. Domestic visibility of design through prizes, fairs and media still relies on the products of the more traditional sectors. There have been, however, recent changes in public exposure and organization in this area. The events of Helsinki Design Week[135] and the related *Designpartners* exhibitions and panel discussions have brought new design to the fore. The Helsinki Design District[136] concept, launched upon the initiative of Design Forum, seeks to create a cluster of design shops and firms in a part of the city centre that has been a nationally significant locus for design and architects' offices for many years. Young designers have established collectives such as Imu Design, which present themselves in group exhibitions. At the same time, independent design management and promotion agencies have appeared, such as the recently established Huippu Design Management agency.[137] They assemble designers and businesses to be promoted both within the country and internationally. In recent years, consumption of the designed experience society was steered and reflected by *Muoto* magazine, which shifted from its former approach of information and debate to become a lifestyle catalogue of the cultural consumption of design.

Finnish design at the end of the first decade of the 21st century cannot be described without first defining the genres of products, environments and services that are involved. This book has sought to provide

▲ Specializing in wrist-worn devices measuring, among other data, heart rate, altitude and barometric pressure, Suunto is an example of a company making long-term, strategic use of design. The equipment shown in the picture is from 2006, Suunto Design Team.

an overview. The number of design disciplines that have emerged over the decades, not to mention the expanding range of designed products and artefacts, makes any concise summary difficult. Perhaps it reflects in a positive sense the growth and diversification of design in Finland from Estlander's day to the present. There is no single 'design' to be described – design is present everywhere.

Postscript

One of the main themes of the present book is design education in Finland since its founding in 1871. The evolution of the original Craft School into the University of Art and Design Helsinki was of particular importance for applied art and design and their operating environment in this small country. In the spring of 2007, Finland's Council of State decided to merge the University of Art and Design Helsinki, the Helsinki University of Technology and the Helsinki School of Economics. The result was the new Aalto University, which began its work in January 2010. The University of Art and Design Helsinki had taken the initiative in this process. The ending of complete academic autonomy, in order to become part of a multidisciplinary entity of education and research combining design, technology and business, is the most significant change that has taken place in the present field of Finnish design.

At the time of writing, design education and research have been taught and practised within the School of Arts, Design and Architecture, one of the six schools of Aalto University, for four years. Students have been able to benefit from the whole range of education offered by this multidisciplinary university. The earlier doubts that technology and commerce, the other main areas of the university, would swallow up design have proven to be unfounded.

The global economic crisis that broke out in the autumn of 2008 and the resulting financial crisis in the European Economic Area have radically altered the setting in which Finnish design, especially within the telecommunications cluster, had thrived since the mid-1990s. Export-based industries focusing on consumer products or investment goods and utilizing design face major challenges. Design must once again find new ways to make its influence felt. This is the aim of Finland's recent government-level programme of design policy from 2013. Around the same time, the European Commission issued the European Design Innovation Initiative's (EDII) report 'Design for Growth and Prosperity', outlining a design agenda for the whole European Union. An international competition was held for the preparation of the report, and the task was given to the Aalto University School of Arts, Design and Architecture. Promoting the visibility of design was decisively facilitated

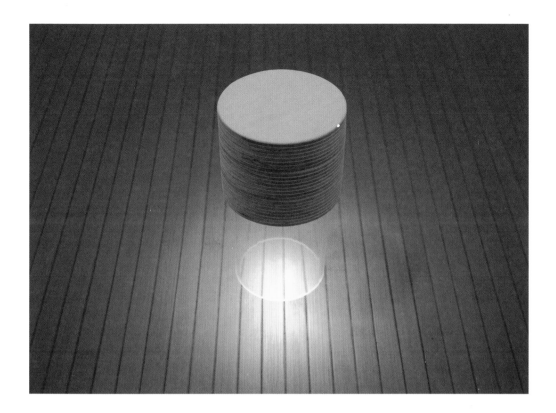

▲ The eternal need for light, traditional wood and new LED technology. The *Foxfire* lamp by Jukka Korpihete, 2008.

by Helsinki being chosen as World Design Capital 2012. This venture, which included all the cities of the Helsinki Metropolitan Area, emphasized the public service function of design in keeping with its overriding theme of "embedded design". Accordingly, the supported and interrelated areas of co-design, service design and participatory design were able to demonstrate their potential in facilitating the quality of everyday urban life for citizens.

The preceding pages seek to show how Finnish design as an integral aspect of society, culture and the economy, has sought to find, under changing circumstances, new models of operation serving the public and private sectors alike. With its perspective on the past, this book is also an introduction to the future.

SUMMARY

The conscious efforts to develop applied art that began Finland in the
1870s coincided with the marked industrialization of the country, at the
time an autonomous Grand Duchy of the Russian Empire. Training in
the field began at the Craft School in 1871, and the Museum of Applied
Art was founded in 1873, followed by the Finnish Society of Crafts and Design in 1875. These main bodies still carry on their work in various forms.
The Friends of Finnish Handicraft, which developed the field over a long
period, began its work in 1879. Fanned by economic liberalism and leg-
islation guaranteeing freedom of occupation, the process of industrialization also drew attention to the possibility of improving product quality through the applied arts. For many years, Finnish industry was mainly based on paper and timber. This situation gave an important role to
handcrafting and workshop production, the main sources of applied
art products until the 1920s. Finland's significant cotton, ceramics and
glass industries looked to foreign examples in design at that time.

Where the applied arts originally underscored their benefits for industry, arts and crafts were emphasized as an area of art-related activity,
especially in relation to architecture. This raised their status, and promoted their inclusion among the arts, while the Finnish Pavilion at the
Paris World's Fair of 1900 marked an international breakthrough. Contemporary arts and crafts combined applications of domestic folk heritage with the latest international trends, such as Art Nouveau and *Jugendstil*. Maintained by a long economic boom that promoted construction and urbanization, arts and crafts developed strongly until the end
of the First World War and training diversified, although it emphasized
applied art as arts and crafts in particular, rather than industrial design.
In 1911, professionals in applied art established the Ornamo *Association
of Ornamental Artists* (now the Finnish *Association of Designers Ornamo*). It
was one of the first professional organizations of its kind in the world.

National independence in 1917 and the closing of the border with
Soviet Russia that soon followed led to stylistic and commercial changes
in applied art and design. The classicism that became the predominant
style of the period was well suited to the new democracy. The neoclassi-

cal Parliament House in Helsinki, which was inaugurated in 1930, was a showcase of the best achievements of Finnish applied art and design, and a demanding project that promoted this field as a whole.

Of the various sectors of applied art, furniture was among the first to use the services of designers trained in Finland. This sector rapidly evolved in the 1920s towards serial production. In arts and crafts, textiles, in particular, flourished and several weaving studios in this sector were headed by designers themselves. Works of applied art designed in Finland still consisted mostly of handcrafted small editions and interior design and decoration bound to architectural design. Finland's large textile and ceramics industries had not yet employed designers in large numbers, and the paper industry had no need for design skills. The basis for the international acclaim that was to be important after the Second World War was already laid at the Milan Triennial of 1933, where prizes were awarded to Finnish works of arts and crafts.

The international modernism that came to be known as functionalism gained ground in the early 1930s in both architecture and design. In furniture, the curved and chrome-plated steel tubing that was characteristic of this style was soon replaced by the ingenious use of solid birch and birch plywood. These were the means with which functionalism was domesticated to suit Finnish materials, manufacturing and tastes, facilitating its broad acceptance in homes. Modernism, however, was mainly a middle-class and urban phenomenon. In the 1930s, Finland was still a predominantly rural country, where the peasant and farmer heritage was still strong. Nonetheless, modernism soon became a predominant mode of design serving the modernization of society as a whole, especially after the Second World War. It was thus committed to improving the quality and functionality of everyday life. The home, its furnishings, appliances and practical aspects were to be the main focus of design for many years to come.

In the 1930s, Finnish industries began to rely increasingly on designers to renew their product lines. The glass industry sought new talent through competitions, the textile industry finally began to consult Finnish designers, and Arabia, the country's leading manufacturer of ceramics, introduced tableware designed in the spirit of functionalism. The furniture industry adopted the means of modernism over a broad front. Background factors were strong economic growth towards the end of the decade, the growing pace of urbanization and the new requirements of consumption of the young middle class. Training and education in applied art, however, mainly rejected modernism, which was regarded as allied too closely with technological progress and the industries fuelled by it. Nonetheless, it became obvious that industries evolving increasingly towards mass production would employ growing numbers of professional designers.

In Finland, the years from the autumn of 1939 to 1945 almost completely ended work in design-oriented sectors along with halting development in other areas of manufacturing. Where possible, there was a focus on arts and crafts during this period, when mostly substitute materials and wood were available. On the other hand, the post-war years of shortages until the early 1950s were, despite austerity, a period that saw the rise of applied art and design. Works of arts and crafts employing ceramics and glass introduced elements of fantasy and beauty into harsh everyday life. The process of reconstruction that had begun also led to the rise of the furniture industry, with a young emerging generation of designers who had completely adopted modernism and also understood the parameters and opportunities of industrial mass production. Design education also approached the requirements of industry. New Finnish applied art was highly acclaimed at the Milan Triennial of 1951. The triennials were to be showcases of successful Finnish applied art and design until the mid-1960s. Over the years, the original arts and crafts emphasis of the exhibits changed along with the development of the field to focus more and more on industrial products.

From the beginning of the 1950s, the growth of the national product and consumer demand along with the improving cooperation between industry and design led to rapid progress in design and the expansion of its applications. The international success of designers and their works provided visibility for the field and cash flow for the companies involved in it. These developments attracted a wider range of industries to apply design skills. Towards the end of the 1950s, the traditional sectors were matched by motor vehicles, home appliances, and before long by home electronics. Also these industries used designers to ensure the quality and sales of their products. The training of industrial designers was begun in 1961 to meet the diversifying design requirements of industry. Alongside industrial design, arts and crafts flourished.

Finnish design, its provision and consumption can be said to have achieved modernist maturity and a significant international profile and audience in the 1960s. As in architecture, here, too, modernism had become the dominant idiom. The traditional sectors of design enjoyed success, and the cooperation of designers with industry proceeded well. Investment in design also affected exports. Designers were also able to take the new predominant material, plastics, into use, applying it to a wide range of uses, such as furniture and kitchen appliances. Design and its professional practitioners were finally in the situation that had already been set as a goal in the late 19th century. They were drawn to industry while being able to demonstrate the benefits of their skills.

In this situation, and especially as industrial design proved its merits in heavy industry and machinery production, plans emerged for closer cooperation between design, education for the field, industry and supporting organizations such as the Finnish Society of Crafts and Design. The goal, of course, was to increase exports, and the opportunities of emerging industrial design were underlined. This, in turn, led to lesser regard for the more traditional sectors of design and their artistic nature. Criticism of the design discourse arose, focusing on technocratic-commercial utility thinking which was felt to have dominated discussion around the turn of the 1970s. A young and radicalized generation emphasized social equality and ecological values as they engaged in worldwide cultural and political protest. In the small designer circles of our small country this led to ideological and generational opposition that undermined the dialogue of the design sectors with other partners.

Improvements to the quality and status of design education were desired as part of the policies of developing design. The Institute of Industrial Art, a successor of the original Craft School, in 1973 became the University of Industrial Arts Helsinki (later University of Art and Design Helsinki and the present-day Aalto University School of Arts, Design and Architecture).

A positive period for design continued until the mid-1970s, when the economic recession that followed in the wake of the international oil crisis adversely affected manufacturing, exports and profitability in industries relying on design. The rising price of oil ended, among other things, the production of plastic furniture, which had been extremely successful. At the same time, however, arts and crafts made a comeback, now through small studios often working in textiles or ceramics on a crafts basis. They were part of a search for alternatives to the product lines of the corporations that dominated the field, while also a response to poor employment opportunities for young professionals in these sectors. Arts and crafts continued their emergence in the following decade, when they became gallery art and impressive textile artworks made for public spaces.

The field of design continued to expand. It now came to include devices and equipment commissioned by the public sector in which both design and use differed from those of consumer goods. The continuous growth of the welfare society increased the need for health-care equipment, among other items. In the 1970s hospital technology became one of the new design-intensive areas of work. The role of the designer – now specifically an industrial designer – was reflected in usability and safety achieved by means of ergonomic thinking. Designers also learned to serve as experts in large, multidisciplinary public projects, such as the planning of the Helsinki Metro. The work of the designer became anonymous, blending into a larger whole. This differed from the individual presence that had marked the post-war decades. In this sense industrial design and its professionals had different aims.

Since the 1970s, design work had been strongly influenced by the emergence of the electronics industry, data communications systems and finally by digitization. The last-mentioned would ultimately revolutionize both the methods and objects of design. The Finnish television industry expanded during the economic boom of the 1980s and in-house designers were employed. Many of this generation of designers went on to establish their own offices that continued to serve the same companies, though now on a commissioned basis. Around the same time, the need emerged for various electronic surveillance, control and data communications systems. Design was needed to provide a point of access to their properties. When wireless data communications technology was adopted in the mid-1980s the path lay open for making mobile phones. Designers were involved with mobile phones from the very beginning, and this sector, which became a flagship of Finnish industry, also grew to become one of the main new areas of design.

In the late 1980s, digitization offered design a new toolkit of computer-based simulation. This spelt comprehensive changes in the nature of design work, making it more efficient and providing easier communication with manufacturers. When these developments were led further in the 1990s by information networks and the Internet, work in design was no longer bound to any specific place or time.

The traditional sectors of design, art and crafts and the above-described rapidly digitized reality of industrial design functioned alongside each other during the economic boom of the 1980s until its last overheated years. When the severe economic recession of the early 1990s abated around the middle of the decade, the structures that had previously supported the various areas of design had changed. Imports of consumer goods for the home, such as glassware, ceramics, textiles and furniture grew in the liberalized global economy and through Finland's membership in the European Union. Around the same time, the production of mobile data communications devices and software, which greatly benefited industrial designers, also emerged and developed. A completely new sector was media design, which combined several areas, such as industrial and graphic design.

In a new international competitive situation that was more demanding than ever before – a parallel to the founding stages of the 1870s – the field of design came to be considered as part of a post-recession national reconstruction project. Decision-makers in design education, research, industry and politics prepared a five-year national design policy programme that was officially approved in 2000 by Finland's Council of State. The important aspect of this programme was that it made design part of the so-called national innovation system, marking a significant step forward for the status, visibility and operating conditions of design.

Finnish design in the first decade of the 21st century still encompasses the field described above, ranging from arts and crafts to furniture, wrist-top computers and papermaking machinery. A long period of economic growth spurred purchases of designed consumer commodities. Most of them, however, such as mobile media devices, are neither designed nor made in Finland. The same is true of ready-to-wear fashions with their extremely quick cycles of adoption. The rise of the Far East to become the workshop of the world spells new requirements. Owing to the ever-faster pace of the media, visibility and distinction in a saturated world market are technically easier to achieve than before. At the same time, the sheer numbers of designer products and their designers call for a strong degree of distinction.

In recent years, the less visible but functionally and economically significant contribution of industrial design has been understood more broadly than before by leading industrial corporations such as lift manufacturers. Design has become, at least partly, an important aspect of corporate decision-making. More broadly, design is regarded as belonging to the so-called creative industries. To promote design, manufacturing and commercialization in these industries, among other goals, it was decided to merge the University of Art and Design Helsinki, the Helsinki University of Technology and the Helsinki School of Economics to create the new Aalto University, which began its work in 2010. In Aalto University the School of Arts, Design and Architecture can benefit from the presence of education and research in technology and economics, hence offering innumerable combinations for the benefit of students. In 2012, Helsinki was World Design Capital. In that year design was more visible than ever before, with numerous projects both private and public that will live on far beyond the event.

Perhaps the most profound change in design practice and education during recent years has been the rapid rise in demand for immaterial design, i.e. participatory design, co-design and especially service design. Service design became rapidly a much-wanted tool for both the private and public sector. At the time of writing, in the spring of 2014, the future occupational vistas for Finnish designers seem to lie within these areas.

REFERENCES

Chapter 1

1 More on terms, see: Ihatsu, 1996 & 1998.
2 Finlayson, see: Niinimäki, Saloniemi (eds), 2008.
3 Arabia, see: Aav, Vakkari, Viljanen, Vilhunen (eds), 2009; Kumela, Paatero, Rissanen, 1987; Tomula, 2004.
4 The Craft School, see: Huovio, 1998.
5 Svenska Slöjdföreningen, see: Ivanov, 2004; Frick, 1978.
6 Finnish Society of Crafts and Design, see: Suhonen, 2000.
7 Carl Gustaf Estlander, see: Pettersson, 2008; Schybergson, 1916.
8 Finnish Art Society, see: Pettersson, 2008.
9 Ateneum, see: Levanto (ed.), 1987.
10 See: Smeds, 1999.
11 Design Museum, see: Leppänen, Svenskberg, Svinhufvud, Vilhunen (eds), 2013; Suhonen, 2000.
12 Armas Lindgren, see: Nikula, 1988.
13 Arthur William Finch, see: Lindströn, Valkonen (eds), 1991.
14 Rafael Blomstedt, see: Suhonen, 2000; Sotamaa, Strandman, Nyman, Suortti-Vuorio (eds), 1999.
15 Werner von Essen, see: Suhonen, 2000; Sotamaa, Strandman, Nyman, Suortti-Vuorio (eds), 1999.
16 Ornamo, see: Hohti (ed.), 2011; Ornamo, 1962.
17 Theodor Höijer, see: Viljo, 1985.
18 See: Suhonen, 2000.
19 Vienna World's Fair of 1873, see: Smeds, 1996.
20 Paris World's Fair of 1900, see: MacKeith, Smeds, 1993.
21 Paris World's Fair of 1889, see: Smeds, 1996.
22 An exhibition of home industries and crafts in Helsinki 1875, see: Smeds, 1996.
23 "General Finnish Exposition" 1876, see: Smeds, 1996.
24 An exhibition devoted to the applied arts in Helsinki in 1881, see: Smeds, 1996.
25 Friends of Finnish Handicraft Society, see: Johansson-Pape, 1981; Priha, 1999.
26 Fanny Churberg, see: Konttinen, 1994.
27 Kalevala, see: Lönnrot, 1835.
28 Karelianism, see: Sihvo, 1973.

Chapter 2

29 Axel Gallén, see: Ilvas, 1996.
30 Eliel Saarinen, see: Hausen, 1990; Tuomi, 2007.
31 Louis Sparre, see: Hämäläinen, Hagelstam (eds), 2010.
32 Eva Mannerheim-Sparre, see: Hämäläinen, Hagelstam (eds), 2010.
33 Iris company, see: Supinen, 1993.
34 Artek, see: Nuortio, 1989; Suhonen, 1985.
35 Herman Gesellius, see: Hämäläinen, Hagelstam (eds), 2010.
36 Iris Room, see: MacKeith, Smeds, 1993; Supinen, 1993.
37 Alvar Aalto, see: Aav, Savolainen, Viljanen (eds), 2005; Jetsonen, 2004; Kellein, 2005; Korvenmaa, 2003; Olafsdottir, 1998; Pallasmaa (ed.), 2003; Ray, 2005; Schildt, 1994, 1997, 2007; Standertskjöld (ed.), 1989.
38 Eric O. W. Ehrström, see: Hämäläinen, Hagelstam (eds), 2010.
39 See: Smeds, 1999.
40 Hvitträsk, see: Hämäläinen, Hagelstam (eds), 2010; Pallasmaa (ed.), 1987.
41 Suur-Merijoki Manor, see: Hämäläinen, Hagelstam (eds), 2010.
42 Kulosaari, see: Kolbe, 1988.
43 Salomo Wuorio, see: Tarjanne, 2007A, 2007B.
44 Lars Sonck, see: Hämäläinen, Hagelstam (eds), 2010.
45 Valter Jung, see: Hämäläinen, Hagelstam (eds), 2010.
46 Emil Wikström, see: Hänninen (ed.), 2002; Suomalainen, 1982.
47 Fiskars, see: Aav, Savolainen, Viljanen (eds), 2004.
48 Nuutajärvi, see: Poutasuo, 1993.
49 Russian Nizhniy-Novgorod exhibition of 1896, see: Smeds, 1996.

Chapter 3

50 Johan Sigfrid Sirén, see: Suomen Rakennustaiteen museo, 1989.
51 Werner West, see: Karttunen, 2006.
52 See: Saarikangas, 2002.
53 See: Strengell, 1923.
54 See: Setälä, 1928.
55 Arttu Brummer, see: Aav (ed.), 1991.
56 Furniture Fair 1927, see: MacKeith, Smeds, 1993.
57 See: Paulsson, 1919.
58 Jac. Ahrenberg, see: Ekelund, 1943.
59 Friends of Finnish Handicraft, see: Priha, 1999.

60 Laila Karttunen, see: Peltovuori, 1987, 1988, 1995.
61 Eva Anttila, see: Salo-Mattila, 1997.
62 Maija Kansanen, see: Tenkama, 1983.
63 Tampella, see: Seppälä, 1981.
64 See: Wiberg, 1996.
65 Erik Bryggman, see: Nikula (ed.), 1991.
66 Exhibition on the Rationalization of Small Apartments, see: MacKeith, Smeds, 1993.
67 Aino Aalto, see: Kinnunen (ed.), 2004.
68 See: Blomstedt, 1930.
69 See: Aav (ed.), 1991.
70 See: Suhonen, 2000.
71 Ilmari Tapiovaara, see: Korvenmaa, 1997.
72 Asko, see: Miestamo, 1981.
73 Finnmar, see: Davies, 1998.
74 Gullichsens, see: Nummelin, 2007.
75 Korhonen, see: Lahtinen, 2011.
76 Paavo Tynell, see: Huusko, 2012.

Chapter 4

77 Michael Schilkin, see: Kalha, 1996.
78 Toini Muona, see: Kalha, 2002A.
79 Dora Jung, see: Palo-oja (ed.), 2007; Fernström, 2012.
80 Tapio Wirkkala, see: Aav, Viljanen, Träskelin, 2000.
81 Göran Hongell, see: Koivisto, 2011.
82 Karhula-Iittala, see: Aav, 2006.
83 Riihimäen lasi, see: Koivisto, 2001.
84 Gunnel Nyman, see: Koivisto 2001.
85 Timo Sarpaneva, see: Sarpaneva, Kalin, Svennevig, 1986; 1995 Sarpaneva, Valtasaari.
86 Kaj Franck, see: Aav, 2011; Jantunen, 2011.
87 Vuokko Nurmesniemi, see: Aav, Viljanen (eds), 2007B; Aav, Kivilinna, Viljanen, 2011.
88 Birger Kaipiainen, see: Kalha, 2013.
89 Herman Olof Gummerus, see: Aav, Viljanen (eds), 2009.
90 Rut Bryk, see: Aav, Viljanen (eds), 2007A.

Chapter 5

91 Eero Aarnio, see: Hai, 2003; Kalha (ed.), 2003.
92 Antti Nurmesniemi, see: Hai, 2002; Nurmesniemi, Bell, Kalin, Kokkonen, Buchwald, 1992.
93 Marimekko, see: Aav, Härkäpää, Viljanen (eds), 2003; Aav, Kivilinna, Viljanen (eds), 2005, 2011; Suhonen, 1986.
94 Armi Ratia, see: Karsi, 1995; Parkkinen, 2005; Saarikoski, 1977.

95 Saara Hopea, see: Untracht, 1988.
96 Yrjö Kukkapuro, see: Aav (ed.), 2008;
Hai, 2001; Kukkapuro, 1983.
97 Olavi Hänninen, see: Aaltonen, 2006.
98 See: Kalha, 1997.

Chapter 6
99 See: Franck, 1966.
100 Jussi Ahola, see: Amberg (ed.), 2000.
101 Design Museum, see: Leppänen,
Svenskberg, Svinhufvud, Vilhunen (eds),
2013; Suhonen, 2000.
102 Yki Nummi, see: Huusko, 2012.
103 See: Sarantola-Weiss, 2003.
104 Maija Isola, see: Aav, Kivilinna, Viljanen (eds), 2005.
105 Annika Rimala, see: Maunula, Tarschys (eds), 2000.
106 Artisaani-shop, see: Priha (ed.), 2011.
107 Anu Pentik, see: Parkkinen, 2006.
108 Oiva Toikka, see: Aav, Vakkari, Viljanen (eds), 2010; Toikka, Dawson, 2007.
109 Kirsti Rantanen, see: Priha (ed.),
2000.

Chapter 7
110 Simo Heikkilä, see: www.periferia
design.fi
111 Design Forum Finland, see: www.
designforum.fi/en
112 University of Industrial Arts, see:
Sotamaa, Strandman, Nyman, Suortti-
Vuorio (eds), 1999; Huovio, 1998, 2009.
113 Stefan Lindfors, see: www.stefan
lindfors.com
114 See: Takala-Schreib, 2000.
115 Sisu, see: www.sisuauto.com
116 Valmet, see: www.valmet.com
117 ED-Design, see: www.ed-design.fi/en
118 Creadesign, see: www.creadesign.fi/
en/creadesign.html
119 LinjaDesign, see: www.linja.com
120 See: Valtonen, 2007.

Chapter 8
121 Muurame, see: www.muurame.com/en
122 Hackman, see: Nukari, 1990.
123 Ilkka Suppanen, see: www.suppanen.
com
124 Harri Koskinen, see: www.harri
koskinen.com
125 Suunto, see: www.suunto.com/en-GB/
About-Suunto
126 See: Valtonen, 2007.
127 Sitra, see: www.sitra.fi/en
128 See: Korvenmaa (ed.), 1998.

129 Tekes, see: www.tekes.fi/en
130 Media Lab, see: mlab.taik.fi
131 Media Centre Lume, see: lume.aalto.
fi/en
132 International Design Business
Management see: idbm.aalto.fi
133 University of Lapland see: www.
ulapland.fi/InEnglish
134 Lahti Institute of Design, see: www.
lamk.fi/english/design/Sivut/default.aspx
135 Helsinki Design Week, see: www.
helsinkidesignweek.com
136 Helsinki Design District, see: www.
designdistrict.fi/news
137 Huippu Design Management, see:
www.huippu.fi

INDEX OF SUBJECTS

INDEX OF PERSONS

SELECT BIBLIOGRAPHY

Aaltonen Susanna (ed.), 2006. *Muovituolista raitiovaunuun: Olavi Hänninen – sisustusarkkitehti 1920-1992*, Multikustannus Helsinki; Gummerus Jyväskylä.

Aav Marianne (ed.), 1991. *Arttu Brummer: taideteollisuuden tulisielu*, Taideteollinen korkeakoulu ja Taideteollisuusmuseo, Helsinki.

Aav Marianne, 1994. *Eva Anttila. Tekstiilitaiteilija. Textile Artist. 1894-1993*, Helsinki.

Aav Marianne, 1999. 'Kansallinen tehtävä'. Ateneum Maskerad. Taideteollisuuden muotoja ja murroksia, 105-132, Taideteollinen korkeakoulu, Helsinki.

Aav Marianne, 2006. *Naisen muoto*, Designmuseo, Helsinki.

Aav Marianne (ed.), 2008. *Yrjö Kukkapuro: huonekalusuunnittelija*, Designmuseo, Helsinki.

Aav Marianne (ed.), 2009. *Arabia: keramiikka, taide, teollisuus*, Designmuseo, Helsinki.

Aav Marianne, 2011. *Kaj Franck: universaaleja muotoja*, Designmuseo, Helsinki.

Aav Marianne, Amberg Anna-Lisa, Fagerström Raimo, Tillander-Godenhielm Ulla (eds), 2012. *Koru Suomessa*, Designmuseo, Helsinki.

Aav Marianne, Härkäpää Maria, Viljanen Eeva (eds), 2003. *Marimekko: Fabrics, Fashion, Architecture*, Yale University Press, New Haven.

Aav Marianne, Kivilinna Harri, Viljanen Eeva (eds) 2005. *Maija Isola: life, art, Marimekko*, 2005. Design Museum, Helsinki.

Aav Marianne, Kivilinna Harri, Viljanen Eeva, 2011. *Marimekkoelämää: väriä, raitaa ja muotoja*, Designmuseo, Helsinki.

Aav Marianne, Koivisto Kaisa, Thiry Michèle (eds), 1995. *Nanny Still: 45 years of design*, Finnish Glass Museum, Riihimäki

Aav Marianne, Savolainen Jukka (eds), 2010. *Modernismi: kirjoituksia suomalaisesta modernismista / Modernism: essays on Finnish modernism*, Designmuseo, Helsinki.

Aav Marianne, Savolainen Jukka, Viljanen Eeva (eds), 2004. *Alvar Aalto: muotoilija, filosofi – 8 näkökulmaa*, Designmuseo, Helsinki.

Aav Marianne, Savolainen Jukka, Viljanen Eeva (eds), 2005. *Luova teollisuus*, Designmuseo, Helsinki.

Aav Marianne, Stritzler-Levine Nina (eds) 1998. *Finnish modern design: utopian ideals and everyday realities, 1930-1997*, Bard Graduate Center for Studies in the Decorative Arts, New York.

Aav Marianne, Vakkari Susanna, Viljanen Eeva, Vilhunen Merja (eds), 2009. *Arabia, Ceramics Art Industry*. Designmuseo, Helsinki.

Aav Marianne, Vakkari Susanna, Viljanen Eeva (eds), 2010. *Oiva Toikka: moments of ingenuity*, Designmuseo, Helsinki.

Aav Marianne, Viljanen Eeva (eds), 2005. *Paavo Tynell ja Taito Oy*, Designmuseo, Helsinki.

Aav Marianne, Viljanen Eeva (eds), 2006. *Suomalaisen lasin juhlaa: Iittala 125*, Designmuseo, Helsinki.

Aav Marianne, Viljanen Eeva (eds), 2007A. *Rut Bryk*, Designmuseo, Helsinki.

Aav Marianne, Viljanen Eeva (eds), 2007B. *Vuokko: Vuokko Nurmesniemi – pukuja ja kankaita*, Designmuseo, Helsinki.

Aav Marianne, Viljanen Eeva (eds), 2009. *Herman Olof Gummerus: muotoilun diplomaatti*, Designmuseo, Helsinki.

Aav Marianne, Viljanen Eeva, Träskelin Rauno, 2000. *Tapio Wirkkala: ajattelevat kädet*, Designmuseo, Helsinki.

Ahde-Deal Petra, 2013. *Women and jewelry: a social approach to wearing and possessing jewelry*, Aalto University School of Arts, Design and Architecture, Helsinki.

Ainamo Antti, 1996. *Industrial design and business performance: a case study of design management in a Finnish fashion firm*, Helsinki School of Economics and Business Administration, Helsinki.

Amberg Anna-Lisa (ed.). 1986. *Lisa Johansson-Pape*, Taideteollisuusmuseo, Helsinki.

Amberg Anna-Lisa (ed.), 2000. *Arjen muotoilua 35 vuotta: teollinen muotoilija Jussi Ahola*, Ahola Design Oy, Helsinki.

Amberg Anna-Lisa, 2003. *"Kotini on linnani": kartano ylemmän porvariston omanakuvana: esimerkkinä Gesselliuksen, Lindgrenin ja Saarisen suunnittelema Suur-Merijoki vuodelta 1904*, Suomen muinaismuistoyhdistys, Helsinki.

Apila-Salo Inkeri, Tefke Erkki, Toikka Oiva, 1991. 'Lasi on pomo: maan vanhin lasipruuki ja kylä tuomitaan kuolemaan', Kotiliesi 1991: 1, 2-6, 71.

Bálint Juliana (ed.), 1991. *Muodon kuvat 1960-1990*, Teollisuustaiteen liitto Ornamo, Tietopuu, Espoo.

Berg Maria, 1986. *Kaipiainen*, Otava, Helsinki.

Blomstedt Pauli Ernesti, 1930. *Vanha ja uusi taideteollisuus. Pienasuntojen rationalisoimisosastojen julkaisu taideteollisuusnäyttelyssä 1930.*

Blomstedt Pauli Ernesti, 1932. *Kansallista ja kansainvälistä rakennustaiteessa*, Pohjoismaiset rakennuspäivät.

Blomstedt Pauli Ernesti, 1951. *P. E. Blomstedt: arkkitehti*, Suomen arkkitehtiliitto, Helsinki.

Bruun Erik, 1967. *Runar Engblom. Muistonäyttely Amos Andersonin taidemuseossa 22.11.-10.12.1967/ Minnesutställning i Amos Andersons konstmuseum 22.11.-10. 12.1967*, Amos Anderson, Helsinki.

Capella Samper Juli, 2000. *Lindfors: rational animal; selected projects from Stefan Lindfors' first 15 years as an artist and designer 1985-2000*, Petomaani, Helsinki.

Connah Roger, 2005. *Architecture in History: Finland*, Reaktion Books, London.

Davies Kevin, 1998A. 'Finmar and the Furniture of The Future: The sale of Alvar Aalto's plywood furniture in the UK, 1934-1939', Journal of design history / Design History Society, 1998, vol. 11 num. 2, Oxford University Press, Oxford. (article)

Davies Kevin, 1998B. 'Scandinavian Furniture in Britain: Finmar and the UK Market 1949-1952', Journal of design history / Design History Society, 1997, vol. 10 num. 1, Oxford University Press, Oxford. (article)

Davies Kevin, 2003. 'A geographical notion turned into an artistic reality': Promoting Finland and selling Finnish Design in Post-war Britain c. 1953-1965', Journal of Design History Vol. 15. num. 2, 101-116, Oxford University Press, Oxford. (article)

Ekelund Erik, 1943. *Jac. Ahrenberg och Östra Finland*, Svenska Litteratursällskapet i Finland, Helsingfors.

Fernström Päivi, 2012. *Damastin traditio ja innovaatio. Tekstiilitaiteilija Dora Jungin toiminta ja damastien erityisyys*, Helsingin yliopisto, Helsinki.

Franck Kaj, 1966. 'Anonymiteetti'. Keramiikka ja lasi 1/1966, Wärtsilä-yhtymä, Helsinki.

Franck Kaj, Kalin Kaj, Wynne-Ellis Michael, Enbom Carla, Räsänen Liisa, 1992. *Kaj Franck: muotoilija*, WSOY, Porvoo.

Frick Gunilla, 1978. *Svenska slöjdföreningen och konstindustrin före 1905*, Nordiska museet, Stockholm.

Fritze Sointu, Kuoppasalmi Maija, 2007. *Dorrit von Fieandt: elämän värit / livets*

färger / colours of life, Helsinki City Art Museum, Helsinki.

Gullichsen Kirsi, Kinnunen Ulla (eds), 2009. *Inside the Villa Mairea: art, design and interior architecture*, Alvar Aalto Museum, Jyväskylä.

Haapala Leevi, Hirvonen Sanna, Vanhala Jari-Pekka (eds), 2012. *Camouflage: nykytaidetta muotoilun maastossa / Visual art and design in disguise*, Nykytaiteen museo Kiasma, Valtion taidemuseo, Helsinki.

Hagelstam Katja, Visser Piëtke, Lamppu Eva, 2011. *20+12 muotoilutarinaa Helsingistä / 20+12 design stories from Helsinki*, WSOY, Helsinki.

Hai Fang, 2001. *Yrjö Kukkapuro: furniture designer*, Southeast University Press, Nanjing

Hai Fang, 2002. *Antti Nurmesniemi*, China Architecture & Building Press, Beijing.

Hai Fang, 2003. *Eero Aarnio*, Southeast University Press, Nanjing.

Hämäläinen Pirjo, Hagelstam Katja (eds), 2010. *Jugend Suomessa*, Otava, Helsinki.

Hänninen Hannu (ed.), 2002. *Emil Wikström: delicacy and strength*, Gösta Serlachiuksen taidesäätiö, Tampere.

Harni Pekka, 2010. *Object categories: typology of tools*, Aalto University School of Art and Design, Helsinki.

Hasu Mervi, Keinonen Turkka, Mutanen Ulla-Maaria, Aaltonen Aleksi, Hakatie Annaleena, Kurvinen Esko, 2004. *Muotoilun muutos – Näkökulmia muotoilutyön organisoinnin ja johtamisen kehityshaasteisiin 2000-luvulla*, Teknologiateollisuus ry, Helsinki.

Hausen Marika, 1990. *Eliel Saarinen: Suomen aika*, Suomen rakennustaiteen museo, Helsinki.

Heikkilä-Rastas Marjatta, 2003. *Muodin vai muodon vuoksi? Couturemuodin ja muotoilun vaikutukset Kaisu Heikkilä Oy:ssä 1950-luvulta 1980-luvun alkuun suunnittelijan näkökulmasta*, Taideteollinen korkeakoulu, Helsinki. (doctoral thesis)

Heinämies Kati, 2012. *Yliopisto istuu: uniikkituoleja arkeen ja juhlaan / Seats of learning: University chairs for all occasions*, Helsingin yliopisto, tila- ja kiinteistökeskus, Helsinki.

Heinänen Seija, 2006. *Käsityö – taide-teollisuus: näkemyksiä käsityöstä taideteollisuuteen 1900-luvun alun ammatti- ja aikakauslehdissä*, Jyväskylän yliopisto/

Jyväskylän yliopiston kirjasto, Jyväskylä. (doctoral thesis)

Hellman Åsa (ed.), 2004. *Taidekeramiikka Suomessa*, Keuruu.

Hohti Paula (ed.), 2011, *Rajaton muotoilu: näkökulmia suomalaiseen taideteollisuuteen*, Avain, Helsinki.

Hovi Päivi, 1990. *Mainoskuva Suomessa: kehitys ja vaikutteet 1890-luvulta 1930-luvun alkuun*, Taideteollinen korkeakoulu, Helsinki.

Huokuna Tiina, 2006. *Vallankumous kotona!: arkielämän visuaalinen murros 1960-70-lukujen vaihteessa*, Yliopistopaino, Helsinki. (doctoral thesis)

Huovio Ilkka, 1998. *Invitation from the future: treatise on the roots of the School of Arts and Crafts and its development into a university level school 1871-1973*, University of Tampere, Tampere.

Huovio Ilkka, 1999. 'Veistokoulusta korkeakouluksi', Ateneum maskerad: taideteollisuuden muotoja ja murroksia: Taideteollinen korkeakoulu 130 vuotta, 308-339, Taideteollinen korkeakoulu, Helsinki.

Huovio Ilkka, 2009. *Bridging the Future: The General History of the University of Art and Design Helsinki 1973-2003*, Tampere University Press, Tampere.

Huusko Anna-Kaisa, 2012. *Muotoilun aarteet: Suomalaisia valaisimia*, WSOY, Helsinki.

Ihatsu Anna-Marja, 1996. *Craft, Art or Design: In pursuit of the changing concept of craft*, Joensuun yliopisto, Kasvatustieteiden tiedekunta, Joensuu.

Ihatsu Anna-Marja, 1998. *Craft, Art-craft or Craft-design: In pursuit of the British equivalent for the Finnish concept 'käsityö'*, NordFo/Joensuun yliopisto, Joensuu.

Ilvas Juha (ed.), 1996. *Akseli Gallen-Kallela*, Suomen taiteen museo Ateneum, Helsinki.

Ivanov Gunnela, 2004. *Vackrare vardagsvara - design för alla?: Gregor Paulsson och Svenska slöjdföreningen 1915-1925*, Umeå universitet, Umeå.

Jantunen Päivi, 2011. *Kaj Franck: esineitä ja lähikuvia / Kaj Franck: designs & impressions*, WSOY, Helsinki.

Jetsonen Jari, Jetsonen Sirkkaliisa, 2004. *Alvar Aalto Apartments*, Rakennustieto Oy, Helsinki.

Johansson-Pape Lisa (ed.), 1981. *Sata vuotta: Suomen käsityön ystävät 1879-1979*, Suomen käsityön ystävät, Helsinki.

Kaipiainen Birger, Peltonen Jarno, Peltonen Kaarina, 1989. *Birger Kaipiainen*, Taideteollisuusmuseo, Helsinki.

Kalha Harri (ed.), 1990. *Ruukuntekijästä multimediataiteilijaan*, Taideteollinen korkeakoulu, Helsinki.

Kalha Harri, 1996. *Marita Lybeck 1906-1990*, Galleria Septaria, Helsinki.

Kalha Harri, 1997. *Muotopuolen merenneidon pauloissa: Suomen taideteollisuuden kultakausi: mielikuvat, markkinointi, diskurssit*, Suomen historiallinen seura/Taideteollisuusmuseo, Helsinki. (doctoral thesis)

Kalha Harri, 1999. 'Sankarien sukupolvi', Ateneum maskerad: taideteollisuuden muotoja ja murroksia Taideteollinen korkeakoulu 130 vuotta, 134-171, Taideteollinen korkeakoulu, Helsinki.

Kalha Harri, 2000. *Kaj Franck and Kilta: gendering the (aesth)ethics of modernism*, Scandinavian Journal of Design History vol. 10/2000, 28-45.

Kalha Harri, 2002A. *Toini Muona & Gunnel Nyman*, Retretti, Punkaharju.

Kalha Harri, 2002B. 'Myths and Mysteries of Finnish Design: Reading "Wirkkala" and the National Nature Paradigm', Scandinavian Journal of Design History vol. 12/2002, 24-47.

Kalha Harri (ed.), 2003. *Oleta pyöreä tuoli: Eero Aarnion 60-luku*, Helsingin taidehalli, Helsinki.

Kalha Harri, 2004. 'The miracle of Milan: Finland at the 1951 Triennal', Scandinavian journal of design history 2004: 14, 60-71.

Kalha Harri, 2013A. *Birger Kaipiainen*, Suomalaisen Kirjallisuuden Seura, Helsinki.

Kalha Harri, 2013B. *Muodon vuoksi: lasin ja keramiikan klassikoita*, Suomalaisen Kirjallisuuden Seura, Helsinki.

Kalha Harri, Tervo Tuija, 1996. *Michael Schilkin 1900-1962*, Hagelstam, Helsinki.

Kalin Kaj, Sarpaneva Timo, Svennevig Marjatta 1986. *Sarpaneva*, Otava, Helsinki.

Kalin Kaj, Viljanen Eeva (eds), 1985. *Bertel Gardberg: taiteilija*, Taideteollisuusmuseo, Helsinki.

Karjalainen Toni-Matti, 2004. *Semantic transformation in design: communicating strategic brand identity through product design references*, University of Art and Design Helsinki, Helsinki. (doctoral thesis)

Karsi Anneli, 1995. *Marimekon yrityskulttuuri: designed by Armi Ratia*, Kampanja, Helsinki.

Karttunen Leena, 2006. *Werner West – huonekaluarkkitehti*, Keravan museo / Formato Print, Kerava.
Keinonen Turkka (ed.), 2000. *Miten käytettävyys muotoillaan?*, Nokia Oyj, Helsinki.
Kellein Thomas, 2005. *Alvar & Aino Aalto design: Collection Bischofberger*, Cantz, Ostfildern-Ruit.
Kinnunen Ulla (ed.), 2004. *Aino Aalto*, Alvar Aalto -museo, Jyväskylä.
Kjellberg Friedl, Hipeli Mirja-Kaisa, 1989. *Keraamikon tie 1924–1970 / En keramikers väg 1924–1970*, Porvoo.
Koivisto Kaisa, 1996. 'Beautiful glass for everyone', Scandinavian Journal of Design History vol. 6/1996.
Koivisto Kaisa (ed.), 1998. *Nanny Still: sana /szo/word*, Suomen lasimuseo, Riihimäki.
Koivisto Kaisa, 1999. 'Goran Hongell, the Finnish glass designer', Scandinavian Journal of Design History vol. 9/1999, 106–119.
Koivisto Kaisa, 2001. *Kolme tarinaa lasista: suomalainen lasimuotoilu 1946–1957*, Suomen lasimuseo, Riihimäki. (doctoral thesis)
Koivisto Kaisa, 2002. 'Designers, Glass Makers and Rationalisation', Scandinavian Journal of Design History vol. 12/2002, 80–91.
Koivisto Kaisa (ed.), 2010. *Riihimäen lasia / Glass from Riihimäki: Riihimäen Lasi Oy 1910–1990*, Suomen lasimuseo, Riihimäki.
Koivisto Kaisa, 2011. *Maailman kaunein: suomalaisen lasin kultakausi 1946–1965*, Tammi, Helsinki.
Koivisto Kaisa (ed.), 2012. *Erkkitapio Siiroinen: Riihimäen Lasin nuori lupaus / A young promising name at the Riihimäki Glassworks*, Suomen lasimuseo, Riihimäki.
Koivisto Kaisa, Laurén Uta (eds), 2012. *Lasia - ja muuta: karahvista kirjahyllyyn / Glass etc.: from carafe to cardboard*, Suomen lasimuseo, Riihimäki.
Koivisto Kaisa, Simanainen Timo (eds), 1988. *Oiva Toikka: Lasia/Glas/Glass: 13.5.–11.9.1988 Suomen lasimuseo*, Suomen lasimuseo, Riihimäki.
Kolbe Laura, 1988. *Kulosaari - unelma paremmasta tulevaisuudesta*, Kulosaaren kotiseuturahaston säätiö, Helsinki.
Konttinen Riitta, 1994. *Fanny Churberg*, Otava, Helsinki.
Korvenmaa Pekka, 1996. *Huonekalupiirtäjästä tuotesuunnittelijaksi: kalusteiden ideoinnista ja tuottamisesta sotien jälkeisessä Suomessa, esimerkkinä Ilmari*

Tapiovaara, Näköalapaikalla: Aimo Reitalan juhlakirja, 1996, 125–133, 198–199, Taidehistorian seura, Helsinki.
Korvenmaa Pekka, 1997. *Ilmari Tapiovaara*, Santa & Cole, Barcelona.
Korvenmaa Pekka (ed.), 1998. *Muotoiltu etu 1 & 2: Muotoilu, teollisuus ja kansainvälinen kilpailukyky*, Suomen itsenäisyyden juhlarahasto, Helsinki.
Korvenmaa Pekka, 1999. 'Tilat ja tuolit – näkökulmia sisustusarkkitehdin ammattikuvaan', Yhteiset olohuoneet: näkökulmia suomalaiseen sisustusarkkitehtuuriin 1949–1999, 106–111, Otava, Helsinki.
Korvenmaa Pekka, 2001. 'Rhetoric and Action: Design Policies in Finland at the Beginning of the third Millennia', Scandinavian Journal of Design History vol 11/2001, 7–15.
Korvenmaa Pekka, 2003. *MORE LIGHT?*, Alvar Aalto: designer, s. 109–134, Alvar Aalto Foundation, Helsinki.
Korvenmaa Pekka (ed.), 2003. *Alvar Aalto architect [Volume 7]: Sunila 1936–54*, Alvar Aalto Foundation / Alvar Aalto Academy, Helsinki.
Korvenmaa Pekka, 2003. *Näkyä vai palvella? Muotoilusta Suomessa 1960-luvulla / To be seen or to serve? Finnish Design in the 1960's*, Oleta pyöreä tuoli: Eero Aarnion 60-luku, 28–51, Helsingin taidehalli, Helsinki.
Korvenmaa Pekka, Pallasmaa Juhani, Treib Mark, Reed Peter, 2002. *Alvar Aalto: Between Humanism and Materialism*, Museum of Modern Art, New York.
Kotro Tanja, 2005. *Hobbyist knowing in product development: desirable objects and passion for sports in Suunto Corporation*, University of Art and Design Helsinki, Helsinki. (doctoral thesis)
Kruskopf Erik, 1989. *Suomen taideteollisuus: suomalaisen muotoilun vaiheita*, WSOY, Helsinki.
Kukkapuro Yrjö, 1983. *Furniture by Yrjö Kukkapuro*, Avarte, Helsinki.
Kulvik Barbro (ed.), 2003. *Q: Designing the Quietness: Contemporary Finnish Design*, JFDA Japan Finland Design Association and University of Art and Design, Helsinki.
Kumela Marjut, Andenberg Rolf, 1993. *Kurt Ekholm. Arabia 1931–1948*, Arabian museo, Helsinki.
Kumela Marjut, Paatero Kristiina, Rissanen Kaarina, 1987. *Arabia*, Wärtsilä / Arabia, Helsinki.

Kälviäinen Mirja, 1996. *Esteettisiä käyttötuotteita ja henkisiä materiaaliteoksia: hyvän tuotteen ammatillinen määrittely taidekäsityössä 1980-luvun Suomessa*, Kuopion käsi- ja taideteollisuusakatemia, Kuopio. (doctoral thesis)
Lahtinen Rauno, 2011. *Modernin synty: Aalto, Korhonen ja moderni Turku / The birth of the Finnish modern: Aalto, Korhonen and modern Turku*, Huonekalutehdas Korhonen Oy.
Lavery Jason Edward, 2006. *The History of Finland*, Greenwood Publishing Group, Westport, Connecticut.
Leppänen Helena (ed.), 2003. *Ruukun runoutta ja materiaalin mystiikkaa. Sata vuotta keramiikkataiteen opetusta ja tutkimusta*, Taideteollinen korkeakoulu, Helsinki.
Leppänen Helena, 2006. *Muotoilija ja toinen: astiasuunnittelua vanhuuden kontekstissa*, Taideteollinen korkeakoulu, Helsinki.
Leppänen Helena, 2013. *Rakastetut Arabian astiat koristelijana Esteri Tomula*, WSOY, Helsinki.
Leppänen Helena, Svenskberg Aila, Svinhufvud Leena, Vilhunen Merja (eds), 2013. *Aate, muoto, materiaali: Designmuseon kokoelmat*, Designmuseo, Helsinki.
Levanto Marjatta (ed.), 1987. *Ateneum 100*, Suomen taideakatemia, Helsinki.
Lindström Anneli, Valkonen Olli (eds), 1991. *Alfred William Finch 1854–1930*, AteneumTaideteollisuusmuseo, Helsinki.
Lindström Aune, 1939. *Fanny Churberg: elämä ja teokset*, WSOY, Helsinki.
Lönnrot Elias, 1835. *Kalevala*, Suomalaisen Kirjallisuuden Seura, Helsinki.
Luojus Susanna (ed.), 2013. *Art Deco and the arts: France-Finlande 1905–1935*, Suomalaisen Kirjallisuuden Seura, Helsinki.
MacKeith Peter B., Smeds Kerstin, 1993. *The Finland pavilions: Finland at the universal expositions 1900–1992*, City, Helsinki.
Mäenpää Pasi, 2005. *Narkissos kaupungissa: tutkimus kuluttaja-kaupunkilaisesta ja julkisesta tilasta*, Tammi, Helsinki. (doctoral thesis)
Mäkikalla Maija, 2004. *Sileää pintaa Bomanin huonekaluissa*, Moderni Turku 1920- ja 1930-luvuilla, 22 kirjoitusta, Turun yliopisto, Turku.
Matiskainen Heikki (ed.), 1987. *Gunnel Nyman*, Suomen lasimuseo, Riihimäki.
Matiskainen Heikki, 2006. *Valto Kokko, muotoilija*, Suomen lasimuseo, Riihimäki.

Matiskainen Heikki (ed.), 2013. *Tapio Wirkkala: a poet in glass and silver,* Suomen lasimuseo, Riihimäki.
Matiskainen Heikki, Kokkonen Jyri, 2004. *Lumpeenkukka: Aimo Okkolin,* Suomen lasimuseo, Riihimäki.
Matiskainen Heikki, Koivisto Kaisa (eds), 2002. *Humppila: lasitehdas tien varrella,* Suomen lasimuseo, Riihimäki.
Mattelmäki Tuuli, 2006A. *Design probes,* University of Art and Design Helsinki, Helsinki. (doctoral thesis)
Mattelmäki Tuuli, 2006B. *Muotoiluluotaimet,* Teknologiateollisuus ry, Helsinki.
Mattila Mirva, 2001. *Antti Nurmesniemi: 50 vuotta muotoilua; 50 years of design,* Veturitalli, Salon kaupungin taidemuseo, Salo.
Mattila Mirva, 2002. 'Changing meanings of a piece of furniture: variations on the theme of a sauna stool', Scandinavian Journal of Design History vol. 12/2002, 93-101, Rhodos, Copenhagen.
Maunula Leena, Tarschys Rebecka (eds), 2000. *ANNIKA RIMALA 1960-2000. Väriä arkeen / Färg på vardagen / Colour on your life,* Designmuseo, Helsinki.
Mauranen Tapio, 2005. *Hopeasiipi: sata vuotta Helkamaa,* Otava / Helkama, Helsinki.
Miestamo Riitta, 1981. *Suomalaisen huonekalun muoto ja sisältö: Suomen suurimman huonekalutehtaan näkökulmasta tarkasteltuna,* Askon Säätiö, Lahti.
Mikkonen Tuija, 2005. *Corporate architecture in Finland in the 1940s and 1950s: factory building as architecture, investment and image,* Academia scientiarum Fennica, Helsinki.
Muona Toini, 1988. *Toini Muona: Arabia 1931-1970,* Taideteollisuusmuseo, Helsinki.
Mutanen Ulla-Maaria, Virkkunen Jaakko, Keinonen Turkka, 2006. *Muotoiluosaamisen kehittäminen teknologiayrityksissä,* Teknologiateollisuus ry, Helsinki.
Na Yuri, 2013. *Craftology: redefining contemporary craft in culture, and sustainability.* Aalto University School of Arts, Design and Architecture, Helsinki.
Naukkarinen Ossi, 2011. *Arjen estetiikka,* Aalto yliopiston Taideteollinen korkeakoulu, Helsinki.
Niinimäki Kirsi, Saloniemi Marjo-Riitta (eds), 2008. *Kretongista printtiin: suomalaisen painokankaan historia,* Maahenki Oy, Helsinki.
Nikula Riitta, 1988. *Armas Lindgren 1874-1929: arkkitehti,* Suomen rakennustaiteen museo, Helsinki.
Nikula Riitta (ed.), 1991. *Erik Bryggman 1891-1955: arkkitehti,* Suomen rakennustaiteen museo, Helsinki.
Nikula Riitta (ed.), 1994. *Sankaruus ja arki: Suomen 50-luvun miljöö / Heroism and everyday: Building Finland in the 1950s,* Suomen rakennustaiteen museo, Helsinki.
Nikula Riitta, 2005. *Wood, stone and steel: contours of Finnish architecture,* Otava, Helsinki.
Norri Marja-Riitta, Standertskjöld Elina, Wang Wilfried (eds), 1999. *20th century architecture: Finland,* Museum of Finnish Architecture, Helsinki.
Nukari Matti, 1990. *Enduring values: Hackman 1790-1990,* Hackman, Helsinki.
Nummelin Esko, 2007. *Kyse on aikamme taiteesta: Maire Gullichsen 100 vuotta 2007 / It's about the art of our time: Maire Gullichsen 100 years 2007,* Porin taidemuseo, Pori.
Nuortio Antti, 1989. *Artekin vahdinvaihto,* Avotakka 1989: 8, 70-72. (article)
Nurmesniemi Antti, Bell Marja-Liisa, Kalin Kaj, Kokkonen Jyri, Buchwald Eva, 1992. *Antti Nurmesniemi: ajatuksia ja suunnitelmia,* Kaupungin taidemuseo, Helsinki.
Nyman Hannele, Poutasuo Tuula, 2004. *Muovikirja: arkitavaraa ja designesineitä,* WSOY, Helsinki.
Ornamo 1962. *Ornamo: viisi vuosikymmentä,* Suomen taideteollisuusyhdistys Helsinki.
Orvola Heikki, Orvola Mirja, Arnold John, 2000. *Heikki Orvola: craft design: lasi, keramiikka, tekstiili, emali,* Pohjoinen, Oulu.
Olafsdottir Asdis, 1998. *Le mobilier d'Alvar Aalto dans l'espacee et dans le temps: la diffusion internationale de design 1920-1940,* Publications de la Sorbonne, Paris. (doctoral thesis)
Palin Tutta (ed.), 2004. *Modernia on moneksi: kuvataiteen, taideteollisuuden ja arkkitehtuurin piirteitä maailmansotien välisen ajan Suomessa: texter om bildkonst, konstindustri och arkitektur mellan första och andra världskrigen i Finland,* Taidehistorian seura, Helsinki.
Pallasmaa Juhani (ed.), 1987. *Hvitträsk: Koti taideteoksena,* Suomen rakennustaiteen museo, Helsinki.
Pallasmaa Juhani (ed.), 2003. *Alvar Aalto architect [Volume 6]: The Aalto house 1935-36,* Alvar Aalto Foundation / Alvar Aalto Academy, Helsinki.
Palo-oja Ritva (ed.), 2007. *Dora Jung: tekstiilitaiteilija, taidekäsityöläinen, teollinen muotoilija,* Tampereen museot, Tampere.
Parkkinen Marja-Leena, 2005. *Love Armi: Armi Ratian henkilökuva,* Otava, Helsinki.
Parkkinen Marja-Leena, 2006. *Anu Pentik: saven sytyttämä.* Otava, Helsinki.
Paulsson Gregor, 1919. *Vackrare Vardagsvara,* Svenska Slöjdföreningen, Stockholm.
Peltonen Kaarina (ed.), 2009. *Tunnista designklassikot,* WSOY, Helsinki.
Peltovuori Sinikka, 1987. *Laila Karttunen ja kansantaide: Laila Karttunen and folk art,* University of Helsinki, Helsinki.
Peltovuori Sinikka, 1988. *Laila Karttusen kirkolliset tekstiilit,* Fredrika Wetterhoffin kotiteollisuusopettajaopisto, Hämeenlinna.
Peltovuori Sinikka, 1995. *Linnut liiteli sanoja: Laila Karttusen kuvatekstiilien problematiikkaa,* Helsingin yliopiston taidehistorian laitos, Helsinki.
Periäinen Tapio, Lindfors Stefan, Enbom Carla, Melander Marco, 1992. *Maamme muotoilua: Suomen itsenäisyyden 75-vuotisjuhlanäyttely 1992,* Suomalaisen muotoilun edistämiskeskus, Helsinki.
Pettersson Susanna, 2008. *Suomen Taideyhdistyksestä ateneumiin: Fredrik Cygnaeus, Carl Gustaf Estlander ja taidekoelman roolit,* Suomalaisen Kirjallisuuden Seura / Valtion taidemuseo, Helsinki.
Piri Markku, 2009. *Elämän työ: Markku Piri / Life-work: Markku Piri.* Libris, Helsinki.
Poutasuo Tuula (ed.), 1993. *Nuutajärvi: 200 vuotta suomalaista lasia / 200 years of Finnish glass,* Hackman, Helsinki.
Priha Päikki, 1991. *Pyhä kaunistus: kirkkotekstiilit Suomen Käsityön Ystävien toiminnassa 1904-1950,* Taideteollinen korkeakoulu, Helsinki. (doctoral thesis)
Priha Päikki, 1994. *Silkkinen seppele: Hanna Loimaranta, tuntematon kirkkotekstiilien taitaja,* Taideteollinen korkeakoulu, Helsinki.
Priha Päikki, 1996. *Women in Finnish textile design: a successful group of artists,* Scandinavian Journal of Design History vol. 6/1996.
Priha Päikki, 1999. *Rakkaat ystävät: Suomen Käsityön Ystävät 120 vuotta,* Kustannusosakeyhtiö Ajatus, Helsinki.
Priha Päikki (ed.), 2000. *Langan varassa: Kirsti Rantasen merkkejä ja merkintöjä,* Taideteollinen korkeakoulu, Helsinki.
Priha Päikki (ed.), 2011. *Artisaani-ilmiö:*

suomalaisen taidekäsityön vuosikymmenet, Aalto-yliopiston taideteollinen korkeakoulu, Helsinki.

Ray Nicholas, 2005. *Alvar Aalto*, Yale University Press, New Haven.

Ryynänen Toni, 2009. *Median muotoilema. Muotoilun mediajulkisuus suomalaisessa talouslehdistössä*, Kuluttajatutkimuskeskus, Helsinki. (doctoral thesis)

Räsänen Liisa (ed.), 1989. 'Muotoilijan tunnustuksia/ Form och miljö', (Kaj Franck), 10, 12–15, Taideteollinen korkeakoulu / Valtion painatuskeskus, Helsinki.

Saarikangas Kirsi, 1993. *Model houses for model families: gender, ideology and the modern dwelling: the type-planned houses of the 1940s in Finland*, Finnish Historical Society, Helsinki. (doctoral thesis)

Saarikangas Kirsi, 2002. *Asunnon muodonmuutoksia: puhtauden estetiikka ja sukupuoli modernissa arkkitehtuurissa*, Helsinki: Suomalaisen Kirjallisuuden Seura.

Saarikoski Tuula, 1977. *Armi Ratia: legenda jo eläessään*, WSOY, Porvoo, Hki, Juva.

Salakari Tuula, 2012. *Suomalaisia tuoleja*, WSOY, Helsinki.

Salo Merja, 2005. *Muodin ikuistaja – Muotivalokuvaus Suomessa*, Taideteollinen korkeakoulu, Helsinki.

Salo-Mattila Kirsti, 1997. *Picture vs. weave: Eva Anttila's tapestry art in the continuum of the genre*, University of Helsinki, Department of Art History, Helsinki. (licentiate thesis)

Salo-Mattila Kirsti, 2000. 'Art textile in architectural space: the Finnish experience', Scandinavian Journal of Design History vol. 10/2000, 70–81.

Sarantola-Weiss Minna, 1995. *Kalusteita kaikille: suomalaisen puusepänteollisuuden historia*, Puusepänteollisuuden liitto, Helsinki.

Sarantola-Weiss Minna (ed.), 1999. *Rooms for everyone: perspectives on Finnish interior design 1949–1999*, Otava, Helsinki.

Sarantola-Weiss Minna, 2003. *Sohvaryhmän läpimurto: kulutuskulttuurin tulo suomalaisiin olohuoneisiin 1960- ja 1970-lukujen vaihteessa*, Suomalaisen Kirjallisuuden Seura, Helsinki.

Sarantola-Weiss Minna, 2008. *Reilusti ruskeaa: 1970-luvun arkea*, WSOY, Helsinki.

Sarpaneva Timo, Kalin Kaj, Svennevig Marjatta, 1986. *Sarpaneva*, Otava, Helsinki.

Sarpaneva Timo, Valtasaari Jukka, 1995. *A retrospective / Timo Sarpaneva*, Helsinki City Art Museum, Helsinki.

Savolainen Jukka, Svenskberg Aila (eds), 2012. *Tulevaisuuden rakentajat / Builders of the future: Finnish design 1945–67*, Designmuseo, Helsinki.

Schildt Göran, 1994. *Alvar Aalto a life's work architecture, design and art*, Otava, Helsinki.

Schildt Göran, 1997. *Alvar Aalto in his own words / Näin puhui Alvar Aalto*, Otava, Helsinki.

Schildt Göran, 2007. *Alvar Aalto – elämä / his life*, Alvar Aalto Museum, Jyväskylä.

Schybergson M.G., 1916. *Carl Gustaf Estlander: levnadsteckning*, Tidnings-och tryckeri-aktiebolagets tryckeri, Helsinki.

Seppälä Raimo, 1981. *Koskesta syntynyt*, Tampella, Tampere.

Setälä Salme, 1928. *Miten sisustan asuntoni*, Otava, Helsinki.

Sihvo Hannes (ed.), 1973. *Karjala: idän ja lännen silta*, WSOY, Porvoo.

Simola Sanna, Mäkelä Marjukka (eds), 2008. *Tunnetko teolliset muotoilijat*, Kustannusosakeyhtiö Avain, Helsinki.

Smeds Kerstin, 1996. *Helsingfors–Paris: Finlands utveckling till nation på världsutställningarna 1851–1900*, Svenska litteratursällskapet i Finland, Finska historiska samfundet, Helsinki.

Smeds Kerstin, 1999. *Teollisuutta Suomeen!*, Ateneum maskerad: taideteollisuuden muotoja ja murroksia, Taideteollinen korkeakoulu, Helsinki.

Sopanen Tuomas (ed.) (Tuomas Sopanen Collection), 2008. *Ryijy elää: suomalaisia ryijyjä 1778–2008*, Tuomas Sopanen, Varkaus.

Sotamaa Yrjö, Strandman Pia, Nyman Hannele, Suortti-Vuorio Auli (eds), 1999. *Ateneum maskerad: taideteollisuuden muotoja ja murroksia / Taideteollinen korkeakoulu 130 vuotta*, Taideteollinen korkeakoulu, Helsinki.

Sparke Penny, 2004. *An Introduction to Design and Culture – 1900 to Present*, Routledge, New York.

Standertskjöld Elina (ed.), 1989. *Alvar Aalto: arkkitehtuuria Suomessa / arkitektur i Finland / architecture in Finland*, Museum of Finnish Architecture, Helsinki.

Standertskjöld Elina, 1996. *P. E. Blomstedt 1900–1935, arkkitehti*, Suomen rakennustaiteen museo, Helsinki.

Stenros Anne (ed.), 1999. *Visions: Modern Finnish Design*, Otava, Helsinki.

Strengell Gustaf, 1923. *Koti taideluomana: esitys sisustustaiteen alkuperusteista*, Otava, Helsinki.

Suhonen Pekka, 1985. *Artek: alku, tausta, kehitys*, Artek, Helsinki.

Suhonen Pekka, 1986. *Phenomenon Marimekko*, Weilin + Göös, Espoo.

Suhonen Pekka, 2000. *Ei vain muodon vuoksi: Suomen taideteollisuusyhdistys 125*, Otava, Helsinki.

Suomalainen Yrjö, 1948. *Visavuoren mestari: piirteitä Emil Wikströmista ihmisenä ja taiteilijana*, Otava, Helsinki.

Suomen Rakennustaiteen museo, 1989. *J. S. Sirén: Arkkitehti 1889–1961*, Suomen rakennustaiteen museo, Helsinki.

Suominen-Kokkonen Renja, 1997. *Designing a room of one's own: the architect Aino Marsio-Aalto and Artek*, Scandinavian Journal of Design History vol. 7/1997.

Suominen-Kokkonen Renja, 1999. *Aalto, Artek ja muotoilu*, (in Alvar Aalto ja Helsinki / Alvar Aalto och Helsingfors) WSOY, Porvoo, Helsinki, Juva.

Suominen-Kokkonen Renja, 2007. *Aino and Alvar Aalto: a shared journey; interpretations of an everyday modernism*, Alvar Aalto Foundation / Alvar Aalto Museum, Jyväskylä.

Supinen Marja, 1993. *A.B. Iris suuri yritys*, Taide, Helsinki.

Svinhufvud Leena (ed.), 2001. *Eva Brummer*, Taideteollisuusmuseo, Helsinki.

Svinhufvud Leena, 2009. *Moderneja ryijyjä, metritavaraa ja käsityötä: tekstiilitaide ja nykyaikaistuva taideteollisuus Suomessa maailmansotien välisenä aikana*, Designmuseo, Helsinki.

Svinhufvud, Leena (ed.), 2009. *Ryijy! The Finnish Ryijy Rug*, Designmuseo, Helsinki.

Takala-Schreib Vuokko, 2000. *Suomi muotoilee: unelmien kuvajaisia diskurssien vallassa*, Taideteollinen korkeakoulu, Helsinki. (doctoral thesis)

Tarjanne Hilla, 2007A. *Seinät kertovat: Salomo Wuorio 150 vuotta – juhlakirja*, Gerda ja Salomo wuorion säätiö, Helsinki.

Tarjanne Hilla, 2007B. *S. Wuorio: helsinkiläinen koristemaalausliike*, Helsingin kaupunginmuseo, Helsinki.

Tenkama Pirkko, 1983. *Maija Kansanen suomalaisen modernin tekstiilitaiteen uranuurtajana: virein luomiskausi 1927–1936*. Taidehistorian pro gradu, Jyväskylän yliopisto, Jyväskylä.

Toikka Oiva, Dawson Jack, 2007. *Oiva Toikka: glass and design*, WSOY, Helsinki.

Toivanen Pekka, Savolainen Anuliina, Metsäranta Pinja (eds) 2005. *Toimistosta tuttu: Martela kuusikymmentä*, Martela.
Tomula Esteri, 2004. *Arabia 1947-1984*, Taideteollisuusmuseon säätiö, Helsinki.
Tuomi Timo, 2007. *Eliel ja Eero Saarinen*, Ajatus, Helsinki.
Turkka Marja, Aaltonen Susanna, 2006. *Muovituolista raitiovaunuun: Olavi Hänninen – sisustusarkkitehti 1920-1992*, Multikustannus, Helsinki.
Turpeinen Iida, Uoti Jaakko (eds), 2011. *TOKYO 50 MCMLXI-MMXI : Taideteollisen korkeakoulun opiskelijaliike viisikymmentä vuotta*, Aalto-yliopiston Taideteollinen korkeakoulu, Helsinki.
Tuukkanen Pirkko (ed.), 2003. *Alvar Aalto: designer*, Alvar Aalto Foundation, Helsinki.
Tynell Helena, 1998. *Helena Tynell design 1943-1993*, Finnish Glass Museum, Riihimäki.
Untracht Oppi, 1988. *Saara Hopea-Untracht: elämä ja työ*, Werner Söderström, Porvoo.
Valtonen Anna, 2007. *Redefining industrial design: changes in the design practice in Finland*, University of Art and Design Helsinki, Helsinki. (doctoral thesis)
Vepsäläinen Jussi (ed.), 2012. *Markku Kosonen: puun aika / time of wood*, Maahenki, Helsinki.
Vihma Susann, 2005. *The Legacy of HfG Ulm*, Scandinavian Journal of Design History vol. 15/2005, 64-75.
Vihma Susann (ed.), 2008-2009. *Suomalainen muotoilu 1-3*. Weilin+Göös, Espoo.
Viitala Janne, 2010. *Liedeltä pöytään: suomalaiset design talousvalut*, Karkkilan ruukkimuseo Senkka Karkkila.
Viljo Eeva Maija, 1985. *Theodor Höijer: en arkitekt under den moderna storstadsarkitekturens genombrottstid i Finland från 1870 till sekelskiftet*, Suomen muinaismuistoyhdistys, Helsinki.
Weston Richard, 1995. *Alvar Aalto*, Phaidon, London.
Wiberg Marjo, 1996. *The textile designer and the art of design: on the formation of a profession in Finland*, University of Art and Design, Helsinki. (doctoral thesis)
Woirhaye Helena, 2002. *Maire Gullichsen: taiteen juoksutyttö*, Taideteollisuusmuseo, Helsinki.
Woodham Jonathan M., 1997. *Twentieth-Century Design*, Oxford University Press, Oxford.

SOURCES OF ILLUSTRATIONS

Abbreviations
MFA: MFA
DM: Design Museum
AUAD: Archives, University of Art and Design Helsinki
LUAD: Library, University of Art and Design Helsinki
P: Photo

Chapter heading illustrations
12–13 Catalogue of mathematical instruments as drawing aids, dated 1 January 1890, Digitized collections of the National Library of Finland.
40–41 Farmhouse interior. First prize in the Farmer series of a competition held by Kotitaide magazine, 1903. Kotitaide 1902, LUAD
76–77 Abloy padlock, brochure, Kone ja silta O.y., Helsinki 1935, Digitized collections of the National Library of Finland.
144–145 Brochure illustrations (no date) presenting contemporary kitchen furniture of the Stockmann department store and the Keravanpuusepäntehdas factory. Digitized collections of the National Library of Finland.
172–174 Design exhibition slogans, Finnish Fair Corporation, photographer unknown.
210–211 Marimekko's first advertisement for Tasaraita t-shirts, photographer Teemu Lipasti, *Annika Rimala 1960-2000*
268–269 The Visio chair designed by Simo Heikkilä and Yrjö Viherheimo for the Vivero company, photographer unknown.
292–293 Fiskars pruner, Olavi Linden, Sune Bruman Sune, Veikko Mäkipelto, Svante Rönnholm, Fiskars consumers, 1996, patent illustration, Internet.

Additional illustrations
p. 12-13 National Library of Finland
p. 18 National Library of Finland
p. 22 MFA
p. 22 MFA
p. 24 MFA, P: Kari Hakli
p. 26 Helsinki City Museum
p. 27 AUAD
p. 29 DM, P: Rauno Träskelin
p. 30 National Board of Antiquities, photographic copy: T. Syrjänen
p. 30 National Board of Antiquities
p. 32 National Library of Finland

p. 33 DM, P: Kimmo Smolander
p. 34-39 National Board of Antiquities
p. 40-41 LUAD, Kotitaide magazine 1902
p. 44 DM, P: Aimo Hyvärinen
p. 46 DM, P: Niclas Warius
p. 47 National Library of Finland
p. 48 DM, P: Rauno Träskelin
p. 52 DM, P: Rauno Träskelin
p. 55 Kotitaide magazine 1902, LUAD
p. 57 MFA, P: Nils Wasastjerna
p. 58 DM, P: Rauno Träskelin
p. 60 DM, P: Claire Aho
p. 61 DM, P: Otso Pietinen (cropped detail)
p. 62 DM, P: Jean Barbier
p. 63 DM, P: Eija Valojärvi
p. 64 Helsinki City Museum
p. 66 DM, P: Rauno Träskelin
p. 67 DM, P: Jean Barbier
p. 68 AUAD
p. 70 MFA, P: Kari Hakli
p. 71 Rauno Träskelin
p. 72 Rauno Träskelin
p. 73 Rauno Träskelin
p. 74 MFA
p. 75 MFA
p. 75 MFA, P: Katja Hagelstam
p. 75 Rauno Träskelin
p. 76-77 National Library of Finland
p. 80 DM
p. 82 AUAD
p. 82 National Library of Finland
p. 85 DM
p. 86 DM, P: Rauno Träskelin
p. 87 DM
p. 89 Finnish Fair Corporation
p. 89 National Library of Finland
p. 90 Kuopio Museum / Tuomas Sopanen, Ryijy elää, P: Kari Jämsen
p. 92 MFA, P: Foto Roos
p. 93 National Library of Finland
p. 94 National Library of Finland
p. 95 Electronics collection of the City of Salo, P: Salla Pesonen
p. 97 Finnish Fair Corporation
p. 97 DM, P: Teigens Fotoatelier
p. 101 Kuopio Museum / Tuomas Sopanen, Ryijy elää, P: Kari Jämsen
p. 106 DM, Alvar Aalto Foundation
p. 107 MFA, P: Ezra Stoller
p. 109 Finnish Fair Corporation
p. 113 National Library of Finland
p. 114 Finnish Fair Corporation
p. 119 National Library of Finland
p. 121-123 DM, P: Rauno Träskelin
p. 124 Finnish Fair Corporation
p. 124 MFA, P: Kolmio
p. 125 DM, P: Rauno Träskelin

LIISA VALONEN

Pekka Korvenmaa Ph.D. is Professor
of Design and Culture at the School
of Arts, Design and Architecture at
the Aalto University. He has published
books and articles on the history of
Finnish architecture and design both
in Finland and abroad.